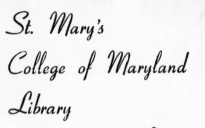

BOOKS BY RICHARD HALL

Zambia
The High Price of Principles
Discovery in Africa
Stanley

LOVERS
ON THE NILE

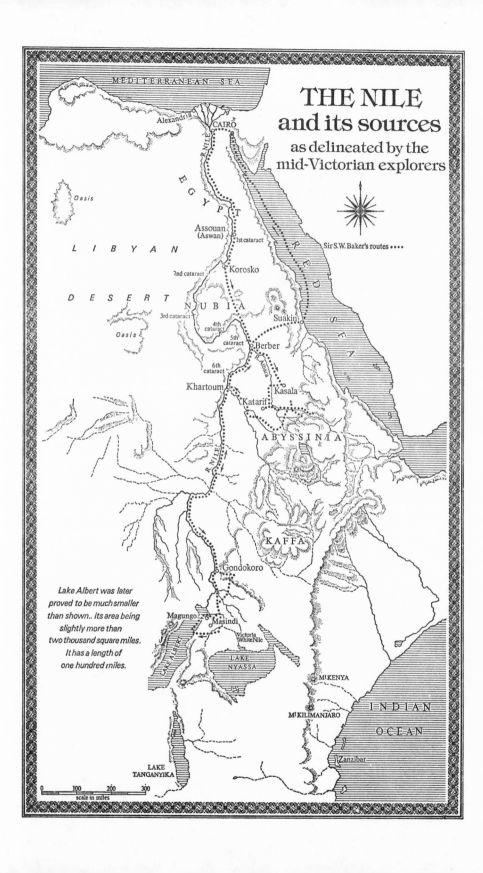

MEDITERRANEAN SEA

THE NILE
and its sources
as delineated by the
mid-Victorian explorers

Sir S.W. Baker's routes ••••

Alexandria
CAIRO

NILE

EGYPT

Oasis

LIBYAN

Assouan
(Aswan)   1st cataract

Korosko

2nd cataract

DESERT

NUBIA

3rd cataract   4th
                      cataract
Oasis   5th
                      cataract   Suakin
                              Berber

                        R. Atbara
                6th
                cataract
Khartoum   Kasala

            Katarif

                      ABYSSINIA

RED SEA

RNILE

KAFFA

Gondokoro

*Lake Albert was later
proved to be much smaller
than shown.. its area being
slightly more than
two thousand square miles.
It has a length of
one hundred miles.*

Magungo   Masindi

LAKE ALBERT

                      Victoria
                      White Nile

            LAKE
            NYASSA

                              Mt KENYA

                                          INDIAN
Mt KILIMANJARO
                                          OCEAN

                              Zanzibar

LAKE
TANGANYIKA

0   100   200   300
      scale in miles

LOVERS
ON THE NILE

*The Incredible African Journeys
of Sam and Florence Baker*

RICHARD HALL

RANDOM HOUSE   NEW YORK

For Carol
who saw it through

Library of Congress Cataloging in Publication Data
Hall, Richard Seymour, 1925-
Lovers on the Nile.
Bibliography : p.
Includes index.
1. Baker, Samuel White, Sir, 1821-1893. 2. Baker, Florence, Lady. 3. Africa, Eastern—Discovery and exploration. 4. Nile River—Discovery and exploration. 5. Africa, Central—Discovery and exploration. 6. Slave-trade—Africa, Central—History. 7. Explorers—Great Britain—Biography. 8. Explorers—Africa—Biography.
I. Title.
DT365.72.A2H34   962   79-5522
ISBN 0-394-50227-2

Manufactured in the United States of America

Contents

'Petherick takes with him a stout bucksome wife! He will be joined by a great friend of mine, whom you perhaps know, Samuel White Baker the Ceylon sportsman. He too takes up a charming little woman with him – I much fear both these ladies may lose health, perhaps life, in their rambles.'

Robert Colquhoun, British Consul General in Egypt, giving latest news of the search for the Sources of the Nile, in a letter to Christopher Rigby, Consul in Zanzibar, 20 July 1861.

Introduction

The Victorian Age never asked many questions about Sam and Florence Baker. To an adoring public they were simply national heroes, models of courage and virtue. At the time, that was enough; as explorers, the Bakers were ranked with Livingstone and Stanley, Burton and Speke.

Florence was celebrated as the first white woman to have made the death-defying journey to the Sources of the Nile. Sam was the only African traveller to be knighted as a direct reward for his discoveries. They were lionized by society and became friends of the Prince of Wales.

Behind this façade of fame, the unorthodox Sir Samuel and his beautiful wife, with her exotic origins, had much to hide. Queen Victoria picked up a hint of the truth – enough to make her refuse ever to receive Lady Baker. But the full, extraordinary story was so resolutely buried that previous books on their lives and adventures have failed to portray the Bakers as really convincing human beings. It has been my aim to draw back the veil and take into account all those facts which the Victorian public was denied.

The task could not have been done without the help of scores of people. My foremost debt is to the present members of Samuel Baker's family, who have granted full access to his unpublished diaries. This permission, not given to any previous biographer, makes it possible to take an entirely fresh view of many important incidents.

Moreover, Mr and Mrs Valentine Baker, Dr John Baker, and Mrs Erica Graham have made available many family letters, private memoranda and photographs. This is not to imply that they will necessarily agree with my interpretations.

I cannot claim to have unravelled completely the secret of Florence Baker's origins. Perhaps after this lapse of time, it was too ambitious a hope. But for help in clearing up many obscurities I am grateful to Dr Istvan Gal in Budapest, Professor Dan Berendei in Bucharest, and Dr Edward Fuchs in Vienna. I am also indebted to Professor George Cushing and Dr Theodore Beynon, both of London University.

Ever since embarking upon this project I have worked closely with Professor James A. Casada of Winthrop College, South Carolina. I have benefited from his suggestions as well as from access to documents he has collected in preparation for a full-length academic study of Samuel Baker.

The archivists and librarians who have helped me in tracking down relevant material are so numerous that I cannot name them all. However, particular thanks are due to Mrs Christine Kelly at the Royal Geographical Society, London, and Mr Ian Cunningham at the National Library of Scotland in Edinburgh. Invaluable research was done in the Public Record Office and elsewhere by Mrs Renée Prawdin.

Several writers, experts in fields bordering upon my own, have put themselves out to answer my queries – especially Charles Chenevix-Trench, Penelope Gladstone, Alan Hankinson and Oliver Ransford. Mrs Mary Lloyd-Morgan gave me an insight into the personality of that briefly-famous member of her family, Kate Dickinson; and Mrs Alex Heape brought to light a revealing letter, written on behalf of Queen Victoria. Mr J. C. C. Houlton has kindly allowed me to use the papers of his ancestor, the railway-builder Henry Barkley.

I should like to thank the *Financial Times*, for being so tolerant during my retreat from today's headlines into nineteenth-century adventure. Finally, I acknowledge with gratitude the work of Lois Warner, my colleague on the paper, in transcribing my original typescript.

AFRICAN NAMES AND SPELLINGS. I have generally kept to the usage of Baker and his contemporaries, seeking period authenticity rather than orthographic precision. Many names have changed: for example, Lake Albert is officially called Lake Mobuto. Much of the action related in this book occurred in what is now Uganda – a far larger place than the tribal kingdom of Buganda from which it has derived its name. A comparison of Baker's map with a modern atlas should help readers to resolve any uncertainties of geography.

RICHARD HALL

CHAPTER I

Stag at Bay

When Queen Victoria and her family went to Balmoral, in the Scottish Highlands, the Prince Consort's keenest pleasure was deerstalking. Sometimes the Queen and the royal children would accompany him and be fortunate enough to see the kill. Victoria recorded in her diary the last moments of one stag which the Prince had brought down: 'The noble animal never rose, but struggled and groaned, so that Albert went and gave him another shot, which killed him at once. It was a most exciting sight . . .'

But if she had chanced, one day in September 1858, to have journeyed over the picturesque mountain route from Balmoral to a glen on the estate of the Duke of Atholl, the Queen could have witnessed a kill that was far more breathtaking. An air of expectancy, a thrill at the prospect of watching some rare and unconventional feat, possessed the knots of people waiting beside their carriages on the gravelled road. It was here, a few miles north of the duke's castle, that Samuel Baker was about to try to fulfil the boast he had made at dinner the previous night.

Baker had promised to show them a novel way to hunt down a stag; as he recalled later, 'the arguments had interested the ladies of the party', so that several now waited, resplendent in their crinolines, and stared as intently as their male companions towards the bare hillside on the east of the glen.

There was no sign yet of Baker, but at such a time of year there were few more agreeable places to pass an afternoon. A fresh stream, the Tilt, cascaded over rocks down towards the woods beyond which the castle stood. Autumn had made the trees into a patchwork of red, browns and fading greens. Silver birches and red-fruited mountain ash hung over the rocky salmon pools.

All at once, Baker was seen in the distance, running and leaping through the heather. Ahead of him, two deer-hounds were chasing a large stag. Although the man on the hillside was strongly built, his fleetness of foot was renowned. When he neared the carriages he suddenly swerved down the hill and raced along the road, because it had become apparent that the dogs would drive their quarry diagonally across the slopes towards the river, there to bring it to bay. As he drew closer to the onlookers, they joined the hunt, running as best they might along the stony road. Baker did not carry a gun, but a large knife was hanging in a sheath from a belt around his tweed breeches.

The doomed stag was standing in a rapid, with the hounds baying from the water's edge. Baker jumped into the water and ran hip-deep downstream, shouting encouragement to the dogs. He had unsheathed his knife, double-bladed and more than a foot long. As the dogs sprang into the torrent, he took hold of the stag by its lowered antlers and raised his knife. One dog had the cornered animal by the throat, another by an ear. With his immense strength, Baker drove the knife in behind the stag's shoulder, until he reached the heart. 'It was a pretty course, which did not last long,' he wrote, 'but it was properly managed, and in my opinion ten times better sport than shooting a deer at bay.'

Deerstalking was so fashionable in the 1850s that his gory success in Glen Tilt enhanced Baker's reputation still further among society in the Highlands. Sam had many other qualities that made him a welcome guest at various lordly homes; he was good humoured, a vivid raconteur, and expert at sketching instant likenesses. The Duke of Atholl, on whose estate Baker rented a large house for much of the year, often invited him to stay. Following the Prince Consort's example, it was the accepted thing when in the Highlands to wear Scottish dress; Baker had the duke's consent to assume the blue and green Atholl tartan, and he cut a good figure in a kilt. If his face could not be called handsome, it was striking – his blue eyes and neat fair beard contrasting with the deep tan acquired during many years in the East.

Although without a title (and secretly displeased at this oversight by Fate), Baker came from a rich family in the West Country of England. The eldest son of a merchant and banker whose fortunes derived from sugar plantations in Jamaica, he had been brought up in a somewhat old-fashioned way: his father distrusted schools and relied mainly upon private tutors to educate his children. So Sam Baker's youth was largely untrammelled by discipline – he learned what he liked, became fluent in several languages, but really preferred roaming the countryside. His sense of freedom was enhanced by receiving a large inheritance from his maternal grandfather, and he rejected any idea of a business career. Nor did he care to enter a university; but he was married when barely out of his teens.

Many of his attitudes and actions were typical of the earlier, pre-Victorian decades of the century. He had been born in 1821 and in the 1840s somewhat cut himself off from the more tight-lipped standards that were developing in England by going to live abroad with his wife and young children. At first he had tried Mauritius, managing a plantation there; then he moved on to Ceylon, where he founded a farming settlement in the mountains, with the aid of a large retinue of English craftsmen. In 1855 illness had forced him to return home; shortly afterwards, his wife died.

Even if he was not fully in sympathy with the growing earnestness he found in England, he was intensely patriotic. After all, one of his ancestors, Sir John Baker, had been Chancellor of the Exchequer to Henry the Eighth. Another was an admiral who had fought some spectacular battles against the French.

His patriotism was all of a piece with the rest of his nature: having a fine bass voice, with which it was said he could sometimes make the windows rattle, he liked to sing rousing airs at drawing-room entertainments. His favourite piece was a martial duet, 'Sound the trumpets!', from *I Puritani*, Bellini's opera based on a story of the English Civil War: Baker appropriately sang the part of a Roundhead hero.

So his less intimate friends must have judged him well pleased with his lot. He had been a widower for several years, it was true, and had four daughters, but if the fancy took him to marry again he could choose almost as he wished from the flocks of well-bred women in the circles where he moved.

Yet Baker's air of well-being was a deception. He was possessed by anxiety. Like an animal pacing behind the bars of its cage, his mind moved ceaselessly to and fro, looking for an escape. The years were slipping by, yet Baker could never find the challenge, the chance for fame, that life seemed resolved to deny him.

He was still trying to shake off a mood of dismay at the latest rebuff to his ambitions, the refusal by Dr David Livingstone to have him as a member of a government-aided expedition to explore the Zambezi region of Africa. As soon as he knew of Livingstone's plans, Baker had written to his friend, the young Lord Wharncliffe, who had political influence: 'I should amazingly like to form one of the party, as you are aware. Will you kindly write to Lord Clarendon and say all you can for me by the next post, as there is not a moment to be lost.' Baker stressed that he would be willing to meet Clarendon, the Foreign Secretary, 'at a minute's notice'.

Wharncliffe had done his best. He began by telling Clarendon that Baker was a very old friend, 'my companion in elephant shooting in Ceylon, and who has written two books about that island'. After praising Baker's physical strength, he called him 'a very well-informed man, having some knowledge of geology, botany and medicine, as well as an eager longing after everything that concerns natural history . . . He has been accustomed to hard out-of-door life in Ceylon for eight years and as a sportsman his character ranked higher than anyone else in the colony . . .'

Within three days the answer came back. Clarendon had passed the letter on to Sir Roderick Murchison, President of the Royal Geographical Society, who after consulting Livingstone said Baker was 'out of the question', because nobody could join the expedition who did not have some useful occupation. Murchison referred sarcastically to Baker as a 'nimrod' – after the name of the mighty hunter mentioned in the tenth chapter of Genesis.

Undeterred at first, Baker had written to the Royal Geographical Society proposing his own expedition to southern Africa, as an 'auxiliary to Livingstone'. He would follow a separate route, take several trusty companions, and to sustain the expedition for two years would put down £2000 of his own money.* Baker had exchanged letters with Livingstone and explained to the RGS that he was now being guided by the doctor's advice; but after a flurry of correspondence, the Foreign Office intervened, telling the society that Baker's presence might antagonize the Portuguese colonists in Mozambique, and make difficulties for Livingstone. In May 1858, writing despondently from the Highlands, where the snow still clung

* This would be nearly £40,000 ($80,000) today.

to the hilltops, Baker said wistfully: 'I wish I were in Walfish Bay.'

Walfish Bay, on Africa's south-west coast, was one of the places from which he had vainly suggested he might start for the interior. His gloom at Livingstone's rejection was aggravated through knowing that John Speke, a young army captain he had first met while coming home from the East, was at that moment exploring in Africa. Reports from Zanzibar said that Speke and another officer, Richard Burton, were trying to find the vast lakes which were said to be the reservoirs of the Nile. The age-old mystery of where Africa's greatest river had its source was all at once seizing the curiosity of geographers and public alike. This mood was exactly caught by an American writer, Bayard Taylor, who had travelled up the Nile to a point where the peoples living beside its banks were no longer Arabs, but black Africans. In a book which had quickly gone through ten impressions, Taylor proclaimed: 'Since Columbus first looked upon San Salvador, the Earth has but one emotion of triumph left in her bestowal – and that she reserves for him who shall first drink from the fountains of the White Nile, under the snow-fields of Kilimanjaro.'

The envy Baker felt towards Speke, who even now might be enjoying that triumph, was sharpened by the fact he had so much in common with him. They came from the same part of the West Country: Baker's father had sold one of his properties to Sir John Dorington, a brother-in-law of Speke. Enthusiasm for big game hunting was something else they shared; Baker recognized in the younger man his own love of lonely places – where as he had put it in one of the books about Ceylon, there was 'no hum of distant voices, no rumbling of distant wheels'. Yet there were also displeasing traits in Speke: he was very excitable, and his conversation tended to be a confused muddle of fact and prejudice.

However, Baker was aware of his own failings, particularly an inability to 'fit in'. As he wrote to one of his sisters: 'You know what I always was – made up of queer materials, and averse to beaten paths; unfortunately, not fitted for those harnessed positions which produce wealth; yet, ever unhappy when unemployed, and too proud to serve . . .' It was this last quality which had kept him from a career in the army; he was well suited for it in other ways, having been fascinated with guns since boyhood. Two of his three brothers were in the cavalry and a few years earlier, during the Crimean War,

Sam had put his knowledge of weapons to good use by inventing a new type of rifle ball that would not jerk out of the barrel of a muzzle-loader being carried on horseback.

At the end of the Crimean War, Sam had gone out to visit his brothers Valentine and James in their quarters at Scutari, near Constantinople. He was at the time in a distracted state of mind, his wife having died a few months earlier; he had asked an unmarried sister known as Min to care for his daughters while he was abroad. The three brothers had made boar-shooting trips into the Turkish mountains and for a time Sam thought of going further, to explore Circassia in the Caucasus region across the Black Sea. 'I have no plans for the future,' he told one of his family. 'I shall wander about and trust to fate . . . Anything for a constant change.'

But the idea of Circassia soon palled. Sam came home again, and cast about for some occupation in which he could be with his children. He was in a quandary, for tolerable options were limited. In early manhood he had spent a year in an importing company owned by his father, which convinced him that he wanted no more of that. Although he had later built up his estate in the hills of Ceylon, in the strict sense of the word he had scarcely worked at any time in his life.

Suddenly, Baker declared that he wished to enter the Church – which was odd for someone who never took much interest in religion and had poked condescending fun at missionaries in his writings about Ceylon. There was also a powerful streak of sexuality in him that would have gone awkwardly with religious ministrations, even in an age of sporting parsons. Writing to reveal this scheme to Lord Wharncliffe, he admitted that it might astonish him; all else aside, thirty-seven was late in life for taking holy orders, although he hoped it would be 'no great obstacle'. The handwriting in his letter was jerky and uncontrolled, and in a later era it might have been suspected that he was close to a nervous breakdown.

Thoughts of the Church were to linger in Baker's mind for some months; a daguerreotype portrait taken in London in 1857 shows him wearing a distinctly clerical garb, although the solemnity of his expression may be blamed on the time a sitter had to stay motionless in those days. (Nobody looks cheerful in mid-Victorian photographs, because it was impossible to sustain a convincing smile for anything up to two minutes.)

Impractical as it clearly was, this talk of becoming a clergyman did allow Baker to maintain a show of purposefulness before his seven brothers and sisters. They all looked up to him, the eldest, as virtually a paterfamilias, someone whose example should be copied. As events would shortly make plain, he was not ideally suited for this role, but it had been thrust upon him by their father's unexpected remarriage after the death of their mother; this event had provoked a temporary rift in the family.

Sam was also being put on his mettle by the achievements of Valentine, the brother who was most like him in character. Although six years his junior, Valentine was already a major in one of the best cavalry regiments, the Tenth Hussars. Lithe and energetic, Valentine had been decorated for his courage at the fall of Sebastopol in the Crimea. He rivalled Sam in his flair with words and his first book had attracted much attention: a study of British cavalry methods, it contrived to be both entertaining and provocative. Loyally, Valentine had inserted a footnote praising the rifle ball 'invented by my brother, S. W. Baker Esq.'.

It was from Valentine, who had fought in one of the Kaffir Wars, that Sam had heard something of the big game hunting to be had in Africa. It was the plethora of wildlife, as much as its blank spaces on the map, which made the 'Dark Continent' so alluring for a traveller with sporting inclinations. Africa's animals seemed to be infinite in number and many species were excitingly dangerous (deerstalking in Scotland could only be tame by comparison, however one went about it).

It was the elephants of Africa which lured Sam, for he had shot more of the Ceylonese variety than any other man living. But when he studied the thick cranium of African elephants he doubted if they would be easy to bring down by the conventional forehead shot from an ordinary gun. With this in mind he had designed a massive muzzle-loader, firing a half-pound shell, which he nicknamed 'The Baby'; unfortunately, it needed so much powder that even he could scarcely use it without being thrown on his back.

There was going to be a time when Baker would confess his regret at having killed so many elephants. But that was in far later years, and for the moment he rejoiced in what he called 'whole hecatombs of slaughter'. Hunting was the one activity in which he was incomparable and it answered a deep emotional want. (It is widely accepted by psychologists that stabbing has strong sexual connotations; so Baker's obsession with killing animals in this way may have reflected unfulfilled urges, canalized in displays of physical conquest.)

Yet although he believed, in a typical pre-Darwinian way, that animals were put on earth purely for man's satisfaction and amusement, some rules must still be kept. After lying in wait at night with two companions by a waterhole in Ceylon, he had written remorsefully: 'This watching by moonlight is a kind of sport that I do not admire; it is a sort of midnight murder; and many a poor brute who comes to the silent pool to cool his parched tongue finds only a cup of bitterness, and returns again to his jungle haunts to die a lingering death from some unskilful wound.' If an animal were wounded in the daytime, it was a matter of honour to track it down; in the dark, that was impossible.

Baker's way of shooting elephants in Ceylon had been spectacularly bold, for he would creep as close as ten feet before firing. Once an angry bull had hurled him in the air, and frequently he narrowly escaped being trampled to death, but was nonetheless scornful of the hunting methods in Africa, where 'according to all accounts, elephants are fired at at thirty, forty and even sixty yards . . .'

Yet for all his eagerness to show how the job should be done, Baker felt so discouraged by the failure of his approaches to Livingstone and the Royal Geographical Society that he had resolved to put aside all thought of Africa for the moment. Fortunately, the chance of making a face-saving journey abroad had just presented itself; there was not likely to be a great deal of danger or excitement, but it could well prove an amusing change from his life at Lochgarry House in the Highlands.

CHAPTER 2

A Girl for Sale

When Sam Baker alighted in mid-November on a London platform, after travelling by train from Scotland, he had taken the first step towards his destiny. Yet his immediate plans gave no hint of that. As usual, when making a brief trip to town, he had booked a room in his club, the Windham; it was much frequented by sportsmen, and famed for its gargantuan dinners. The Windham was also in the middle of London, in St James's, and thus convenient for settling the minor details of the journey he was about to make.

Travelling across Europe to Constantinople in 1858 was not the sort of trip which any member of the Windham would consider to be more than a pleasant excursion. The first part, to Austria and Hungary, was elementary, because there were now railways all the way. Nor was there the slightest reason for concern about the rest, for although there might be no steamers on the Danube in mid-winter, even the wildest parts of Eastern Europe had become far better known since the Crimean War. It was always possible to get through. Baker must have fancied himself perfectly prepared for any eventuality on the way to Turkey.

All his arrangements went on smoothly, until at the end of November Baker found that he must depart quite suddenly. He could not even wait to say farewell to his eldest daughter Edith, who was ten. 'I am so sorry my dear child that I am obliged to leave just as you will be coming to London,' he wrote. His letter sent all the girls his love and kisses, as well as some inconsequential paternal advice on how they should wash their faces before going to bed: 'Lukewarm water is horrid, but hot water is the thing for comfort.' With that, Baker turned all his thoughts to the journey. Although he must be away for Christmas, there was every reason, at that moment, to feel confident of being home again in the spring.

The excuse for being so precipitate about setting off was that Baker had a companion, someone far keener than himself to be down at Dover, boarding a cross-Channel steamer. The Maharajah Duleep Singh, in his suite in Claridge's Hotel, could hardly bear to linger a moment more before savouring a taste of freedom. There had been a notable lack of untrammelled fun until now in the life of the young Indian, because he had been kept in Britain under strict surveillance since the annexation of his hereditary kingdom, the Punjab, during his childhood. On recently reaching the age of twenty, Duleep Singh had forced the grudging authorities to accept that he might travel abroad with whom he liked. When he met Baker, so engagingly informal and entertaining, the maharajah felt he had found the ideal escort and protector. His enthusiasm for the Danube expedition knew no bounds.

The attractions of the relationship on Baker's side are less obvious. The maharajah was seventeen years his junior and looked rather effete. Moreover, the author of *Eight Years Wanderings in Ceylon* took a view of non-Europeans that was typical of his time.

But the time also revered kings and princes. A ruler by right of birth was always entitled to honour, whatever his hue or however afflicted by fate. The aura of regality would still cling to such a person, even though he were totally deprived of power – and that was especially so in the case of Duleep Singh. For of all the high-born victims of the British occupation of India (and there were many) he was incomparably the grandest – that small, excitable creature who now waited to set off with his three servants and a fine array of luggage on the evening train from London Bridge station. He was the hereditary ruler of an historic kingdom the size of Italy.

The wealth that had once been in his Punjabi Treasury was the envy of the East; its glory was the Koh-i-Noor diamond, whose possession was a talisman of sovereignty. Down the centuries, Moguls, Persians and Sikhs had struggled for it, until Lord Dalhousie, the governor-general of the Punjab after its annexation, took the jewel away by night in a chamois leather purse and despatched it to Queen Victoria. So the stone and the maharajah both came to Britain, and both were, on the surface, transformed. The Koh-i-Noor was cut down in Amsterdam to fit into the imperial crown; and Duleep Singh was turned into a Christian. The Queen was much reassured by his baptism, because she felt religion must subdue the intemperate instincts in his blood; he had long been separated from his mother, the Maharani Chunda Khour, but her nickname was remembered: 'The Messalina of the Punjab'.

Although prone to fits of hysterical laughter, Duleep Singh had tried his best to play the part Fate had given him. During many visits to Windsor Castle and Buckingham Palace through his adolescence he listened politely to all the exhortations of the Queen and the Prince Consort. He made friends with the Prince of Wales, three years his junior. Under the tutelage of Sir John Login, a high-minded Scot, the maharajah picked up the sporting habits of the British nobility. He was given a stipend adequate to indulge them. Every autumn as he grew older he rented Menzies Castle in Perth-shire, an easy journey from Balmoral, and entertained there quite handsomely. Lochgarry House was twenty miles away, but in those thinly-populated parts Samuel Baker was almost a neighbour, and that was how they met.

The ostensible motive they both had for going off on a long winter tour was a general discontent with the quality of shooting to be had that year in Scotland. As *The Field* said in an editorial: 'We observe an almost unanimous determination on the part of sportsmen not to revisit the Highlands for two or three seasons.' It added that some enthusiasts were going as far afield as Scandinavia and Germany to find game. The informant was probably Baker, a regular contributor; a letter from him published on 9 September had bemoaned the decline in the grouse that year: 'I can walk over some 2000 acres without moving more than two or three broods.' Even so, he and a companion – William Price, a Liberal member of Parliament – had contrived to kill 355 birds, not to mention 91 hares and rabbits.

Now the maharajah and his mentor declared themselves to be after bigger quarry, the wild boar of Serbia and bears of Transylvania. First they would go to the capital of the Habsburgs, then eastwards to the twin Hungarian cities of Buda and Pest. The maharajah also looked forward with enthusiasm to meeting an Austrian baron renowned for his skill in stuffing birds; Duleep Singh loved falconry and was making a collection of trophies.

After touring the Balkans, the pair would travel on to Asia Minor, which Baker was familiar with from his trip to Turkey nearly three years before. More sport might be had there. Finally, they would go by way of Greece to Rome, where the maharajah hoped to rendezvous with Bertie, the Prince of Wales. The prince would be spending the spring in Rome, under the tutelage of his Latin master – it was the latest of several edifying tours arranged for the heir to the throne by his father. Also waiting in Rome would be Lady Login, wife of Duleep Singh's erstwhile guardian; she was chaperoning a young Indian princess whom she thought the maharajah might be persuaded into marrying.

So all in all, it was an itinerary laden with possibilities; despite their wide disparity in ages there was an undeniable appeal to Baker's ego to be travelling with a celebrity in whose welfare the Queen herself was known to take the closest interest. In his farewell letter to Edith, her father had told her to look at a picture of the maharajah – 'exactly like him' – in the latest issue of the *Illustrated News of the World*. The engraving covers a whole page of the magazine (a short-lived rival to the *Illustrated London News*) and shows Duleep Singh in all his Eastern finery, wearing bejewelled ear-rings, a turban adorned with strings of pearls, and richly embroidered Sikh costume. He had a small beard and moustache, and full lips; the eyes stared imperiously, or perhaps with a touch of wildness.

The picture was accompanied by a biographical sketch. This was largely taken up with reciting the traits of Duleep Singh's forebears, including his mother – 'lowest and most profligate habits' – and his father – 'low excesses and debauchery'. In contrast, 'His Highness has adopted the English dress and habits, and is excessively fond of field sports, and takes far more interest in athletic exercises than is customary among Orientals'. Even so, the article implied, he might not need much encouragement to regress to the ways of his parents.

It was perhaps this possibility that had provoked Queen Victoria to try to stop Duleep Singh going away with his new friend. Although Baker came from the well-to-do squirearchy, was of mature years, and possessed distinguished friends, the Court had no hold over him. Moreover, was he utterly without moral blemish? Lady Login subsequently wrote that Baker was 'an habitué of eastern cities'; perhaps she was confusing him with the notorious traveller Richard Burton, or perhaps she had merely heard of his visit to Constantinople, the enticements of which became better known during the Crimean War. Certainly, strong pressure was put on the maharajah to take an equerry, but he was so adamant that he would only go with Baker that it was decided nothing could be done.

At a dinner in Windsor Castle, a fortnight before the journey to Eastern Europe was due to start, the Queen had sat with Bertie on one side of her and Duleep Singh on the other. 'He certainly is very attractive,' she wrote about her guest in her diary. The following day, she made notes of what she had been told of the maharajah's character by Sir Charles Phipps, her private secretary. The verdict ran: 'Extremely high principled and truthful with most gentleman-like and chivalrous feelings, but rather indolent, and not caring to learn or read, this, due probably to his Indian nature.'

However, as the *Illustrated News of the World* told its readers, living in Britain was teaching Duleep Singh many of the manners of the upper classes. For instance, no sooner had he and Baker stepped ashore from the steamer at Ostend than he adopted a popular stratagem used when abroad by gentlemen who wanted to follow their inclinations unobserved. He assumed a false name: Captain Robert Melville. He simply borrowed this from one of his friends, an Oxford undergraduate named Ronald Melville, the son of Lord Leven.

The maharajah was eagerly looking ahead, knowing that the next few months offered the chance of liberties and pleasures until now denied him. Yet as their train steamed across the Rhineland, his companion looked back to adventures in Germany as a student, when he was Duleep Singh's age. For him, those days had also been a taste of freedom – the brief interlude between his boyhood and a return home to be married, at the age of twenty-two, to a country vicar's daughter. So for Baker, this new journey to Europe may have seemed to offer the prospect of reliving a carefree past. Perhaps it was that mood, that romantic nostalgia, which made him act as he did in the bizarre encounter awaiting him – the meeting which would change the whole direction of his life.

But now, as Baker and the maharajah made their comfortable progress towards Austria, they looked forward to nothing more than lighthearted adventure. There were overnight stops in several cities along the route – Hanover, Magdeburg, Berlin and Breslau – for in those days a train journey across Europe was leisurely, echoing in many ways the styles of the lately-outmoded stage coaches; they came to Vienna at the start of December. In its 'new arrivals' column the daily *Wiener Zeitung* rather inaccurately recorded their presence: 'Samuel W. Barker, rentier in London; Robert Melville, ditto.' The term *rentier* was used freely of all those who were patently persons of property, having no cause to work.

In the capital of the Austrian Empire, the fancy for travelling *incognito* did not long survive. The maharajah, dressed in his Indian finery, had an audience with Emperor Franz-Josef which was reported in all the newspapers. He went to meet the bird-stuffing baron, then accompanied Sam Baker on a boar-hunting party arranged in their honour near Vienna by Duke Esterhazy. The newspapers grew rather confused and one said that the maharajah's companion was really called Sir Robert Melville; this bestowal of a knighthood must have given Baker some secret pleasure.

In London, an item in the *Daily News* had already played havoc with earlier attempts at secrecy: 'Duleep Singh is at Vienna under the travelling name of Captain Melville. His Highness has chartered a steamer belonging to the Austrian Steam Navigation Company and is going down the Danube on a shooting expedition.'

After a few days in Vienna, the two travellers moved on to Pest, taking quarters in the Queen of England Hotel overlooking the Danube. On the far bank was the towering outline of Buda, the twin town. For fear of another uprising by the Hungarians, the Austrian rulers kept a powerful force in Buda Castle and had built a citadel close by. Ten years before, there were desperate battles here as the Hungarian nationalists struggled against their overlords. While only half-built, the one bridge across the river had been taken and retaken by rival armies – much to the consternation of an Englishman, Adam Clark, who was in charge of its construction. After the fighting, Clark had settled down in Pest with an Hungarian wife. Baker and the maharajah called upon the Clarks.

There were few other formal engagements, but a hitch developed about the journey down the Danube: a steamer could not after all be hired, because of ice. Conveniently, the time did not drag, because the Hungarians were able, then as now, to make the best of life despite foreign domination. The city was called the 'Paris of the east'. It had many theatres, an opera, and cafés where gipsy music was played until the early hours. For Duleep Singh, all this was quite a new experience.

The maharajah was emotionally impetuous and took a fancy to almost any pretty young woman who came his way. In Scotland, he had developed a grand passion for a Scots girl who was one of the Grosvenors, a family of aristocratic Whigs with the Marquess of Westminster at their head. Nothing came of that, nor of his earlier attempt to propose to a landowner's daughter during a tour of Sardinia. So it was inevitable that now – enjoying new freedom – he would waste little time in forming some liaison. In Pest he picked up what the Austrian newspapers would shortly call a 'bride'. But the status of any girl willing to set off at short notice on a hunting trip in all-male company must have been far more basic.

The transport arranged by Baker – who seems to have under-estimated the difficulties of such a voyage in midwinter – was spartan and unorthodox. It was a corn-boat, of the kind used on the Danube in warmer months to carry grain downstream. The boats were roughly built and were simply broken up when they reached their destinations. In the short time available the selected craft was modified to make it more comfortable, and a team of oars-men was hired, but by any measure it was a reckless venture. In letters home Baker confessed that 'all kinds of miseries and dangers' were prophesied. But he went on bravely: 'It was of course cold, but we had three good stoves on board, lots of wood and champagne, two casks of splendid beer and wine on deck, three English servants of the maharajah, fowls, turkeys, guns, etc., therefore we were always jolly.' His is the only surviving account of the trip, and discretion forbade any mention of the extra female member of the party.

After 250 miles, a halt was made at the river port of Semlin. Christmas and New Year were spent here. It was a regular stopping-place for the Danube steamers, had several hotels, and was a border post at the limit of the Habsburg Empire. On the opposite bank of the river was the fortress of Belgrade, controlled by the Turks. Semlin was used as a centre for hunting forays by Baker and his young companion.

But on 16 January 1859, an item appeared in the Vienna *Fremden-Blatt*: 'The Maharaja Duleep Singh, well known in English fashion-able circles, has chosen unto himself a bride at Pest. They are now resting at Semlin. The marriage will take place at Galatz and after the ceremony the young couple will proceed to India. According to rumours circulating about this prince, he is said to have an income of twelve million crowns.' A similar report was in another Vienna newspaper the next day. Neither named the girl, nor was there any mention of Baker: he may have been away shooting.

It took four days for the news of the maharajah's romance to be picked up by the *Frankfurter Journal*, a paper much inclined to court and society intelligence. Two days later it was reprinted by three London dailies. The mention of a wedding in Galatz was completely logical: this port on the Lower Danube would have been the first place on a voyage downriver where a couple intending to be married could find a British consul to perform the ceremony. In fact, no marriage ever took place.

What Baker thought of the maharajah's inamorata is never revealed. Writing later to the Duchess of Atholl, he said there was not 'the slightest foundation' for rumours in the papers that Duleep Singh was to be married to 'a Wallachian lady of high rank'.

By mid-January, the party was once again on the river, with an alarming part of the journey ahead. This was the passage through the rapids known as the Iron Gates. It was 'exhilarating', said Baker, when the boat went through the rapids at 'rocket-like speed'. The maharajah's thoughts must have been rather different. With his amorous involvement and the freezing weather, he did not, moreover, show any disposition to stop to go in search of boar or bears. 'Our sport has not been good,' Sam later wrote to his sister Min, the one who was looking after the children, 'the maharajah being, as I expected, of too soft a texture for the successful pursuit of large game in midwinter in a wild country.' He did not refer to any of the less rugged aspects of the journey, least of all to what befell him soon after a crash with an iceflow forced the abandonment of the boat near a town named Widdin.

The town was the main Turkish fortress in that part of the Balkans. When Baker and the maharajah went ashore it was their first contact on the tour with the Ottoman Empire – and one that was scarcely encouraging. From the river, Widdin was impressive, with its minarets and massive fortifications, but a closer look revealed all the decadence and failure of will pervading the lands still held by Turkey to the south and west of the Danube. Starving dogs scavenged in the icy gutters and rubbish was piled haphazardly outside the houses. Few buildings had glazed windows. The place was terrorized by the Albanian militia, underpaid and living like brigands, who were valued by the Turks as a means of subduing the Bulgarian peasantry. The mood in the town was

26

uneasy, for the Turks had been under heavy political pressure that winter in the Balkans, with disturbances to the north in Serbia and across the Danube in the vassal state of Wallachia: Baker's claim that he and Duleep Singh were suspected of spying is credible enough, because a corn-boat making an erratic and dangerous journey in midwinter could surely be up to no good.

Unprepossessing though Widdin might be, both Russia and Austria kept consuls there. The British ambassador in Constantinople, Sir Henry Bulwer, was repeatedly suggesting to London – but in vain – that he might follow their example. The town, under the military command of a pasha, was strategically placed to control a large sweep of the Danube, and was the headquarters of an administration holding down much of what is now Bulgaria.

The eyes of Europe had been on Widdin ten years before, because it was here that the Hungarian patriot, Lajos Kossuth, first took refuge after the collapse of his short-lived republic. With him had come many of his fleeing compatriots, including five thousand soldiers. But soon, when Kossuth left, the spotlight moved away and the Turks of Widdin returned to their normal preoccupations. Significant among these was the buying and selling of slaves. From time to time, the dealers would offer an array of boys and girls, each fit for service of one kind or another. It happened that while Baker and the maharajah were in Widdin, an auction took place.

They went to the sale, for there was little else to divert them in Widdin. Perhaps the Turks imagined that the younger of the two visitors would, because of his colour, be the more amused – to see white people being bought like cattle. Yet it was Samuel Baker who stared transfixed at the barbaric scene, and at one in particular of those hapless victims paraded before the crowd of Turkish merchants and officials. In these dire surroundings he had set eyes upon the person who was going to be the love of his life, his companion in adventures that would make his name familiar to millions.

The emotions which had caught hold of him in the slave auction can merely be guessed at. He never spoke or wrote about that moment; only she described it, many years later, in her old age. We cannot tell whether Sam Baker was moved by pity, or desire. Possibly he was shocked, beyond all else, that a frail, golden-haired girl – so like his own daughters – was trapped in this real-life nightmare, only a step from a misery from which escape would be impossible. She cowered before the onlookers, a beautiful piece of property, nothing more.

Sam Baker began to bid in that auction at Widdin – a gesture that his friends at the Windham Club would have found incredible, pitting his money against the system of the Ottoman Empire. He had decided to acquire a slave . . .

It was a headstrong act, whatever his first motive. To take part in a slave auction was to appear to condone it – at a time when the campaign against slavery was stirring emotions throughout Europe and America. But Baker may have had less rigid inhibitions, since slave-owning was in his family tradition. His father liked to argue that the blacks on the Baker plantations in Jamaica were far better off than English factory workers; it was a diehard defence.

Even in the Ottoman Empire, during the half-hearted reforms after the Crimean War, there had been a show of forbidding slavery. Yet any Turk who so desired (and most did) could still buy a young girl or boy whenever he wished. Inside the frontiers of the empire, which stretched from the Adriatic to the Persian Gulf, slaves were circulated according to market needs. A merchant in the Balkans might have in his retinue several black slaves of both sexes, whereas Ismail Pasha, the ruler of Egypt, chartered a British ship named the *Kangaroo* to bring him consignments of white Christian slaves supplied through his agent in Constantinople. Although Europe's conscience was aroused by the slavery in the United States, less heed was given to what was happening in Turkey, the ally of Britain and France. But the cruelties that encompassed oriental bondage defied general belief. Burton and other travellers gave blood-curdling accounts of the trade in eunuchs; and when a female slave became pregnant by her master, she would often be either crudely aborted or condemned to having her child taken away at birth and killed. Anyone such as Samuel Baker, after living in Constantinople, would have understood what part slavery played in Turkish society.

Although Islam is less aware of colour than is Christianity, there was a *cachet* for wealthy Turks in having white girls in their harems. It was the custom for a rich man to give his son several pretty girls from the Caucasus as a birthday present. Shortly after the Crimean War the *Morning Post* of London reported that there was 'an absolute glut in the Turkish market' of 'white human flesh'. Most of the girls came from Georgia or Circassia, but frequently the flow was interrupted because of military onslaughts on Caucasus by Russia.

Supply problems would have a severe effect on prices. Sometimes a white girl would fetch only £5 (less than £100 in today's terms), but a shortage could push the going rate much higher for a well-made virgin aged between twelve and eighteen. The merchants would then look to the less normal sources, such as Greece and the wilder parts of Serbia and Albania. They clutched at societies thrown into upheaval by the wars that were endemic in the Balkans, at refugees who had lost the protection of their original nationality. There were many such defenceless groups within their reach in the years following 1848 – Europe's 'Year of Revolution'. In some Bulgarian districts, each family had to give up one child: it was called the blood tax.

During the uprisings throughout the Habsburg Empire, and especially in Hungary, thousands of Slavs escaped across the Danube into the deceptive tranquillity of Turkey's vassal states. The girl whom Baker was about to buy was one of these, a particle of the flotsam of 'Turkey in Europe'.

She was in her teens, slim and small, her hair loosely braided at the back of her head. He paid over the price at which the bidding stopped. Then she was *his* slave.

What were the girl's reactions to her rescue, in the ominous surroundings of Widdin, by the Englishman who had appeared by such marvellous chance? Florence would only say, in the years afterwards: 'I owe everything to Sam.' But one thing is certain: her life really began when she became his property – and his mistress – for some never-revealed amount of Turkish lire.

CHAPTER 3

Together to Africa

They left Widdin at once and crossed over the Danube into Wallachia. The expedition was at an end – the corn-boat was wrecked and Baker had a new preoccupation. As for Duleep Singh, the cold and desolation of recent weeks were making him want nothing more than a quick return to civilization. So the crew were left to await the first steamer back to Pest; the maharajah's ephemeral fiancée was also presumably abandoned with them.

Three coaches were hired for a 200-mile dash across the Wallachian steppes to the city of Bucharest. 'We were five days jolting at full gallop over a wild country of frozen deep ruts without the semblance of a road,' wrote Baker. 'Your backbone nearly sticks into the cushion.'

In Bucharest came an abrupt parting from the maharajah, who pressed on by coach with his escort of servants. By 11 February 1859, Duleep Singh was in the comfort of the Hotel d'Angleterre in Constantinople, but so shattered by the journey that he even refused a dinner invitation from the ambassador, Bulwer. Then he made his way across the Mediterranean to Italy. When Lady Login reached Rome, she was intrigued to find the crestfallen maharajah already there, after 'hurrying away from Constantinople'. She wrote in her diary, with a sly satisfaction, that the expedition 'had been rather a fiasco' and that Baker had failed to prove himself a 'wise counsellor to a young and inexperienced charge'.

She made no reference to the newspaper reports of the maharajah's romance, doubtless hoping that he might now accept her advice on a suitable wife. In fact, Duleep Singh would in time choose himself a child-bride, the daughter of an Abyssinian slave, from an American mission school beside the Nile. It would be a sudden romantic attachment which curiously echoed the situation in which his erst-while mentor now found himself in Bucharest.

At first, Baker must have simply enjoyed the thrill of excitement at being alone in an unknown city with a disturbingly attractive girl. For the moment, he had no need to make any vital decisions about her. It was some months yet before he was due to be back with his daughters at Lochgarry House. There should still be opportunities to go boar shooting and he might even take Florence, as he now called her, along with him. But it must have been clear that ulti-mately he would have to make a choice – one which might mean turning her loose to the renewed uncertainties of life in the Balkans.

What looked to be out of the question was ever taking her back to Britain. Even Baker's strong sense of the absurd could not encompass the prospect of introducing her to his family as a bargain acquired in a Turkish market. He might somehow avoid going into that matter; but she spoke no English, and was by no stretch of the imagination what his own people would describe as 'wife material'. It might have passed through his mind eventually to find her a modest position somewhere, perhaps as a governess. But that would depend upon being able to part from her. Such were the pressures of Victorian society that this same choice was still to weigh upon him six years later, after they had been through momentous adventures together.

But who *was* Florence? Sam began to piece together a pitiful story. The first clues dated back to when she was a small child. She remembered 'shots, knives, yells, corpses and fire': all her family were massacred during an uprising in 1848. Florence survived be-cause she was hidden away, and was afterwards cared for by a woman retainer. The family name was Sass, and her home had been in Transylvania – somewhere in one of the German-speaking en-claves along Hungary's southern boundaries, and now part of Romania. Her first names were Florenz Barbara Maria – she was a Catholic – and she knew the date of her birth: 6 August 1841. But by the time Sam found her the surname she was using was Finnian.

Although rare, the name Finnian is Armenian, so it is likely that she was given into the care of a Catholic Armenian family in Hun-gary – ever since the middle of the seventeenth century the Turkish persecution of the Armenians had driven many thousands to flee through the Balkans, beyond the borders of the Ottoman Empire.

Some 50,000 settled in Transylvania and were well regarded by Empress Maria Theresa. According to Florence, the name of her adoptive father was Matthew (Madteos in Armenian), but nothing is definite about him except that he was dead by the time she was in the hands of the Turks. The years leading up to her extraordinary rescue by Baker must have been full of misery and degradation. She never felt she belonged to Eastern Europe after Sam found her; her mind was clamped tightly against the past. Apart from one romantic gesture on a distant shore, Florence was to renounce forever her Balkan background. Sam Baker became her sole hope, his quintessential Englishness her touchstone.

On Sam's part, his personality seems to have found a new fulfilment in Florence. Although his thirteen years of married life had produced a crop of daughters (and two sons who died in infancy), his relationship with his wife seems to have been no more than respectably humdrum; in his books on Ceylon, where most of the marriage was spent, she is never once mentioned – although there is much about the male companions with whom he was forever away hunting. Now he was making a totally different choice.

The gulf in years between Florence and himself, the complete disparity of their backgrounds, the sheer inability to talk to one another except in German (which Sam had rarely used since he was twenty) – all this leaves little room for doubt as to the mainspring of their liaison. Florence could have been, at first, only the servant to his repressed instincts. However, events would soon prove her more self-assertive than that. As she would reveal again and again in Africa, she was not by nature timid. She would also be able to display, even in the tightest corners, a sense of humour that matched his own.

Baker must have sensed such qualities in her very early on. Certainly an intimate alchemy soon sprang up between them. Try as he might, he would never be able to leave her. Yet the first pretext he hit upon to avoid a parting was mundane enough: he applied for a job in Eastern Europe on a railway project.

In a letter to his sister Min, written a few days after reaching Bucharest, he revealed his plan for working with a British company which was preparing to build a line from the port of Constanza, on the Black Sea, to the Danube east of Bucharest. He knew something about the railway because one of its directors was William Price, the

MP with whom he had shot grouse in Perthshire six months earlier;
it happened that Price was more than merely a friend – his sister-in-
law was Baker's stepmother. So there was a fair reason to hope
that a job with the Danube and Black Sea Railway would be forthcoming. Its senior engineer, Charles Liddell, was in Bucharest
when Baker arrived there.

'I have made up my mind to undertake the management if he can
come to terms,' Baker told his sister. 'I remain here two or three
weeks until I receive answers to letters to Price. My future depends
on the reply. Should I become the director here I am afraid, my
dearest Min, that I shall not be able to return home . . .'

Such a decision must have seemed to his family a remarkable
volte-face, coming from someone who until that moment had spurned
all regular employment. Perhaps conscious of how surprised they
would be, Baker was at pains to make his potential job sound grander
than it was: he did not say that, despite the title of managing
director, he would be saddled with every sort of administrative
chore that might impede the engineers. He emphasized instead that
he was applying for the consulship in Constanza – at that moment
nothing more than a Turkish fishing village bordered by newly-dug
earthworks for the railway. In his letters he envisaged bringing out
silver and china for the director's residence, which he expected
would be big enough to have spare rooms for guests. Admittedly, the
lands around the Lower Danube did not have much to commend
them. 'Fleas as big as bantam cocks and bugs as large as turbots,' he
reported to Min. 'Bucharest is a mass of filth, the streets everywhere
are five inches deep in black mud . . .'

His first letters home were full of the verbal pyrotechnics which
came so easily to him. But there was never a hint of the new influence
in his life. Min and his daughters would wait seven years before Sam
told them about that. Indeed, when he started living with Florence,
she was so enwrapped by his need for secrecy that she might, in a
sense, have indeed been immured in some Turkish harem.

Yet even in Bucharest, a city somewhat off the beaten track, there
was a British eye-witness to the start of his amatory adventure – and
one incidentally who knew Lochgarry House well and shared all
Baker's enthusiasm for the Perthshire moors. A melancholy and
hypochondriac Scottish bachelor in his late fifties, Robert Colquhoun
had endured a quarter of a century as Britain's consul amid the

longueurs of the Wallachian capital. When Baker toyed with the hope of being the consul in Constanza, he at once called to meet Colquhoun. As Sam wrote in a letter to his brother Valentine, there was much nostalgic talk about the best salmon fishing spots in their favourite part of the Highlands – because Colquhoun happened to own a house only a few miles from the Forest of Atholl. Yet the consul took a bleak view of the involvement with Florence, and in due course would give vent to his criticisms.

Although neither he nor Baker could know it then, their paths were to cross again: for despite being in the 'November of his career', when he must have lost all hope of advancement, Colquhoun had recently heard that he was to become Her Britannic Majesty's consul-general in Egypt.

Whatever Colquhoun may have thought of Baker's scheme for applying to be a consul, it came to nothing. Even so, when the railway did offer the managing directorship, Baker quickly accepted. Early in March, he wrote to his eldest daughter saying that it had been a struggle to take such a step, because it would mean staying away from England far longer than he imagined when on leaving. But he was sure, said the letter, that his daughters would not forget him. He then set off for Constanza.

Although there was little enough to see, it was a town with a history. In Roman times it was called Tomis, and the poet Ovid – notorious for his *Ars Amatoria* – spent his last years in exile there; today a statue of Ovid stands in a square overlooking the quay where in 1859 sailing ships landed supplies for the railway builders. 'In making the excavation for the railway we discover antiquities every day,' Baker wrote soon after arriving, 'such as marble sculpture, coins, Roman houses . . .' The British navvies imported to spearhead the construction work were obstructed by a city wall built by Trajan, so it was unceremoniously smashed asunder. A Roman bath, lined with white marble, was shattered when workmen tried to hack it from its foundations.

Baker also found that he was involved in a more modern fragment of history, albeit an esoteric one: the railway was going to be the first completed anywhere in the Ottoman Empire. Its object was to create a short cut between the Lower Danube and the Black Sea and Mediterranean, as well as to carry grain and other crops to the coast from Wallachia. At the outset, he was all enthusiasm for the project and his part in it – looking after the accounts, paying wages, ensuring that contractors for wooden sleepers and stone made deliveries on time, negotiating with local merchants and buying up the vineyards and orchards through which the line would pass. In April he wrote to one of his sisters: 'My office is being built as fast as possible and I am daily expecting the arrival of bookkeepers and clerks. Imagine my being anxious for the completion of an office! I mean to make this a model concern, if I can . . .'

But his efforts were being watched with a jaundiced eye by four young brothers who were in charge of the construction. Jack, George, Robert and Henry Barkley were the sons of a Norfolk parson; the eldest, Jack, had already spent six years in various engineering jobs in Turkey and was still only thirty. Self-taught and self-confident, the Barkleys were typical of a wave of young Englishmen who in the wake of the Crimean War were hoping to make their fortunes in the Middle East. Such ambitions were constantly hindered by the deviousness and lethargy of the Turks, who rightly saw progress as a time-bomb that would shatter the remains of their empire: in letters home, the Barkleys dwelt constantly on the failings of the Sultan's functionaries.

Now they had a new topic. Henry Barkley broke the news: 'We are expecting a Mr Baker, the great elephant shooter, as managing director . . . If he is a nice man he will be a great addition to our party.' But a sour note soon creeps into the letters, for it was scarcely surprising that the Barkleys would resent this socially superior newcomer with connections on the company board. 'I am afraid he does not know very much of the work he will have to do,' wrote Henry, 'and gives Jack a lot of trouble in teaching him . . . He is mad about shooting and fishing and has sent home for lots of dogs and fishing tackle.' The letters leave the impression that Baker was doing his best to be amiable, but that his colleagues found little good in him. The Barkleys saw him as a challenge and were combining to make him feel unwelcome.

From Henry Barkley comes the first mention of Florence – even if a very oblique one. This reveals that within a few weeks of Sam's arrival in Constanza she had come down from Bucharest to live with him. A letter to the Norfolk parsonage dated 4 May 1859 tells of returning from a trip and 'finding Jack in solitary state as he is not fond of having much to do with the Bakers'. The last two words are

35

heavily underlined. The Victorians – their Queen setting a formidable example – used underlining in their letters for emphasis; they also employed it for innuendo, to draw attention to something that was too indelicate or confidential to describe in plain terms. The Barkleys would have had scant doubt that the girl their new managing director had brought into their English enclave at Constanza was not his wife. Although there is a great deal of gossip in the letters on other new arrivals, there is a frigid silence about her, and only hostile remarks on him.

Henry Barkley was of literary inclinations, and years later he was to publish two books of reminiscences about his younger days in Eastern Europe. By the time the books appeared, the Bakers were world-famous, but nonetheless he evades making any reference to them. Barkley cannot even bring himself to relate how Baker swam out to sea during a storm off Constanza in the December of 1859, to rescue a shipwrecked sailor seen clinging to a spar – although he does tell of watching from a clifftop as two ships were pounded to pieces by the gale. Typically, Baker did more than just look on.

For all his strength and ability as a swimmer, he was risking his life in the icy water. Years afterwards, in a novel, he was able to exploit the incident in a vivid ten-page re-creation: a girl named Polly (the original is unmistakably Florence) watches fearfully from the cliffs while her husband Paul struggles amid raging seas, to save a child on a raft.

It is from this fictionalized portrayal of Sam and Florence that it is incidentally possible to derive some idea of their physical bonds. In one scene, Paul is trying to comfort Polly after her own baby has died: 'They were now sitting at the table, his arm around her waist, while, as her head rested upon his shoulder, he tenderly wiped the tears from her large blue eyes and warmly kissed her forehead.' At another time, she clings to him 'in a paroxysm of joy that almost approached madness'. One cannot expect to find any direct accounts of how Sam and Florence behaved intimately towards one another – the age they lived in did not permit it – beyond his admission that his love for her was 'perhaps more intense than is often bestowed on women by their husbands'.

So although the efforts of the Barkleys to ostracize him were discouraging – and his job less satisfying than he might have hoped – Baker gave evidence of being happier than ever before in his life.

With a degree of vivacity and humour never apparent in his writings before, he launched into a series of long essays about everything around him. Regardless of brigands, wolves and extremes of climate, he wandered through the wildest parts of what is now Romania, making notes and illustrating them with ink sketches and watercolours. These essays, fourteen in all, were published in *The Field*, as a sequel to a series by Baker about Ceylon printed some months earlier. At first, they bore the nom-de-plume 'Phantom', but then began appearing over his own name – perhaps because the style was inimitable. Using only a sentence or two for each, he vividly portrays the vagabonds, peasants and huntsmen he meets.

Once he mentions that he has sent the editor a picture of a Wallachian post-cart at full speed: 'You cannot see the cart, only a small portion of a horse here and there . . . the rest is dust – not a difficult style of drawing.' The editor clearly agreed – it was not published. He goes shooting in a swamp with a village boy as his companion and discovers that the swamp is full of frogs: 'They, like all people enjoying a monopoly, are assuming and bumptious, popping up their ugly heads in crowds as I go splashing after wild ducks.' He relates how his long boots became so firmly stuck in the black mud that he was driven to climbing out of them: 'Accordingly they were extracted and slung over the shoulders of my Wallachian lad, both he and I voting boots an encumbrance.'

He also finds occasions to be serious. In one article he writes perceptively about bird migration, then speculates on the vision of birds and how they find their food. Another contrasts the rich landowners with the villagers in Wallachia: 'Card-playing and gambling are the prevailing vices of the principality; and the wealthier classes are generally addicted to dissipation in all its branches. Not so the peasantry, who are a quiet, well-conducted people, not industrious, but excessively clean in their dwellings.' Then there is a long and moving description of the plight of the Tartar refugees, fleeing by ship from Russia and landing at Constanza, only to die in their thousands from epidemics as they travel inland to new settlements.

The frontier between the busy and well-ordered lives of the railway community and the haphazard cruelties all around was fragile. Constanza was under the direct administration of the Turks, who called it Kustendjie. While Sam and Florence were living there, six captured brigands were decapitated in the market square and their

heads put on show. Life was ephemeral and the dead were soon forgotten: near the two-roomed house with which Baker finally had had
to be content, a mass grave was uncovered and proved to contain
the remains of French soldiers killed when a powder magazine blew
up four years earlier, during the Crimean War. Life was endlessly
fascinating yet sad: 'Indolence, cruelty, avarice and sensuality have
succeeded in rendering comparatively barren the fairest and richest
land in Europe,' wrote Baker.

By this time, however, his mind was roaming far from the Dan-
ubian plains. In the middle of 1859, copies of the London newspapers had arrived in Constanza with first accounts of a stirring feat
of exploration. John Speke was back in Britain from Central Africa.
He and Richard Burton could confirm that the great inland seas
described in classical times by Ptolemy really did exist. After an
exhausting journey they had reached Lake Tanganyika – and Speke
claimed to have discovered, while journeying alone, a vaster stretch
of water, which he loyally named after Queen Victoria and declared
was the Source of the Nile.

The British, recently thrilled by Livingstone's journey across the
continent, were equally as excited at this African adventure of two
more compatriots. Speke became a national hero and the 'Nile fever'
took a firm hold on the public. Beside the Black Sea, it quickly in-
fected Baker. At the inland end of the half-completed railway was a
village called Tchernavoda ('Black Water'), where he sometimes
passed the time by shooting vultures. There the Danube is a mile
wide; and beside Europe's longest waterway, Baker's dreams began
about that great and mysterious river whose source lay in the heart
of the Dark Continent. He was, moreover, conveniently close to
Egypt, land of the Nile – politically as well as geographically, since
it was a part of the Ottoman Empire. His face was turning towards
Africa once more.

By the end of 1859 the London newspapers were detailing Speke's
plans for a second journey, to push his discoveries further. He wanted
to start once again from Zanzibar, explore the African lakes, then
turn northwards and follow the Nile from its headwaters to the
Mediterranean; when the Royal Geographical Society asked the
public for funds to supplement £2500 from the Treasury, money
flowed in. Baker started to think of going in the opposite direction,
southwards from Cairo: somewhere along the course of the Nile he

might bump into Speke. He also envisaged all those African elephants – for years he had been yearning to have a go at them.

By the beginning of 1860, he was bowing out of his job with the railway company; Jack Barkley was writing to the British embassy in Constantinople in a style that showed he had the reins firmly in his hands. But as Sam was still engaged in negotiating for the company, he and Florence were able to keep their house above Constanza harbour.

In May 1860, Baker left Constanza and made a trip to London, by the river and rail route through Vienna. He went to sever his contract with the company, but the journey had a wider purpose: to clear the ground for a long expedition in Africa. Yet he avoided telling his children – or even his brother Valentine – what he meant to do. It might have been different if John Speke had still been in London, so that their projects could be discussed and dovetailed; but on 27 April, Speke had sailed from Portsmouth, en route for Zanzibar. Baker also shunned Speke's sponsors, the Royal Geographical Society; instead he decided to go to one of the exclusive 'Monday Evenings at Home' arranged by the Honourable Henry Murray.

A retired rear-admiral, Murray lived in Albany, the Piccadilly apartments reserved for bachelor gentlemen, and his weekly get-togethers were much patronized by hunters and explorers. After his eighteen months' absence from Britain, this was an ideal place for Baker to renew his sporting contacts. No women were admitted to Murray's rooms and in his bedroom was a set of parallel bars upon which his more athletic visitors displayed their agility. One of his contemporaries wrote of Murray, who was nicknamed 'The Skipper', that he had 'a mixture of bluffness with an almost womanly gentleness and courtesy'. The son of a Scottish earl, he had been put in the navy at the age of thirteen and became an enthusiast for flogging to maintain discipline. Although regarded as 'not remarkable for force of intellect', Murray had written a travel book about Cuba and the United States called *Lands of the Slave and the Free*.

Murray was an unparalleled source of news about the exploring fever of the day – who was going where, and the facts collected by expeditions just home again. Another reason why Baker was keen to strike up a friendship with 'The Skipper' was that his brother, Sir Charles Murray, had important friends in Egypt. Sir Charles had been for eleven years the consul-general there. One of the family's claims to fame was that Sir Charles had sent home from the Nile the first hippopotamus ever seen in Britain; the antics of this celebrated beast were a great delight to the Queen when she visited the Zoo in Regent's Park with her children.

On the evening he went to apartment D4 in Albany, Baker was gratified to encounter William Cotton Oswell, a wealthy elephant hunter. Oswell had accompanied Dr Livingstone on his early explorations and they shared the honour of having been the first white men to reach the Upper Zambezi. The plans Baker outlined so impressed Oswell that he lent him one of his favourite hunting weapons, a massive No. 10 double-barrelled shotgun. Baker was pleased to add it to his already sizeable armoury. 'The Skipper' was also enthusiastic: he lent Baker a naval telescope and helped him buy equipment.

By the beginning of June, the former managing director was back at Constanza. Henry Barkley wrote home: 'Baker has come out but nobody of our party has seen him, and as he is *nobody* now we don't want to.' Taking Florence with him, Sam moved some distance inland and lived with the Tartar refugees. Writing in *The Field* from the village of Medjidiah, halfway along the railway line, he said: 'I returned to this country from England in six days and shall devote myself to the sports of this country till the winter.' One of his hobbies, he said, was hunting wolves.

In October there was a lavish opening ceremony for the £500,000 railway. A party of directors arrived from London and at their head was William Price, representing the company chairman, Sir Samuel Cunard. Although Price was a relation by marriage, Baker kept his distance from the festivities; his name is nowhere mentioned in a closely-printed full page account of the occasion that appeared in the *Levant Herald*, an English-language newspaper published in Constantinople. Yet he was still tidying up loose ends. Just before the opening, he sold a two-masted sailing ship which had been used to ferry supplies for the line; a careful balance sheet in his notebook shows that a good profit was made out of her.

In the middle of the next month, Sam and Florence took a steamer down the Black Sea to Constantinople, which he had last known when staying across the Bosphorus at Scutari, in the camp of the Twelfth Lancers. From an hotel in a busy part of the city, Baker began an outpouring of letters typical of his gusto when he was possessed by an idea.

One of the first went to Richard Burton, who had not gone back to Africa with Speke, since the two were now at loggerheads; Baker asked if Burton might care to go up the Nile with him. Next he wrote to Sir Roderick Murchison, president of the RGS, requesting African maps. Then on 20 November he addressed himself to the society's officials, laying bare his ambitions for visiting Khartoum and the little-known regions of the Sudan. He said he was 'going to spend a few years in working his way through those spots, keeping as much along the White Nile as he could, till he could get no further'. He appealed for the loan of scientific instruments; as for a chronometer, he had already asked a friend for one. The response was not particularly warm. A note attached to the letter says bleakly: 'Mr Baker is not a Fellow of the Society and declined to become one when asked.'

Eventually, the society did draw up some plans for him. When sent them, he was adjured to limit himself to travelling along the eastern tributaries of the Nile, beside the borders of Abyssinia. This would effectively rule out his joining in the search for the Nile sources. Any idea of a meeting with Speke, he was firmly told, should be regarded as 'sub-servient'. The RGS officials clearly wanted to keep Baker out of Speke's route; another expedition might create trouble with the tribes. Baker meekly accepted these instructions, for the time at least. He knew, after all, that some of the best elephant country in Africa was to be found in the regions to where he was being directed.

Another letter from Baker went to John Petherick, who could fairly claim to know more about the Upper Nile than any other Briton alive. After fifteen years in Egypt and the Sudan, Petherick had returned to Europe to buy more guns for hunting, to publish a book on his travels, and to find a wife. Petherick was a massively-bearded Welshman, trained as a mining engineer, who had turned to ivory trading after settling in remote country south-west of Khartoum. After holding for years the honorary title of 'Vice-consul for the Sudan', he had managed while in Britain to have himself upgraded to a full consul, with a modest salary. Yet although his speeches to the RGS had earned some acclaim, Petherick was a contrary and awkward personality; living so long on the fringes of civilization may have put him out of touch with contemporary ways. During his tortuous negotiations with Whitehall about the consulship, he was likened by Lord Russell, the Foreign Secretary, to a hippopotamus, or a wild horse.

Baker and Petherick had chanced to meet in the previous May in Admiral Murray's apartment in Albany. The Welshman's ambitions were being much stimulated by life in London – he was already talking of making a rendezvous with Speke somewhere on the Upper Nile not far north of the equator; a public subscription was being raised to help him on his way. But in writing to him from Constantinople, Baker avoided offering any hint that he might also have designs upon the legendary lands of the Great Lakes. Instead, he gave Petherick the idea that elephants were at the forefront of his mind: 'I do not intend to limit myself to time; but I shall (D.V.) pass two or three years in the elephant districts, and try to combine an extensive exploration with my old amusements . . . If you could give me a letter to anyone in Khartoum who could put me up to the right men and the right plan for a first go at the elephants, I should be exceedingly obliged.'

Petherick was still in Britain, making arrangements in his laborious fashion for travelling back to Africa (although it must be conceded that he was also preoccupied with getting married). Baker ended by asking: 'What are your movements personally? and when do you expect to return to Khartoum? I shall look forward with much pleasure to meeting you somewhere in those parts . . .'

Amid all his letter-writing, Baker found time to pen a final piece from Turkey for *The Field* – and in it toyed with the thought of what life might be like if you owned a harem. 'Let us for a moment imagine ourselves in his position, surrounded by a multiplicity of beauties – dark eyes and blue, black hair and every shade towards gold . . . ravishing forms that we read of in eastern novels. Five and twenty wives going out shopping, and you pay the bills! Can any man of feeling conceive anything more horrible?'

Then from his hotel window – and presumably with Florence at his side – he watches a party of Turkish wives in a carriage having goods brought out to them from a shop by their eunuchs: 'Being by nature wicked, I very improperly watched their selections.' The purchases included silk stockings and white kid gloves. Then one of the wives chose a crinoline. 'I had an intense longing to see her try it on,' wrote

Baker, and speculated that she might even wear it inside her harem trousers. Such racy frivolity must have startled his foxhunting readers in Britain. Had she seen it, the piece might also have done much to confirm Lady Login's deepest suspicions about Baker's moral sobriety.

There is a great deal more in the article. The scenes of Constantinople spring from the faded pages of *The Field*: sellers of sweetmeats, captains of merchant ships in tall hats and tail coats, eunuchs on horseback, an Armenian funeral, drunken sailors, dogs sleeping in the road . . . it was the work of someone entirely carefree and happy. Sam was about to take Florence into the mountains, to Lake Sapanga, where they would spend the second anniversary of their encounter in Widdin. Writing about it thirty years later, he made this interlude at the lake sound – perhaps quite unwittingly – like a honeymoon.

The road to Sapanga began at the port of Izmit, a ten-hour journey by steamer from Constantinople. From there they went on horseback, with pack animals carrying their baggage behind them and Sam's two pointers trotting along the verges. The road was primitive, so that their horses often floundered into mud two feet deep. After twenty-four miles they reached their destination, a town surrounded by groves of vines and fruit trees, and settled into the quarters which would be their home for the next two months. Sam had hired two rooms and a kitchen on the first floor of a private house. 'The ground-floor was occupied by a cow and her calf; this looked propitious, as the milk was close at hand.' Through the gaps in the floor they could see, hear and smell the animals below.

The air was cold and a few days after their arrival snow fell. Sam went into the hills alone with his gun, chasing wild boar through the drifts. But every Friday, the Mohammedan Sabbath, scores of men from the town would make a rendezvous with him outside the walls and join in beating the oak forests for roe-deer and boar.

When he was not out hunting, Baker planned for the adventures ahead. He wrote to Valentine, asking him to send out to Alexandria a battery of polygroove rifles, as well as 250 pounds of gunpowder and a large box of tools. He ordered a medical chest, including large amounts of quinine to combat the malaria which was going to be the greatest hazard he and Florence would face in the Sudan. There was also the matter of money: although he was quite wealthy, Baker knew that his expedition would soak up a substantial part of his resources. He wrote to the family company which looked after his inheritance and asked it to make unlimited funds available in Alexandria through the Bank of Egypt.

In a series of letters from Sapanga he then broke to his family the news that they would not be seeing him for several years. 'I am going to Khartoum, and thence, God only knows where, in search of the sources of the Nile. I shall very likely meet Speke, who is working his way up from Zanzibar . . . You know that Africa has always been in my head.' He told Lord Wharncliffe that he was eager for the journey, although he realized the risks involved. To his sister Min he put forward the *apologia* of every explorer: 'A wandering spirit is in my marrow which forbids rest. The time may come when I shall delight in cities; but at present I abhor them . . . my magnetic needle directs me to Central Africa.' It was not the full story, but enough, he judged, to make Min and his daughters think fondly of him until he came home again.

CHAPTER 4

On the Abyssinian Frontier

When he began his journey up the Nile, Baker started a diary. Its first words, dated 15 April 1861, are: 'Left Cairo at 6 a.m. with a spanking breeze.' Foolscap sized, with brown cloth covers, his journal was not a new one, but already contained notes made in Ceylon many years before and some from his time on the Danube. So he turned it upside down and began from the back, writing in two columns. He used a small, flowing hand, markedly different from the jerky style of his earlier years.

Before that dawn departure from the Egyptian capital there had been many things to do. Sam kept having last-minute inspirations about items that might come in handy during the years ahead, because he and Florence knew that they must as far as possible carry their own world with them. Letters must also be written: one to Petherick, now on his way out from England and due in Alexandria in a fortnight, asked him to look out for some barrels of gunpowder that had failed to arrive on time and forward them to Khartoum. Finally, there was a call upon Robert Colquhoun, the lugubrious consul-general whom Baker had last met in Bucharest. The meeting had its awkward side, because Colquhoun reproached him about Florence – for not making her his wife before carrying her out into the wilds. If Sam should succumb to disease in some lonely spot – and the death-rate among African travellers was stupendous – her plight would be desperate, her fate unthinkable. She would have no nationality or status that might do something to protect her. But Sam rejected any idea of marriage, just yet. Whatever Florence might have thought was of less account. After all, her plight had been far more desperate two years earlier. She had nobody but Sam, so where he went she must go.

Yet Florence was never going to be a mere camp-follower. She was acquiring many wifely skills, and although Sam considered himself to be *ne plus ultra* when it came to cooking, he could not rival her in needlework. By now she knew a lot about guns and shooting: most of Sam's weapons were far too heavy for her small frame, with a recoil that would knock her backwards, so he taught her how to use a light but effective rifle made for him at his boyhood home in Gloucester by a gunsmith named Fletcher.

As they glided up the Nile in their *dahabiah* (a vessel like a small *dhow*, with a diagonal lateen sail), they speculated about their ultimate goal, more than 2000 miles away. Sparkling under the bows was Africa's longest river – and one that cradled humanity's oldest known civilization. They stopped at Luxor, so that Sam could stroll ashore and shoot pigeons and quail for the boat's larder. He thought little of modern Luxor, its huts being 'built in with the mighty ruins of ancient Thebes as the swallow fashions his nest of clay upon the grey walls of a ruined abbey'. Yet he was stirred as always by the wonders of the past: while in Ceylon he had spent days painting watercolours of the lost cities he came across in the jungle during hunting trips.

Even beyond Luxor, they were still on a stretch of the Nile frequented by the more adventurous tourists of the day. At Aswan, a party of young men came aboard asking for *baksheesh* (gifts), and all were completely naked. 'I could not help thinking,' remarked Baker jocularly in his diary, 'how much young ladies must learn by a journey up the Nile which affords such opportunities for the study of human nature.'

After a month of sailing south they sent their boat back to Cairo and began a forced march across the desert in temperatures reaching more than 110 degrees in the shade. This was the direct overland route, avoiding cataracts and a great curve of the Nile. They travelled with sixteen camels – themselves, two servants and a great deal of baggage. From his years in the tropics, Baker was able to contend with the heat, but Florence could not. 'F. very ill with fatigue and heat,' he noted. 'But there can be no halt in the desert; dead or alive with the caravan you must travel . . .' At an oasis they had two jugsful of water with which to wash. After they had done with it, an

Arab outside the tent snatched their bowl and drank all its soapy contents, crying, 'Thanks be to Allah!'

Near the end of the journey, Florence was so overcome that Sam knew they must stop, whatever the risks from delay. In the dusk he made good use of the halt by going out and shooting two desert gazelles for their meat. Three days later they reached the Nile again just north of the Arab town of Berber, where they pitched their tent under a tree. With relief they lay down on their Persian carpets and gazed around them.

Since Egypt and the Nile regions acknowledged the suzerainty of the Ottoman Empire, its red crescent flag was hanging over the nearby army barracks. Baker went next day to present his *firman* (letter of authority) from the Pasha of Egypt for the inspection of the local governor, who asked where he was going. 'To the source of the Nile,' replied Baker grandly. The governor and his officers tried to dissuade him: 'The White Nile is the country of the Negroes, wild ferocious races . . . the climate is deadly; how could you penetrate such a region to search for what is useless, even should you attain it? And how would it be possible for a lady, young and delicate, to endure what would kill the strongest man?'

As it happened, Baker had already abandoned his plan for going straight on southwards to Khartoum. He would turn east, to the borders of Abyssinia, and survey the little-known rivers that rose in its mountains – just as the Royal Geographical Society had instructed him. After a year or so, he would make his way along the course of the Blue Nile to Khartoum – and then begin the journey to the equator, to the magic fountains. Should Florence go too? When they reached Khartoum it would be time enough to decide that.

The words of the governor of Berber on the matter were undoubtedly reasonable: no woman had ever attempted such a journey. Baker must also have pondered intently on what might happen if Florence became pregnant in some wild and distant place – although it is hardly surprising that the subject is never hinted at in his private diaries. It was common knowledge that David Livingstone's decision to take his wife with him on one of his early explorations had ended in the death of her baby; after that, he had travelled alone. The factor must have loomed so large that it merits study.

Contraception was, of course, not unknown – in particular, the male use of thin membranes taken from animal intestines. This means would have been readily available in Africa to a big game hunter. But leaving aside the improbability of total abstinence, there was no method then available to ensure that Florence would avoid any risk of conception in the years of travel that must lie ahead. So was Baker merely reckless and uncaring?

Faced by a curtain of silence, we nonetheless know this: even in later times, when there was every reason for Florence to want children, she would never have any. (Although her fictional counterpart Polly, in Baker's novel, bore a son who died in infancy, it would be rash to read much into that.)

After they had lived together for two years, Sam may have come to assume that Florence was unlikely to become pregnant. There is also the possibility that before they met she had been subjected to some treatment which had made her sterile. What may be said for certain is that in their case, love was never dictated by the Victorian ideal of procreation, although both were fond of children.

One evening before they left Berber, where she swiftly recovered from the nightmare in the desert, Florence was visited by the wives of the leading men of the town. Neither she nor Sam could yet speak Arabic, although they were learning it, but the soirée hardly called for intricate conversation. The wives wanted to examine all her possessions – the wide hats to keep off the sun, her long dresses with leg-of-mutton sleeves, her sewing, the crockery, even the two metal bedsteads in the tent. While all this was going on, Sam retired and sat under a nearby tree. Before the visitors left, Florence handed out small presents from the stores bought in Cairo. It was her first performance as the 'Sitt' – the lady of the English traveller. For his part, Sam was intrigued by the amount of perfume used by Arab women and claimed he could smell a party of them from a hundred yards away when downwind. He noted down how they crouched naked over a sunken fire containing incense, and held out their robes like a tent over the hole to capture all the fragrance.

Before leaving Berber, Sam reached his fortieth birthday. But the diary ignores this unwelcome landmark, the day's entry only saying briefly: 'Packed up but camels not ready.' There is, however, a note about twenty-eight pieces of luggage left for Petherick – who was travelling several weeks behind them – to take on to Khartoum. The Welshman was to express some chagrin about this mountain, which included three portmanteaux, seven deal cases and three barrels of gunpowder; but it would have been impossible for Sam to take so much along the rough tracks leading to Abyssinia.

As they followed the course of the dried-up Atbara river, their journey was little better than during the march across the desert. Shaking off an attack of malaria, Baker wrote that the only moment he enjoyed was in the morning, while having his bath; he envied the camels their ability to endure such harsh conditions. Watching the way they ate the roughest of foliage, he decided that they would breakfast luxuriously off 'a copy of *The Times* and a walking stick'. Once again, Florence was broken down by the weather; now she also had fever. One morning as they neared the Egyptian outpost of Cassala, she suffered a paroxysm brought on by the heat and malaria. Sam laid her on the sand under a tree, and sat watching for several hours until she collected the strength to be helped on to a dromedary. Later he sketched the way they travelled – Florence sitting pensively on her camel with one hand under her chin, while he sat scowling on his animal with his fingers thrust into his belt.

But at last the weather was changing with the approach of the rains. Baker noted that the wild geese had paired, birds were busily making nests and a cool wind was blowing from the south. It was then that they reached a place named Sofi, where Sam decided to set up a camp on the banks of the Atbara, which was now in full flood. Here, for five months, he and Florence were to have their first home in Africa. In appearance, Sofi was not prepossessing, and its history was far from happy: the old town had been destroyed by Egyptian troops – a final act of revenge against local tribesmen for having killed a general and all his retinue in the night by setting fire to bales of straw stacked around his tent. As soon as they knew Baker was not Egyptian, the townspeople gave him and his entourage an amiable reception.

For the equivalent of two shillings (slightly under £2 today), he bought a circular house and had the roof transported on the shoulders of thirty men to his selected riverside spot. The walls were erected, made of sticks and plaster, and the thatch lowered on to it. Florence was delighted with this abode, fourteen feet in diameter. The two travelling bedsteads were set up under their green mosquito nets, and on a dressing table covered with a piece of chintz she laid out brushes, scent and a mirror. Other possessions were put in baskets hung from the ceiling; a table used for dining and writing stood against one wall. Sam arranged his eleven guns and sundry pistols in a rack facing the door. 'In the course of a week we had formed as pretty a camp as Robinson Crusoe himself could have coveted; but he, poor unfortunate, had only his man Friday to assist him, while in our arrangements there were many charms and indescribable little comforts that could only be effected by a lady's hand.'

Around their house, they laid out walks of white sand leading down to the river and planted beds of wild flowers. Sam made a table and two chairs from bamboo. The paths were marked out with stones and rocks – one of which was big enough to be used as a seat. Sam carried it alone, showing off the strength he so revelled in. 'My vanity was touched by the fact that it required two Arabs to lift it from the ground.'

There was one European already at Sofi – a German stonemason named Florian Mouche. He had come to Africa with a party of Austrian missionaries, then decided to live out in the wilds, shooting and selling skins and tusks for a living. In the previous season, he told Baker proudly, he had killed more than fifty hippos in the Atbara river. But the guns he used were of poor make and in bad condition. He had paid the price for this when one exploded, blowing off his thumb. The loose flesh and pieces of bone were cut away by Florian's African servant. Baker remarked drily that the whole hand would have most likely been amputated 'had he enjoyed the advantage of European surgical assistance'. Another German, Johann Schmidt, stayed from time to time with Florian; he was a carpenter who had also deserted the missionaries for the attractions of wandering in the Ethiopian foothills. In his isolation, Florian was glad to see the two newcomers, with whom he could sit and talk in his native tongue.

For a while, the new arrivals merely revelled in their new-found comfort. But Sam gazed through his telescope – given him by Admiral Murray in Piccadilly – at the animals across the river, and made his plans for hunting expeditions. Already he had shot several hippos, watching with cool curiosity the way they tumbled over and over after the bullets hit them, then sank to the bottom; after several hours they would rise, distended, to the surface, where they were hooked by the local people and dragged to the river bank to be cut up. Fascinated by the way everyone fought for the best steaks, Baker made a bloodthirsty sketch of a typical scene. He and Florence soon began to appreciate the flavour of hippo meat and the fat was used for all their cooking.

The array of game around the Atbara seemed infinite. Huge herds of giraffe came down to the bank to drink at dawn and dusk. Crossing the river was easy, using as a ferry the large tin bath that was part of their impedimenta. Baker shot several of the giraffe, then felt a certain remorse.

After lions had roared all night near the camp, he and Florence went out to look for them, she carrying the little double-barrelled Fletcher. But the lions were deep in a thicket, crunching the bones of a newly-killed buffalo. It was impossible to get a shot at them there and they would refuse to be lured out. Far more forthcoming was a hyena that ventured right into the tent when Sam and Florence were on an expedition. In the darkness, she leant across and tugged at the sleeve of his nightshirt; the hyena was silhouetted against the moonlight. Taking hold of the Fletcher, which lay loaded between the beds, Sam sat up and shot the animal dead.

But a hyena was a far cry from the ultimate prize. One day, Baker was visited by a group of men whom he was longing to encounter. They were Hamran Arabs, famed for hunting elephant and other large game while armed only with swords and shields. They sat with Baker, admiring his guns and showing him their razor-sharp swords, which they used two-handed when tackling an elephant. Their host listened to them telling of their experiences and felt 'exceedingly small', for when it was a matter of getting close to a quarry he had now met his match – the Hamran *aggageers* confronted every kind of beast in the manner of antiquity, without the aid of rifles. He had never dared face anything more than a wild boar in such a fashion: the Hamrans made his feat in killing the stag in Glen Tilt seem insignificant.

One of the visitors was badly lame, having fallen on his sword while at close quarters with an elephant and cut himself right through his kneecap. 'There is a freemasonry among hunters,' Baker wrote afterwards, 'and my heart was drawn towards these *aggageers*. We fraternized on the spot . . .' It was agreed that when the weather was right he would join them in the open forest-land to the south. There they would show him how they chased an elephant to bay, then jumped from their horses to slash the tendons of its back legs, so incapacitating it for the kill. They might also lead him to buffalo or rhinoceros. So much the better.

Sam spent the rainy months making notes about the people and animals of the region. His diary is broken up by sketches of animals, insects, fish, swords, lances, musical instruments and maps . . . While he was fishing, Baker would carefully study the habits of the monkeys, how they called to him with a special cry, to find out who he was. Having watched them digging, he concluded: 'If a monkey could only light a fire he would be a reasonable animal.' Florence had a pet monkey called Wallady, whose antics were endlessly amusing. There was also a tame toad to which they grew attached. It lived in one of Sam's shoes and ate up all the white ants in the hut, so that it became 'immensely fat'; it was so much a part of the family that it would come out of the shoe to be stroked.

When any creature had been shot, it likewise became an object for study. The diary relates how after killing a bustard, Sam opens it up and finds the stomach contains scorpions, large ants, various beetles and a lizard. A dead hippo is disembowelled, then Baker stretches its intestines out on the ground: they measure thirty paces. Everything must be diligently measured – a camel is 7′ 3½″ to the top of its hump, the sword of a local sheikh is 3′ ½″ long, 1⅞″ wide.

One drawing in the diary is a self-portrait, showing Sam's workaday clothes made by Florence. He has short trousers, drawn just below the knee with cords, and a short-sleeved shirt tied at the front. The cotton was dyed with the brown juice of mimosa fruit. Around his calves he wears laced gaiters to keep off the thorns; Florence had made them from supple gazelle leather. An accomplishment upon which Sam prided himself, apart from cooking – 'I make a very good kind of half-pudding, half-cake with doura flour, eggs, milk and hippopotamus fat' – was cobbling shoes. He completed four new pairs from the skins of animals he had killed, as well as repairing all their old shoes. He gave the most attention to a venerable pair of brogues in which he had walked over the Highlands.

The entries in the diary about people vary widely, according to the degree of aggravation some recent encounter has provoked. 'These Arabs are the most lying, perfidious, mean, dirty scoundrels on God's earth. They are all alike, therefore it is no use kicking the posterior of an individual.' But soon afterwards he gives one of his servants the money to go on a pilgrimage to Mecca. Everyone is delighted and the man comes to kiss Sam goodbye. 'I was sorry to lose him,' says the note in the diary.

Exasperation followed when another of his servants, Achmed, was forcibly operated upon for a swelling in the groin. Attracted by shouting and screaming, Baker found Achmed biting, kicking and struggling while a knife was being wielded around his genitals. 'Great doctors are the Arabs – dogs are treated for distemper by being thrown from the top of the house to the ground.' Even more dramatic was the method of immunizing dogs against rabies: one night Sam and Florence jumped up from dinner on hearing a fearful howling and barking, to discover that all the dogs in the village had been tossed into the flames of a hut that had been set alight. 'As I approached, first one and then another dog ran screaming from the flames, until a regular pack of about twenty scorched animals appeared in quick succession, all half mad with fright and fire.'

But if Baker thought little of the local medical techniques, he soon acquired a great reputation himself as a *hakim* or doctor. He seems to have treated most minor ailments with laxatives from his box of specifics, and found it rather agreeable that the villagers esteemed him for being a 'master of their bowels, as I set them going and stop them at will . . .'

A trickier challenge was presented when a hunter named Jali with whom Baker was friendly was brought in with a broken thigh. The injury was caused by an elephant, which trod on him after he had fallen from his horse. After setting the thigh, Baker began making splints from branches found on the river bank. He chose one piece of wood that reached from under Jali's armpit to just beyond his foot, and another that fitted along the inside of his broken leg. Florence collected cloths and made nearly two hundred feet of bandages, a layer of which was then swathed around his body from shoulder to hip, and down to his feet around the broken leg. The trusting Jali was next encased in more bandages soaked in gum from the mimosa tree. When the gum dried he was held stiff, as if in a rigid armour plating.

After keeping an eye on his patient for several days, Baker had a bed rigged up on a camel. In this, Jali was carried to his home village.

Six weeks later he sent a message to say that he had been cut out of his bandages and was ready to go hunting again.

When women came to Baker for treatment, it was usually for barrenness. He would give them a few pills and tell them that the gift of children was the will of Allah. In his diary, the habits and appearance of the local girls commanded Baker's regular attention. He was likewise interesting to them – to test his reactions they would bathe naked in the river in front of him. More than game to play his part, Baker would commission them to collect small fish which he could use as bait, and they would spend hours chasing and screaming at the water's edge. 'I have only seen one woman,' wrote Sam, 'with really well-developed calves and thighs.' Such limitations did not deter him from keeping an appreciative eye open for 'handsome Abyssinian girls' or a 'very pretty' servant who washed the clothes by dancing naked on them.

He learnt that in the Sudan the vagina of a small girl was often sewn up to leave only a small hole, both to ensure chastity and to give her future husband greater satisfaction. At a time of childbirth, the mouth of the vagina was cut open to its full size, then resewn soon afterwards. Later, he was to discover much more about this practice, whose horrific cruelty obviously fascinated him.

There is a greater subject to which the diary frequently returns: slavery. Everyone they met had a retinue of slaves – the country depended on the system. For Sam and Florence, memories of Widdin were now well in the past, yet only the merest chance had saved Florence from becoming the property of some bey or pasha, lost for life behind the veil of Islam. Here all around were slavery's victims. In Sofi, they rented a woman called Masara to grind corn. The monthly fee for Masara was one Maria Theresa dollar (a large coin, minted in Vienna, used as currency throughout north-east Africa and roughly at par with the US dollar). Masara had a daughter, a good-looking girl of eighteen. 'This woman's love for her daughter is delightful to witness; her daughter is the moon in her long night of slavery. Without her, all were dark and hopeless.'

When another woman servant was acquired for thirty-five dollars and given her freedom, she imagined that Baker was buying her as a wife, so threw her arms around him and kissed him eagerly. Florence looked on as he disentangled himself and explained that she was only wanted as a cook. This new member of the expedition's

54

labour force came from the Galla, a tribe whose women were greatly sought-after as slaves. Baker's description of them does not merely reveal a lot about his feelings, but is an example of his flair for vivid writing:

'I visited the establishments of the various slave merchants; these were arranged under large tents of matting, and contained many young girls of extreme beauty, ranging from nine to seventeen years of age. These lovely captives, of a rich brown tint, with delicately formed features, and eyes like those of the gazelle, were natives of the Galla, on the borders of Abyssinia, from which country they were brought by Abyssinian traders to be sold for the Turkish harems. Although beautiful, these girls were useless for hard labour; they quickly fade away and die unless kindly treated.

'They are the Venuses of that country, and not only are their faces and figures perfection, but they become extremely attached to those who show them kindness, and they make good and faithful wives. There is something peculiarly captivating in the natural grace and softness of those young beauties, whose hearts quickly respond to those warmer feelings of love and that are seldom known among the sterner and coarser tribes. Their forms are peculiarly elegant and graceful – the hands and feet are exquisitely delicate: the nose is slightly aquiline, the nostrils large and finely shaped; the hair is black and glossy, reaching to about the middle of the back, but rather coarse in texture.

'These girls, although natives of Galla, invariably call themselves Abyssinians and are generally known under that denomination. They are exceedingly proud and high spirited and are remarkably quick at learning. At Khartoum several of the Europeans of high standing have married these charming ladies, who have invariably rewarded their husbands by great affection and devotion. The price of one of these beauties of Gallabat was from twenty-five to forty dollars.'

The passage sheds light on the racial nuances of the time. For all Baker's feudal methods with servants – his tendency to 'admonish them with a little physical treatment' – strong bonds grew up with those who stayed with him throughout the months of wandering along the Abyssinian borders. An especial favourite was a high-spirited young Arab called Bacheet, who fancied himself as a hunter and would often accompany Sam on expeditions. Once he was given a double-barrelled pistol to chase an aggressive bull hippo from one side of a river to the other, where Baker was lying in ambush with a rifle. After shouting at the beast with no effect, Bacheet scrambled down the steep bank and fired the pistol at close range, but missed – the sound so annoying the hippo that it snorted and made for its attacker. Bacheet fled up the bank, to roars of laughter from a crowd of onlookers – including Florence – on the far side of the river. From the top of the bank Bacheet fired his second barrel at the hippo, which was eventually cozened into a position where it received a fatal shot from Baker behind the ear.

Bacheet was also trained to wait at table, where he committed a *faux pas* that much diverted Baker – whose action in eventually devoting almost a page of a book to the anecdote tells a lot about Victorian attitudes and sensibilities. It happened at a time when a plague of flies made mealtimes difficult, because the cups and glasses were continually full of struggling insects. Wishing to be helpful during one breakfast, Bacheet put his fingers in Florence's teacup and hooked out several flies, dead and alive. Sam remonstrated, telling him to use a teaspoon, but to wipe it first to make sure it was clean. Next morning Bacheet 'suddenly took a teaspoon from the table, wiped it carefully with a corner of the tablecloth, and stooping down beneath the bed most carefully saved from drowning, with the teaspoon, several flies that were in the last extremity within a vessel by no means adapted for a spoon. Perfectly satisfied with the result, he carefully re-wiped the teaspoon upon the tablecloth and replaced it in its proper position.' Bacheet was rebuked for being an 'ignoramus' and an 'impossible animal', through not knowing a chamber-pot when he saw one; but otherwise the incident was treated as splendid fun.

Although Bacheet's grasp of the way to deal with flies may have been a matter for ridicule, he was to prove himself more assured with elephants. The moment for him to act as bearer of the huge muzzle-loader nicknamed the 'Baby' came at last, when Baker was to accompany the fearless Hamran *aggageers* in hunting the vast herds south of Sofi. In preparation, clothes were dyed in colours that would merge with the scrubby forests of the elephant country, and Baker checked his armoury. In the course of these operations he carefully inspected a rifle sent out for him to Egypt by Valentine. Although made by a famous London company, the weapon aroused Baker's suspicions because of its heavy recoil; he decided to make a test with a maximum charge of gunpowder, by tying the gun to a tree and firing it with a long fishing line attached to the trigger. When the line was pulled the rifle burst into fragments, destroying the stock up to near the shoulder plate; anyone firing it with a full charge would have been killed instantly.

The adventures with the *aggageers* confirmed to Baker that their courage was unparalleled. He had learned, in Ceylon, to steel himself as an elephant advanced head-on, to wait until the huge beast was upon him, then put it down with a shot through the forehead. Yet on the first hunt in Africa he was incredulous and appalled to watch his companions jump from their horses, sword in hand, and attack a huge bull about the legs while one rider dashed to and fro to distract the animal's attention. The *aggageers*, for their part, were delighted to have a well-armed white man in the hunt, and were so confident of his ability to kill anything that at the first opportunity they drove a whole herd to where he and the German mason, Florian, were standing.

Then Baker made his alarming discovery – the African elephant could not be stopped by a forehead shot from any gun that he possessed. (The only exception would be the huge 'Baby' – which the Arabs called 'Child of a Cannon'; but this had just recently jumped out of Baker's hands on being fired and hit him so hard in the face that his nose bled profusely.) The knowledge that the skull of an African elephant was heavier boned might have been valedictory, had not repeated hits induced the leader of the herd to turn aside, with the rest following. Even so, Baker was able to mark up five kills in the day, with Florian scoring one despite his reliance upon a decrepit single-barrelled gun 'so fond of shooting that it was constantly going off on its own account'.

(Baker prophesied that calamity would ultimately befall Florian unless he used better weapons. Some years later, he was to be proved right, when Florian was killed by a lion which embedded its claws in his skull.)

Sam and Florence began to travel on horseback with the *aggageers* into country never visited before by Europeans. On these journeys, watercourses were carefully mapped and geographical points marked by instruments and dead reckoning. There were also constant adventures on these trips.

One day, during the march, the Arabs captured two young baboons from a large troop by chasing them across open ground,

57

then picking them up while still mounted. They did this to amuse Florence, but as soon as the captives were tied up they began thrashing them with strips of bark from a mimosa tree. Sam vainly appealed to the Arabs to stop, for in his terms it was distinctly not fair play, but they explained that it was the only way to make the baboons *'miskeen'* (humble). Finally, Florence brought the whipping to an end, so with the animals bound and slung and flung in front of their captors' saddles, the march continued. Half a mile later, Baker saw among the trees a large antelope, which he shot and wounded. One of the *aggageers* then pursued the animal and cut its throat after hamstringing it.

The antelope was being skinned when the distant cry of buffalo was heard. Hurriedly, the hunters set off, leaving Florence and a few men in a clearing with the baboons and antelope carcass. In the attack on what proved to be a large herd of buffalo, the delighted *aggageers* managed to capture alive a half-grown bull, which they would keep in captivity until they could sell it to the agent of some European zoo.

The mêlée turned some of the herd towards the clearing where Florence was waiting. When Sam galloped back, she was standing with a rifle to her shoulder, while a bull buffalo stamped the earth fifty yards off, preparing to charge. At the sound of horses' hooves, the animal turned and disappeared into the trees. As for the baboons, one had slipped from its bonds while unwatched and the other had strangled itself in a struggle to follow suit.

After nine months of travelling, during which Baker also had his first encounters with lions and rhinoceros, the country of a chieftain named Mek Nimmur (the Leopard King) was reached. Operating from a mountain retreat, Mek Nimmur waged guerrilla warfare against the Turkish forces in the Sudan, as his father had done before him.

Although Mek Nimmur was reputed to be a dangerous brigand, Baker was eager to meet him and sent a message to say so through a party of the chieftain's men. The meeting with them occurred by chance, for while on their way to raid for cattle they rode down into a dried-up riverbed where Sam and Florence were encamped. After some initial wariness, Mek Nimmur's followers grew more trusting and went back to their leader with the white man's gifts. A few days later, a musician arrived to welcome the strangers into the Leopard

King's domain, which was 'the asylum for all the blackguards of the adjoining countries, who were attracted by the excitement and lawlessness of continual border warfare'.

The musician himself astounded Baker by an immaculate and dandified appearance in such wild surroundings. He rode on a snow-white mule and wore skin-tight white pantaloons, looking at first as though he had 'forgotten his trousers, and had mounted in his drawers'. The king's musician carried a large umbrella and wore two silver-mounted pistols in his belt. Playing on a kind of violoncello called a *rababa* – of which Baker made a careful drawing in his diary – the visitor sang a long paean in praise of Baker, recounting many bold deeds never in reality performed: one of these was the rescue of Florence from a tribe which had kidnapped her – a feat during which the carnage was immense. 'He sang of me as though I had been Richard Coeur de Lion,' wrote Baker, who was less pleased when one of the Arab hunters said it was the custom to pay heavily for such musical tributes. After relinquishing a handful of Maria Theresa dollars, Sam gave short shrift to a second musician who arrived a few hours later to repeat the performance.

The meeting with Mek Nimmur, under a large tamarind tree, was something of a disappointment. He turned out to be extremely dirty and unkempt, and complained of an illness which Baker recognized to be syphilis. While they talked, a horse stood ready saddled nearby in case Egyptian troops might appear and the Leopard King should be forced to flee for his life. Baker offered to take peace terms to Khartoum, towards which he was just about to head. Mek Nimmur declared himself ready to promise that, if he were left in peace, his men would never again raid west of the Atbara river.

Now began a trek down from the highlands, towards the Blue Nile. As the lower altitudes were reached the heat grew intense and swarms of insects covered everything. It was impossible to eat without swallowing flies. The diary becomes dotted with savage references to Baker's dislike of Africa and how he wanted to get away from it. Perhaps he was preparing himself for news that Speke had completed the 'Search for the Nile', leaving nothing more to be done in the south. Certainly, if Speke were on schedule, he should now have got to Khartoum. But as they neared the junction of the Blue and White Niles, where Khartoum lay, a messenger arrived from Petherick: there were still no tidings of Speke.

The messenger did bring letters, however, from England, so Sam sat with Florence and read the news of his daughters, of Valentine – commanding officer of the Tenth Hussars – and the other members of his family. He told her as well about two major events in the outside world. In America, the Civil War was raging. In Britain, the Queen's consort, Prince Albert, was dead.

CHAPTER 5

The Gateway to
Black Africa

In all the world there was no town of consequence more remote than Khartoum. Its sheer existence, 1500 miles southwards from the Mediterranean, was a phenomenon shot through with contradictions. Although it was an assertion of Ottoman sovereignty far inland along Africa's greatest river – even beyond Khartoum itself, to the very limits of geographical knowledge – few Turks ever ventured there. The place had been founded through the imaginative resolve of a brilliant Albanian careerist, Mehemet Ali, who earlier in the nineteenth century sought to make all the lands bordering the Nile his personal fief. Nonetheless, the men who exercised power from Khartoum over the Sudan – a huge, largely unmapped region with no firm frontiers – were always known as Turks. Most of them were in reality Armenians or Circassians, men from those races whose acumen and subtlety bore them to the top in so many of the domains paying allegiance to Constantinople.

When Sam and Florence reached Khartoum in the middle of June, 1862, they were unprepared for the revelations awaiting them about the ways in which the 'Turks' made use of their authority. They were soon to discover why it suited Khartoum so well that only a handful of outsiders found their way to the town every year – and those mainly European big game hunters, not prone to asking awkward questions. They little expected what they would find, because in those parts of the Sudan where they had spent the past year Turkish authority was limited to military sorties for levying taxes or putting down rebellions.

Baker concluded that the Sudanese they had met so far were argumentative and 'saucy', but culturally intriguing – and sometimes personally admirable. He had made firm friends, for instance, with a sheikh aged eighty-five who always ate two pounds of butter a day and was still physically a Hercules. It impressed Sam that the sheikh was just taking a new bride of fourteen. 'There may be a hint here for octogenarians' was the diary's comment on the butter.

Another sheikh was judged noteworthy because of his social habits. He sat on a divan and occasionally 'relieved the monotony of his position' by grandly lifting up the carpet to spit under it, then blew his nose on his fingers and wiped them on the wall 'which bore the marks of similar handwriting in innumerable places'. But in the evening the sheikh sent his visitors a splendid meal. Such Arabs displayed a combination of courtesy and extreme haughtiness which Baker thought one would only see in England on the stage; it rather took his fancy.

There was one significant bond between these country people in their dusty villages and their feline rulers in Khartoum – that of religion. Anyone able to say in Arabic 'There is no God, but God, and Mahomet is the Prophet of God' qualified as a believer and could not be enslaved: that fate was reserved for infidels, such as blacks and Christians.

Since Khartoum stood at an ethnic watershed between the Arabs and the African tribes, those of the latter race encountered until now by Sam were all slaves, transported up from the south. They seemed rather like the Irish peasantry, good-natured enough when contented, but ready to cut your throat without compunction if they coveted your property.

Had he never gone to Khartoum and so learnt at first-hand about all the horrors it spawned, Baker's comfortable judgements on the Sudanese *status quo* might have stayed intact. He had been briefly touched, of course, by the plight of such people as Masara, the woman hired to grind corn – nor could he forget how close Florence herself once was to being sold into bondage. But Florence was white; he felt that blacks were well suited to slavery, through being inherently inferior. Even though it was distasteful to be offered a black man for £20, and to learn that a woman, if ugly, could be bought for £5 – the price of a donkey – the case for 'benign slavery' had not been demolished by what he had seen during the first year of his African travels.

62

Yet if Khartoum was about to transform the preconceptions of a lifetime for Baker, that did not mean he would start regarding black men as his equals. Such an idea was a fallacy propounded by missionaries and liberals: even Charles Dickens could rebuke Harriet Beecher Stowe, author of *Uncle Tom's Cabin*, for 'making out the African race to be a great race'. What Khartoum did was to reveal to Baker how slavery must always spread an evil miasma, poisoning all who came in contact with it.

For all that, to a newcomer approaching across the desert or by river, the town showed a deceptively agreeable countenance. Its white-walled houses, surrounded by palms and tropical fruit trees, were scattered along the verdant water's edge. The skyline was broken by the pinnacle of a minaret and the triple domes of a Coptic church. Dominating the panorama was the palace occupied by the Turkish governor-general and nearby stood the army barracks. There were many boats to be seen, for despite being a three-months journey from Cairo, the town's position at the meeting-place of the greenish mountain waters of the Blue Nile and the muddy, mile-wide expanse of the White Nile had over the years enticed a polyglot community of merchants.

In Arabic the name Khartoum means 'elephant trunk', after the shape of the narrow spit of land where it was built. The link with Africa's greatest wild creature was fitting – because it was upon ivory that the trade of Khartoum was originally sustained. The early traders fanned out, to east, south and west, in search of the tusks so eagerly demanded by Europe for making ornaments and billiard balls. Sometimes they took their own hunters along with them, but mainly they relied upon bartering with the African tribes for their stores of tusks. They might also deal in gum, ostrich feathers, and skins. Khartoum was renowned as a collecting point for another commodity the outside world was avid to buy – living wild animals to fill the zoos.

Underpinning every such activity was one about which the Khartoumers would deny knowing anything, although all played a direct or indirect role in it. Slavery was dictated from the very top, because the Turkish rulers needed constantly to re-stock the Khartoum military garrison, eight thousand strong; malaria, plague and other endemic maladies caused a one-in-three wastage of men every year. What more appropriate way of keeping up the strength

63

could there be than enslaving the Sudanese natives? It was an established tradition. Twenty years before, Mehemet Ali had told one of his first governors-general in the Sudan: 'You are aware that the end of all our effort and expense is to procure Negroes. Please show zeal in carrying out our wishes . . .'

Drilled and disciplined by a nucleus of ferocious Balkan mercenaries, the troops well knew their fate if they tried to desert. To keep them content, as a substitute for pay, they themselves could capture slaves and do with them what they would. There was nothing in the Koran to debar a slave from owning a slave.

Such niceties were not at once apparent to Baker. What at first affronted him was that 'Old England' seemed to have so little standing in the place. The doyen of the European community in the town was unquestionably Georges Thibaut, an elderly white-bearded Parisian who had been trading in the Sudan for almost forty years. Thibaut had somehow remained immune to the diseases that regularly wiped out his rivals; he wore Turkish clothes, was a confidant of the governor-general, and nobody dared offend him. In the past he had enjoyed moments of fame, as when he took to London the first giraffes ever seen in Britain and marched them through the East End from the docks to the Zoo. But now Thibaut was content to bask in the honour of having just been made French consul for the Sudan. 'A man of honour and experience' was how the despatch to the Quai d'Orsay from the French consulate-general in Egypt had described him while recommending the appointment. His days of adventuring on the White Nile were past, but at the right price there was nothing he could not arrange in Khartoum.

The francophobia aroused in Baker by Thibaut's supremacy was the proper emotion at that time for any patriotic Englishman. There was a passionate belief that France was conspiring to destroy British influence throughout the lands of the Nile. The very symbol of French ambitions was the Suez Canal, now being built by Ferdinand de Lesseps, a cousin of the French Empress Eugénie; the frenzy induced by the canal was expressed by the magazine *Punch*: 'Great Britain will indeed, become Little Britain; her Eastern commerce will be annihilated . . . The sun of England will set forever . . .'

Sam's misgivings had been aroused the moment he and Florence arrived at the British consulate, which was John Petherick's house. It was a large rambling place, distinguished only by a crudely-

painted lion-and-unicorn crest over the door. Inside, it most resembled a menagerie, because an Italian collector of wild animals
had left there a lion, a hyena, two wild boar, an antelope, two
ostriches and several lesser creatures; these were all tied up in
various courtyards. Looking after the establishment was Petherick's
former mistress, a local woman now relegated to the rank of house-
keeper. The consul and his new English wife, Katherine, were gone.
In the course of a long and affectionate letter to 'dear Val', Sam said
that he had heard that Petherick was paid £400 a year as consul. If it
were true, every patriotic Englishman had a right to grumble. On
the other hand, since Khartoum was so far off the beaten track, perhaps it did not matter much that the consulate was so primitive.

Although dismayed by the consulate, Sam was perhaps also
relieved that the Pethericks were now somewhere far to the south
on the White Nile. (They had reached Khartoum by the Nile route,
and left again, while he was in the east.) It saved him from having
to explain the precise status of Florence, whose existence he never
mentioned in his various letters to the consul. Petherick would doubtless have taken the broad view; with his wife, the reaction might
have been very different. In one letter, Baker had asked: 'Will Mrs
Petherick accompany you up the White Nile?'

Kate Petherick, a woman of diverse talents and considerable spirit,
was not the type to be left behind. Also with Petherick were two
young doctors. One was a Scot, James Murie, recruited in Britain
for the expedition; his work as a naturalist was notable enough to
have earned him a footnote in Darwin's *The Origin of Species*,
published three years earlier. The other doctor was an American,
Clarence Brownell, who had been lingering uncertainly in Khartoum
with vague ideas of walking across Africa, until being invited to
join Petherick's party.

Reports from the traders coming back down the Nile said that
Petherick was having an arduous time. The winds upon which he
must rely to carry his sailing boats against the current were now
blowing in completely the wrong direction, from the south.

Petherick was paying the penalty of dallying too long in Khartoum,
and so missing the north winds. His Sudanese crews were also paying
the penalty, because they were having to drag the boats with ropes
from the river banks. Not long after Sam and Florence reached
Khartoum, news arrived that Petherick's slow, rain-sodden progress

had claimed its first white victim: Brownell had died of malaria, and been buried beside the Nile, his grave marked by the metal plate that once had been outside his surgery in East Hartford, Connecticut.

Without the advantage of Petherick's guidance, Baker was cautious in reaching any conclusions about the Khartoumers and their methods of acquiring wealth: 'Pages might be written on the slave trade of the White Nile, but I am silent until I become a witness ...' Yet for all his anti-Gallic prejudices, it was a French traveller, Guillaume Lejean, who first pulled back the curtain.

When Lejean arrived in Khartoum a few weeks after Sam and Florence he was on his second visit, and had a mandate from Emperor Napoleon III to make a full report on the Nile regions. He took this duty very seriously: a wiry, deeply-tanned man of thirty-five, formerly a consul in one of the Red Sea ports, he had quarrelled with his counterparts in Egypt because they did not seem to be giving him enough co-operation. He wore a short pointed beard and liked to stand Napoleon-style, with one hand in his coat. Patriotically, Baker's first comment in his journal on Lejean was: 'Looks vermin.' However, they soon became friends, and later Lejean was highly complimentary in his own writings about the Englishman. He praised Baker as a 'lively conversationalist' and capable traveller, who had achieved the feat of living for a year on the Ethiopian borders without losing either his own skin or that of his *'jeune et très-jolie femme'*. The Frenchman was so taken with Florence that he could not resist recounting an apocryphal story about this 'valiant and devoted Hungarian' – how she had saved Sam with a lightning shot from her rifle, just as he was going to be disembowelled by a rhinoceros at which he fired and missed. But it was only a tale he heard second-hand, admitted Lejean, so he could not vouch for it.

What Lejean said about all he saw on his previous trip– which had taken him as far up the White Nile as boats could go – was in contrast expressed in unequivocal, pungent terms. He told of captives from many different tribes being brought northwards in vilely crowded boats; sometimes the death-rate on the journey reached 50% and the survivors might be sold for as little as £2 a head. From Khartoum, those slaves who were not pressed into service locally would be shipped down the Nile to Cairo and from there to all parts of the Ottoman Empire.

The traders grew ever more rapacious. At the end of every year, when the wind blew from the north, armadas of boats would set out from Khartoum. The more successful operators had *vakeels*, or headmen, who would be left with groups of armed followers at encampments along the river. These bands would make raids against the local tribes, seizing men, women and children. Sometimes they would round up vast herds of local cattle, the sole wealth of the riverine tribes. The animals would only be handed back if a chief could produce a set number of slaves – so driving him to make war upon his neighbours.

The goal of the most venturesome slave ships was Gondokoro, which Lejean had visited; a few miles beyond this last mark on the map the White Nile raced through cataracts that barred any further advance. Ten years earlier, Austrian Catholic missionaries had boldly sailed to Gondokoro and established a mission there; but they were long since gone, because the mortality among the priests from malaria had proved unbearable. All that remained as monuments to their sacrifice were the mission church, with a huge cross above it, and lines of lemon trees whose fruit lay neglected on the ground. It was said that the Austrians had not made a single convert.

The traders following in the wake of the missionaries had made the outpost a sink of viciousness. The surrounding Bari tribe, once friendly and trusting, were now notorious for their treachery. The Bari women loitering around Gondokoro were prostitutes, its men would commit any crime for alcohol.

'The missionaries should have taken away their cross,' said Lejean, 'for since they left it has only seen the scum from Khartoum.' When he visited Gondokoro a Maltese trader, Andrea de Bono, was there. His welcome was hardly friendly, and Lejean soon realized that an impartial observer was considered an enemy. De Bono was sufficiently notorious on the Nile that some word of him had even filtered back to London, to the offices of the Anti-Slavery Society; although for the moment the society's energies were almost entirely taken up with events in the United States, it publicized what little it could discover about the Sudan slave trade.

However, De Bono could feel relatively safe from interference, because although as a Maltese he was a British subject, he was in a business partnership with Ahmad el-Aqqad, the government recruiting officer in Khartoum. According to Lejean, the boat De Bono regularly used, the *Zeit el Nil*, was a 'real stud-farm'; every man aboard kept one or more Negro concubines.

Lejean had asked De Bono about the slave trade; he denied any personal involvement, and even claimed that he wanted to organize a private army to wipe it out. His nephew, Amabile Mussu, was more brazen. Although only twenty, Mussu inspired fear all along the river. Once, while trading with a petty chief, he was enraged to hear that a rival Khartoumer had tempted him with a better offer. Mussu ordered his eighty armed followers to round up all the men in the village and bring them as captives to the boat. Once there, they were held hostage until their families bought their freedom with pieces of ivory hidden in their huts. Finally, one man was left whose family could find nothing to offer for him. Mussu cut off the man's hands, nose, tongue and genitals, made a necklace of them, then freed his mutilated, but still living, victim.

Lejean had many similar stories about other traders. One visited an old chief who did not recognize his loaded gun for what it was, but mistook it for an Arab pipe. The chief asked if he might smoke the 'pipe' and put the end of the barrel in his mouth. The trader was amused; he ordered one of his men to bring a piece of live coal, set off the charge of gunpowder, and blew the African's head off. Then there was the fellow Frenchman who had told Lejean that, after quarrelling with a favourite black concubine, he ordered her to be given six hundred strokes with a whip. 'I can assure you that she could not walk for months,' he boasted.

After Baker had been for several weeks in Khartoum he began to realize the truth of all Lejean had said. He wrote in his diary: 'As the water of a river deposits its impurities upon meeting the salt waters of the sea, so we find the dregs of the human race at those points where savage life receives the pollution of semi-civilization.' He complained of never seeing any Khartoumer reading a book, nor with anything more instructive in his hand than a cigarette and a glass of absinthe. The 'European community' was all-male, for none of its thirty or so members – with the unique and recent exception of Petherick – had a white wife. In the Turkish manner they kept a retinue of African girls who raised their children after their own tribal customs.

What Florence thought of this dissolute society is unknown, for nothing that she may have written at the time has survived. But later she branded the slave traders as 'fearful scoundrels'. She said bitterly: 'I really hate the sight of them, whenever I see one of them it reminds me of olden times.'

The traders clearly had much in common with the Turkish administrators; for example, life tended to be short for both of them. Despite the shimmering greens, yellows and blues of their embroidered robes, the elaborate rituals with which they ran their affairs, the rulers of the Sudan were doomed men, and knew it. Most had been sent there from Egypt as a form of banishment, for over-blatant corruption or some other offence, and feared they must stay in that hot, unhealthy place until they succumbed to some disease. Understandably, they did not trouble themselves unduly with their appointed tasks: if an animal, a donkey or a dog, died in one of Khartoum's rubbish-laden roads, it lay where it fell, until it was putrescent and black with flies. Justice was only fitfully administered, and then in most brutal fashion.

A punishment for which Khartoum was infamous involved putting an offender in a cell for several days with a group of Albanian soldiers – who were said to enjoy such practices – to be incessantly sodomized. The Turks in Khartoum could satisfy their sadism and lust in most unbridled ways, and male homosexuality was openly practised. The local governor gave a letter of protection to the town's best-known male prostitute when his own brothers, out of shame, threatened to cut his throat.

Shortly after Sam and Florence established themselves in the British consulate – as Petherick had suggested to Sam in a letter – a new governor-general arrived from Cairo with an escort of 1800 soldiers. A former Circassian slave, Musa Pasha Hamdi 'combined the worst of Oriental failings with the brutality of a wild animal'. Unlike some of his more indolent predecessors, Musa was avid for acquiring wealth by any method and sent out raiding parties to all points of the compass from Khartoum to levy extra taxes. When Baker went to pay his respects to Musa, he proudly took with him a map of the rivers along the Abyssinian borders and presented this to his host. Lejean commented acridly: 'Musa would have preferred it if Baker had given him a young Abyssinian girl.' When Mek Nimmur's peace offer was mentioned, it was rejected out of hand.

At the end of Baker's visit, the governor-general remarked that a sale of mules was about to take place at the entrance to the council chamber and invited him to attend. While the auction began, there was a knot of spectators, wondering how the wealthy Englishman, who was known to need animals for his coming expedition, would react to Musa's blandishments; the onlookers included Georges Thibaut. Baker later described in his diary what happened: 'No person bidding except a government officer and myself, I soon discovered that I was being "run up", the mules being government property – at length when I bid 210 piastres the Governor himself shouted "215!". Well done dignity, when the Governor-General of the Sudan sells his own donkeys in public. Of course, I ceased to bid, and no one else attempting a purchase not one mule was sold and they were led away; the only "sell" being the Governor himself. The miserable assumption of importance of these Turkish officials, combined with their pettifogging grasping after piastres, was thus ludicrously displayed in public.'

But if Musa enjoyed small success with Baker, he was managing to extort vast sums from some far wealthier new arrivals in Khartoum. Indeed, these playthings of the pasha's avarice were the richest Europeans the Sudan had ever known. What is more, they were women, unaccompanied by any males except a few complaisant menservants. Their presence alone made 1862 an extraordinary year in the Sudan, white women having rarely ventured there before – and now there were five, counting Florence and Katie Petherick. The 'Dutch ladies', as they were called, dumbfounded the Khartoumers less by their femininity than by their readiness to fling money around.

They consisted of Harriet Tinne, a widow aged sixty-three, her spinster sister, Adriana van Capellan, and her beautiful and wilful daughter, Alexine Tinne. Old Madame Tinne had been left a huge fortune by her husband, an Anglo-Dutch merchant whose wealth came from West Indies sugar. She was a baroness in her own right. Alexine was her only child, with an inheritance that made her a millionairess by twentieth-century standards. It had been Alexine's idea, after an unhappy love affair, to travel up the Nile, and despite the heat, the mosquitoes and the strangeness of it all, her mother seemed to enjoy the journey. In a letter to the Queen of the Netherlands, a close friend, she told how she was relishing the 'damn-me don't care sort of life'.

When the Tinnes had first reached Khartoum they could not find a suitable house to live in, so they made their own encampment beside the river. The first person to visit them there, even before the tents were erected, was Thibaut. Whatever they might want during their stay, he said, they should let him know about. As the representative of France, he was at their service. Harriet Tinne was enchanted, for the Netherlands had no consulate in Khartoum to which they might turn for advice; the British consul would undoubtedly have been helpful, because she was a British subject through the nationality of her late husband, but he was absent. She was also fascinated by Thibaut's resplendent Turkish attire and his attentiveness; he even seemed able to use the barge of the Khartoum governor when he came to the camp.

Alexine was suspicious of Thibaut and would not speak to him, but her mother overruled her. Thibaut organized matters quite effortlessly and took the ladies to meet all the most important Turks. Life in Khartoum did seem amazingly expensive to Mrs Tinne, but the French consul was meticulous in producing the bills. Even in Egypt, she had noted in her diary, 'money flew so fast there was no keeping account'. The Tinnes were never deterred by the cost of what they wanted, and hearing that the first steam-powered vessel ever seen in Khartoum had just arrived, they stopped at nothing until it was hired for their use.

One sadly sceptical onlooker at their activities was Lejean. In his subsequent writings he carefully avoided naming his compatriot, but said that Alexine (whom he rightly regarded as the driving force of the expedition) had surrounded herself with *coquins* (rogues) who had extorted money mercilessly. He recorded that the Tinnes travelled with 'royal luxury' in the Sudan, spending the equivalent of 450,000 francs. This had added enormously to the problems of more modest expeditions up the Nile.

Lejean recounted how Alexine paid 'an exorbitant price' to buy the freedom of the slaves aboard the vessel of one Khartoum trader, then wept with rage when they fled without expressing any gratitude. 'A great ignorance of the black, little better than an animal,' he observed bleakly.

It is to Harriet Tinne that we owe another early pen-portrait of Florence. She wrote in her diary: 'A famous English couple have arrived. Samuel and Florence Baker are going up the White Nile to find Speke. They have been travelling in Ethiopia and I hear she has shot an elephant!! She wears trousers and gaiters and a belt and a

blouse. She goes everywhere he goes.' As with Lejean and the
rhino, Harriet was wrong about the elephant. She was also making
a generous assumption about Florence's status – but Khartoum was
certainly not a place where anyone would take too close an interest
in their neighbour's marriage lines.

It was only by chance that Harriet was still in Khartoum when
'the famous English couple' made their appearance. Her Egyptian
cook had developed an abscess on his throat when the steamer was a
few days south of Khartoum, so she had put her sister and daughter
ashore at a trading station, and brought him back for treatment.
Harriet was eager to be off again and noted in her diary that she
feared Baker might ask for a tow from the steamer.

This worry was unfounded, for it was to take Baker almost six
months to make ready for the White Nile journey. He and Florence
were still in Khartoum at the end of November, 1862, when the
Tinnes and their astounding retinue – including several ladies'
maids – steamed triumphantly back after a 2000-mile round trip to
Gondokoro. Nothing much had gone amiss for them, except that
their most reliable janissary (guard) had fallen overboard and
drowned. Being of a literary turn of mind, they wrote a poem about
him – and another, nine verses long, relating their various adventures
on the White Nile.

Baker was inclined to view the Dutch ladies with a mixture of
jealousy and masculine superiority. Although far from poor, he
could in no way rival the casualness with which they spent money.
With wages in Khartoum at their existing levels, he could not afford
to employ more than fifty men to go with him up the White Nile,
and everyone declared this to be inadequate if he intended to press
through the warlike tribes beyond Gondokoro. The way in which
Harriet and Alexine behaved tended to compound his troubles by
inflating prices. There was also the possibility, absurd as it might
sound, that the Tinnes were his rivals in exploration. In a letter
home to his brother John, he said: 'They are bent upon discovering
the source of the Nile. They must be demented. The young lady is
now by herself with the Dinka tribe and the mother goes up by
steamer tomorrow. They really must be mad . . . all the natives are as
naked as the day they were born . . .'

He mentions that Alexine Tinne, now facing such unmentionable
hazards in the Dinka country, is only twenty-four (in fact, twenty-

seven), but forbears to add that he is about to take into even wilder parts a girl of barely twenty-one. Yet he was secretly anxious on that score, noting in his diary that the Tinnes had all been afflicted with fever: 'A dangerous climate for ladies to travel through.' Perhaps he felt in some degree reassured that Katherine Petherick was staying the course, despite the appalling mishaps which – according to boats returning from the south – the consul's expedition was still experiencing. For some unaccountable reason, Petherick had turned aside when within 150 miles of Gondokoro and begun a march westwards through swampland, towards a lonely depot where he maintained a team of ivory traders. In the rainy season, it was an action that invited disaster.

In other ways, Petherick was also courting trouble. On the voyage south he had arrested two slavetraders, put them in irons and sent them back to Khartoum to be tried. Such behaviour was unheard of, and the whole trading community was in uproar. It was one thing to express, for the benefit of outsiders, your distaste for slavery, quite another to put in jeopardy a fellow Khartoumer's livelihood. Petherick had never shown any strong feelings about 'the trade' until now, but on making him a full consul the Foreign Office had ruled that all cases of slavery must be firmly dealt with: the appointment of which he was so proud was putting him in a quandary for which he lacked the necessary adroitness.

Baker was quick to gauge that Petherick was overreaching himself. 'There is a direct conspiracy against him,' he wrote. One man the consul had clapped into irons was his own agent, an Arab named Abd el Majid. He was coming downriver after leaving supplies in Gondokoro for the long-awaited Speke, met his master and was found to have slaves hidden below decks. On his arrival in Khartoum the prisoner was immediately freed on the orders of Musa, the governor-general. The second man arrested by Petherick was the notorious young Maltese, Amabile Mussu; he was also released, at the request of Thibaut, who stood security for him. It seemed to Baker typical of the pervasive corruption in the Sudan that the French consul should obtain the freedom of a British subject imprisoned by the orders of his own consul. What he did not mention, and probably did not know, was that the Maltese was Thibaut's putative son-in-law – a fact that made Petherick's behaviour even more reckless. Swiftly, the tables were turned with a document accusing Petherick of slave-trading himself; almost all the Europeans in Khartoum put their signatures to it.

Although Baker was sorry for his compatriot – far out of reach and unaware of what was being contrived against him – the furore was certainly adding to his own headaches. Few men wanted to go with him up the Nile, because of the sudden hatred of all things British; it was much more rewarding to be hired by someone ready to tolerate some measure of freelance slaving and cattle-raiding when the chance arose. Even his interpreter and major-domo, Mohammed, who had been with him ever since Cairo, now deserted to join a party of slave-hunters. Baker was not especially sorry to see him go, because of his tendency to hide whenever there was trouble or danger; nonetheless, it was a disagreeable portent.

Baker became so worried that he even sent a letter to Colquhoun in Egypt, asking if the authorities there might be persuaded to allocate him a troop of soldiers and two boats. Colquhoun was on leave in Scotland, but his deputy, Saunders, took the matter up – without much optimism. In a despatch to the Foreign Secretary, Lord Russell, he explained: 'I could hardly hope that the local government would be willing to afford such assistance to a private traveller . . .' He was right. The Egyptian prime minister, Cherif Pasha, said he thought 'le Capitaine Baker' should be able to get everything he wanted in Khartoum. Cherif brushed aside the argument that it would be impossible to win the friendship of the tribes south of Gondokoro if one had to rely upon an escort of 'the reprobates as are usually engaged by the ivory hunters of Khartoum and who practise slave hunts systematically'. The Egyptians, and beyond them their titular overlord, the Turkish sultan in Constantinople, were perfectly content for the moment to leave matters as they were in the Sudan. At a time when the British consul in Khartoum seemed bent on causing trouble, they were not going to lift a finger to help one of his compatriots, who might further disrupt the indispensable supply of black slaves.

At the start of a long letter to Wharncliffe, written two months after arriving in Khartoum, Sam said he was awaiting the monsoon, due in October, and expected to be in Gondokoro, en route for the equator, by the end of November. That schedule was quietly forgotten, and as the weeks slipped by, he and Florence fell into a routine for occupying the hot, heavy hours in the middle of the day when nothing moved in Khartoum. They would sit in the main court-yard of the consulate, on a shaded platform called a *rakooba*. Florence would do her needlework, while Sam occupied himself with cleaning his many guns and the trophies of their year's hunting – heads, tusks, spears, African musical instruments, skins, the feathers of rare birds . . . Many of these must be sent home before the next stage of their journey.

There was also much correspondence. Sam wrote five long letters to Admiral Murray, 'The Skipper' in Piccadilly, giving detailed accounts of his adventures so far; politely, he remarked how useful he found for spotting game the telescope Murray had lent him. He knew Murray could be relied upon to pass on his news to everyone who mattered. He drafted a letter to *The Times*, and 'The Skipper' saw to its publication (25 November 1862); it attacked the 'wretches of Khartoum' for being 'infatuated with manhunting', called them 'banditti' and said their atrocities were beyond description. Its angry tone must have startled some of his friends.

Another record of what had been achieved so far went to the Royal Geographical Society; a sample of wild cotton was also sent to the society, because Baker was fully conscious of the fears pro-voked by the American war that Britain might have to find new sources of supply for its textile mills.

The hiatus in Khartoum also gave time to record all the facts that could be harvested locally on African geography and the customs of the people. At last, Sam was able to learn everything he wanted to know about the traditional methods for constricting the entrance to a girl's vagina. He devoted a column of his closely-written diary to the excruciating details. 'Thus do these beastly savages mutilate themselves,' he ended, 'not only to ensure chastity before marriage, but to increase their lustful desires afterwards.'

Lejean was probably the source of this information; his stories were described in the diary as '*piquante*'. When he left Khartoum during October, to head in the direction of the Red Sea, social life became even more trammelled. Such unexpected diversions as occurred generally came from the animal kingdom – especially from a variety of huge black ant that infested Petherick's home: 'It bores up through the earthen floors and suddenly takes the room by storm, running up one's trousers and stinging like a wasp.'

One day a larger assailant appeared while Sam and Florence were

sitting on the *rakooba*. After a commotion outside where the wild
animals were kept in pens, a wall suddenly collapsed and a boar
lurched through the dust. It had broken out of its sty. After survey-
ing the courtyard it charged towards the platform. Sam reached out
for the only weapon within reach – the massive horn of a rhinoceros
he had shot some months earlier. It weighed about ten pounds and
he held it in both hands until the boar began to mount the steps.
From a range of a few feet he hurled it at the animal, hitting it
straight between the eyes – so that it rolled down the steps, stunned
and kicking convulsively. Servants then ran up, tied the boar's legs
with ropes and dragged it away to be locked in a storeroom. 'I was
rather proud of my shot,' wrote Baker, 'as I seldom threw a stone
at an enemy without hitting a friend by mistake . . .'

By early in December, the consulate was even more noisy and
smelly than on their arrival six months earlier. Sam was now
assembling his transport animals for the expedition: twenty-one
donkeys, four camels and four horses. Also being accumulated were
untidy heaps of stores, including ten tons of grain.

At last he had recruited forty-five men to form his escort and was
holding gun-drill every day to 'bring them into discipline'. It was
satisfying to have a private army, so much so that Sam designed
uniforms for the men and had these run up by a local tailor. In the
diary he painted an illustration in watercolours of how a *choush* –
'non-commissioned officer' – would look: a brown cotton shirt and
jacket, with red facings as a mark of rank, and a brown felt cap; the
wide trousers came just below the knee in the Turkish manner.

Yet despite the uniforms and the drilling, it was plain that such
men would be fiendishly hard to control. Baker threw a party for
them, with a huge amount to eat and drink, to put them in a good
humour, and paid the usual five months' wages in advance. 'They
promised fidelity and devotion, but a greater set of scoundrels in
physiognomy I never encountered.' So he was pleased by the appearance in Khartoum of the German carpenter, Johann Schmidt,
whose companion Florian was still hunting in the Abyssinian foothills. When Schmidt expressed a readiness to join the expedition,
Baker at once signed him on.

The German showed himself energetic and practical, until suddenly
his health gave way. He lost weight and began coughing, so that
Sam and Florence urged him to think again about making the

journey: it seemed as though he was developing some type of 'galloping consumption'. But Schmidt would not be deflected. The climate of Khartoum did not suit him, he insisted, and a change of air, on the White Nile, was exactly what he needed. That could be true, decided Sam and Florence as they went on with their packing.

Baker hired a sailing boat and two barges for carrying his force to Gondokoro. Masts to bear the British flag were nailed over the sterns. The forty boatmen hired to take the vessels to the south and bring them back to Khartoum were solemnly warned against any temptation to pick up slaves.

Everything was ready. Baker now made his will. He left money to Florence, so that if he died and she managed to find her way back to Khartoum, she might have a chance to extricate herself from the dangers that would confront her there. The will was witnessed by Petherick's consular agent, Hallal el Shami, an Egyptian whom Sam decided was one of the few honest men in the Sudan. But like Johann Schmidt, the young Egyptian was suffering from chest trouble; he kept sneezing and 'stuffing his nose' with large doses of powder from a box. Sam noticed the label on the box: 'Warranted not to misfire. Patent anti-corrosion percussion caps.'

The date of departure was 18 December 1862. It was a lucky day, according to Arabic belief, but after the animals had been taken on board an official suddenly arrived from the office of the governor-general. It was announced that before the three boats could leave, a toll must be paid for every person in them. Baker at once ordered the British flags to be hoisted and retorted that he was neither a Turkish subject nor a trader. If any officials tried to detain him, he would throw them into the water. The challenge was not taken up, and Khartoum was soon lost to view.

CHAPTER 6

Rendezvous in Gondokoro

While his boats with a strong wind behind them pushed their bows into the current of the White Nile – its colour reminiscent of an English horse-pond – Baker's imagination also sped under full sail. His vision was of a stirring rescue, in which he played the hero's role. Somewhere on the equator, so he fancied, John Speke was in a tight fix, surrounded by savages. In his hour of need, Speke could never dream that succour was coming from Sam Baker, the man he had last seen nine years before on a steamer from India to Aden; and the sight of a pretty woman among his relief force might fairly make Speke doubt his eyes.

Admittedly, in this phantasm Sam's mind was leaping far ahead. There was a journey of several weeks, at the very best, to Gondokoro, followed by hundreds of miles of wild country to the equatorial forests where the Nile sources were said to lie. The sombre possibility was inescapable, that it might already be too late to rescue Speke. Africa seemed to have swallowed him up since he left Zanzibar in the autumn of 1860, a time when Sam and Florence were only just making their way from Constanza to Constantinople. At the latest, he should have appeared on the Upper Nile a year ago – emerging into the Sudan from the lake regions like a genie from a bottle.

Also, what of Petherick, the bearer of orders from the Royal Geographical Society to place supplies at Gondokoro for Speke, then to push on southwards to look for him? It might now be that Petherick was likewise dead, together with his wife and all his party. A report reaching Khartoum as Baker was about to leave said the expedition had been wiped out in the swamps by hostile tribesmen.

That was quite possibly a lie – yet who could tell in such a country?

In his letters home, Baker had talked of being 'as strong as a horse' after nearly two years in Africa, but he knew it was a risky boast. The ever-present threat was malarial fever, which attacked him every few weeks with varying intensity and once or twice had prostrated Florence so desperately that he feared for her life. The Austrian consul in Khartoum, Dr Josef Natterer, finally succumbed to it only two days before they departed. The further south you went the more virulent the malaria seemed to become: out of seventeen Catholic missionaries sent to Gondokoro, fever had claimed fifteen. At that period, quinine was just being introduced as a remedy; its value was limited.

In hopes of avoiding the 'bad air' of the swamps bordering the river – which was often more than two miles wide – Baker ordered that they must always anchor at nights in midstream; although he did not realize the significance, this also lessened the attentions of the true assassins, the mosquitoes – the 'nightingales of the Nile'.

As though to emphasize how death was always lurking Johann Schmidt grew steadily weaker, so that within a few days of sailing a note of alarm creeps into the diary entries: 'I much regret that I allowed Johann to accompany me from Khartoum; I feel convinced he can never rally from his present condition.' Christmas Day was passed in gloom, as Baker made notes about the scenery: dead trees reared up from the stagnant water, with solitary cranes sitting on the branches; water plants drifting with the current became jammed together into green, mushy islands on which the spectre-like storks voyaged from unknown lands. The country all around was flat and uninteresting – the only reason for going ashore was to collect firewood; Baker would use the iron sponging-bath as a rowing-boat to do this job.

As 1862 neared its close, the life of Johann ebbed away. Florence sat beside his bed, hour after hour, talking to him in German. He spoke sometimes of Krombach, his home village in Bavaria, but he had no relations still alive. Johann was bleeding from the lungs and Baker took his turn to sit beside the bed in the cabin of the *dahabiah* and bathe the dying man's face. Flies sometimes walked across his glazed and unseeing eyeballs. Early on New Year's Eve, 1862, as he tried to talk he repeated the name of his village, then spoke his last words: *Ich bin sehr dankbar* – 'I am very grateful.' Baker made a cross from the trunk of a tamarind tree and beneath it in the moonlight the German carpenter was buried. The account of Schmidt's death in the diary has a heavy border inked in around it.

Enveloped in melancholy, the three boats renewed their journey southwards. Day followed day with little to relieve the tedium. At night, Baker would stand on the deck and listen to the barking of dogs in distant villages, the snorting of hippos . . . He wanted nothing more keenly than to have this part of the journey completed, because he hated thinking of his horses, camels and donkeys being confined in the boats. He was also irritated by the lack of skill shown by the sailors in handling the square sails of the boats. When they tried to tack in the meandering river, it usually meant being banked on the lee marsh, after a great deal of shouting and screaming. Still, he would be relieved of the sailors after landing at Gondokoro and persuaded himself that, despite the loss of Johann Schmidt, his private army of forty-five men was 'knuckling under'. This he attributed partly to his own show of physical prowess just after leaving Khartoum, when he had clouted the Sudanese captain of a boat which collided with one of his craft and smashed its oars.

On the matter of violence, Baker entirely disagreed with Francis Galton, a luminary at the Royal Geographical Society, whose manual of advice for travellers in foreign parts said that personal strength was unnecessary for maintaining command. 'I believe it adds more to the success of an expedition than anything, provided it be combined with kindness of manner . . . I am not sure that this theory is applicable to savages exclusively.'

By now, both Sam and Florence were also over a hurdle that once had so impeded them in making the most of their followers – they could speak Arabic, in a rough and ready fashion. Moreover, Florence possessed an ally who reported to her every day what the men were talking about and where their grievances lay. His name was Saat, a black boy aged about twelve who had attached himself to her in Khartoum.

Saat's story was an exemplar of all the anarchy and suffering caused by slavery. He came from a place he called Fertit, and there, at the age of six, was captured by Arab raiders while watching his father's goats. One of the raiders put him in a sack on the back of a camel, with the warning that unless he stopped screaming his throat would be cut. Eventually, at a trading station on the Nile, he was sold, then taken to Cairo to be put in the army as a drummer-boy. The army rejected him as too small, but before the dealer decided what next to do with him, Saat ran away to an Austrian mission house. He was given asylum, gained a rudimentary education, then was sent back up the Nile to Khartoum. From there he was despatched to yet a third mission, nearer to his home; but in six months most of the white priests were dead of malaria. With the survivors, Saat returned to Khartoum, where he was put in a Jesuit 'school' with small African boys from all over the Sudan. This first attempt at Christian education in the Sudan soon withered, because the Austrian teachers found that their pupils learned nothing and stole everything. It was decided to turn all the boys loose to fend for themselves – the Austrian missionaries by this time despairing of salvaging anything from a bold endeavour that had cost them huge sums of money and a terrible toll in lives.

Once more in peril, Saat was clever enough to flee into the British consulate. While Florence was pouring tea in the courtyard, Saat suddenly appeared and knelt beside her. He begged to be taken on as a servant. The boy was put in the charge of the cook, for there was a quality about him that made it hard to tell him to go away. Next morning Sam and Florence took him to the mission, which said he had been the most honest boy in the place.

So Saat was accepted as part of the retinue; soon he was to become something more, because Florence adopted him almost as her own child. She made his clothes, taught him to sew, and gave him lessons every night after dinner. Saat's qualities outweighed his looks: according to a mention in the diary he had a mouth rivalling a crocodile's and when he ate soup it 'vanished like water in the desert'. Years later, Sam was to recall: 'We were very fond of this boy; he was thoroughly good.'

Six years in mission hands had produced a wide gulf between Saat and the blacks encountered when stops were made at waterside villages south of Khartoum. The appearance of such peoples as the Nuer and Dinka made Sam bring out his pencils and paints. His first real encounter with an African chief came when the *dahabiah* was visited by a Nuer chief named Joctian, accompanied by his wife and daughter, wanting presents. They were given bracelets and beads. 'The women perforate the upper lip and wear an ornament about four inches long of beads upon an iron wire; this projects like

81

the horn of a rhinoceros; they are very ugly.' Joctian sat proudly while his host drew a picture of him, sitting on the divan in the cabin of the boat. Sam asked him the purpose of a spiked iron bracelet – at which the chief pointed proudly to scars on his wife's back and arms. This information gave the impetus for a diatribe in the diary about the 'poor blacks' and their deluded supporters in England. 'He was quite proud of having clawed his wife like a wild beast,' writes Baker, who speculates that Florence's pet monkey must be more civilized than the chief. Yet the utter poverty of the Dinka tribe stirs his sympathy: 'I have never pitied poor creatures more than these destitute savages. Their method of thanking you for anything is by spitting on your hand.'

There were moments when the blacks could stir feelings other than disgust and pity. The diary contains an account of seeing a good-looking young daughter of a Dinka chief, completely naked, with 'everything exposed'. The word 'everything' is underlined. Baker noted that few girls wore more than ornaments around their hips that tinkled like bells. There was silence, however, about the naked Dinka men, whose appearance has always astounded travellers.

A month after leaving Khartoum, the expedition had sailed beyond the Dinka regions and was three-quarters of the way to Gondokoro. By taking observations of the noon sun, Baker calculated the position as 6° 39' north of the equator. For some days his boats had been in convoy with those of a Circassian, Khurshid Aga, a former officer in the Turkish army. Khurshid lived in some style and sent presents across the water to his European travelling companions; he was also one of the most relentless slave traders in the Sudan. Before long the convoy passed the point where the Pethericks had abandoned their ships in the middle of the previous year and set off eastwards; there was still no news of them.

The boats came, on 23 January, to the last guttering embers of Austrian evangelism on the Nile, the station of St Croix. It was in charge of a tired, embittered, lay missionary, Franz Morlang. He came from the Dolomite Alps, and although still in his early thirties had worked for eight years in the Sudan. A letter delivered by Baker confirmed his orders: to close St Croix and return to Khartoum. The grand design encouraged by Emperor Franz-Josef himself was ending in unrelieved failure. Morlang was momentarily cheered by the arrival of 'Herr Baker with his wife, donkeys, camels, etc.' He also welcomed the slaver Khurshid Aga, to whom he sold the entire mission estate – mainly mud huts and a graveyard – for three thousand piastres (£30). What caught Baker's eye was a horse which had belonged to a German baron, Wilhelm von Harnier. The baron, a daring sportsman, had been killed shortly before by a buffalo which had trampled him to death, and he lay in the mission cemetery with the ill-fated priests. Baker bought the horse, which he decided to call 'Priest'. In recording in his diary that the horse had fetched a thousand piastres, Morlang asserted that the purchaser was Scottish; perhaps before going ashore at St Croix, Sam had donned his kilt – a garment he occasionally put on when keen to make an impression. Although Morlang's record of their meeting is brief, Baker carefully noted the Austrian's verdict on his erstwhile black charges: 'Utterly unfeeling, ungrateful, idle, lying, thieving ...' On the other hand, Morlang branded the traders as robbers, who 'pillaged and shot the tribespeople as they chose'.

During the two days Sam and Florence were at St Croix, there was much talk about Petherick, whom both Morlang and Khurshid Aga knew well. (Khurshid had been on the scene when the consul had arrested the young Maltese, Amabile Mussu.) There was scepticism about Petherick's claim to have travelled down the western side of the White Nile all the way to the equator; that was four hundred miles beyond Gondokoro. Taken together with Petherick's inexplicable behaviour since leaving Khartoum ten months earlier, these conversations did much to lower him in Baker's estimation. The Circassian might have reason enough to damage the consul, but this was scarcely the case with Morlang.

The frankness of the Austrian on other matters was startling, for over a bottle of wine he volunteered that the missions were really a pretext for spying out the country, in hopes of founding a Habsburg colony. This well suited Baker's aversion to Catholics in particular and men of the cloth in general. 'Well done, Jesuits!' he wrote. '*In vino veritas*. Bravo, humbug!'

In the last few miles before Gondokoro, the scenery suddenly changed. The Nile was flanked by steep hills, covered in evergreens, and the marshes were no more. Their mood lighter, Sam and Florence stepped ashore and arranged for the animals to be landed from the boats. It was 2 February 1863. Their first enquiries were about Speke; but he had not arrived and there was no reliable news of his whereabouts. This was alarming, for he was long overdue. Yet if he were still alive, and still trying to reach Gondokoro, now was the moment for him to appear, during the two months of the year when the winds bore the traders upstream from Khartoum to collect their cargoes. He would know that to come at any other time was to risk finding the place virtually deserted.

Their own elation at having arrived was soon tempered by a closer look at Gondokoro. It was 'a perfect hell', wrote Sam. The place was not a town, but a string of camps along the river in which the traders' roving bands would gather with their slaves and ivory and wait for vessels to take them downstream. Gondokoro was without a Turkish garrison and every crime, from murder downwards, knew no check.

It also stank. The thermometer registered close to 100 degrees Fahrenheit and the camps reeked of ordure, bodies and rotting food. Flies and rats feasted everywhere. The men in the camps diverted themselves by drinking, tormenting the slaves and quarrelling. All were armed and shooting affrays happened incessantly. A bullet from nowhere killed a boy sitting on one of Baker's vessels, hitting him in the head and scattering splinters of his skull across the deck. To terrorize the local tribes, prisoners bound hand and foot were now and then carried to a cliff and pushed over into the eddying river where the crocodiles waited.

People outside the slave trade were unwelcome in the place. Sam and Florence discovered that large groups of slaves were being held in forest camps until the white newcomers were out of the way, and then would be driven down to Gondokoro for shipment. If an inquisitive Englishman stayed around too long, then a seemingly accidental shot could remove the hindrance. The boy whose skull was shattered might be an augury.

Yet it was impossible to leave before getting some definite news of Speke. The first clue came in a report brought from the interior by a group of Africans, that two white men were being held as prisoners by a distant black king. The white men had wonderful fireworks, but both had been very ill; perhaps one was dead.

There was surely a kernel of truth in this tale, since it told of *two* white men: Speke had with him, as his assistant, another army officer, James Grant. How to reach them now presented itself as a greater conundrum than Baker ever expected, because the tribes to the south of Gondokoro were so goaded by the traders that any traveller was sure to be identified with them and attacked. Repugnant though the idea was, Baker's best hope seemed to be to attach his force to the large private army of the trader Andrea de Bono; this was expected in Gondokoro soon and would return to its advance camp – somewhere towards the lakes – after depositing ivory and slaves for shipment to Khartoum. From de Bono's camp, the way forward was across a *terra incognita*, to African kingdoms whose tenuous links with the outside world were not northwards, down the White Nile, but south and east to the Indian Ocean.

Baker could not decide where John Petherick might fit into this scheme of things. He and his party had not, after all, been annihilated in an ambush, if the reports in Gondokoro could be trusted. These said that the consul was somewhere due west, across the river, but making slow progress. All the whites with him were thought to be sick. Moored beside the river bank was a handsome *dahabiah* that Petherick had sent down from Khartoum a year before to await Speke; some of the men encamped beside it were preparing to go off and search for the missing consul. But what had he been doing? It seemed extraordinary that the Pethericks had still not arrived in Gondokoro, despite having set off even before Sam and Florence arrived in Khartoum.

Sam decided to send off an encouraging letter with the men going to look for Petherick. Among other news, he told how the Tinnes were planning to make another expedition and hoped to reach the equator by way of a place called Mundo: 'There should be a public house built on the equator, where travellers could stop for a glass of beer: it is becoming a fashionable tour.'. He followed this piece of whimsy with solicitous enquiries after the health of Kate Petherick, who he felt sure must have had a trying journey through the rains. There was no direct mention in the letter that Sam had Florence with him – just an oblique hint in the closing sentence: 'I cannot tell you our disappointment upon arrival at Gondokoro at hearing that you were still astray.'

The feelings Baker had towards the consul at this time were undoubtedly mixed. It was Petherick who was charged with the duty of helping Speke – and £1000 had been raised by public subscription to sustain his efforts; so the most logical course would be, when Petherick's party eventually turned up at Gondokoro, to merge the two expeditions. The combined force could then set out to rescue Speke and Grant. However, on Petherick's dilatory performance so far, the chances of reaching them while they were still alive might not be good.

The temptation to seize the initiative began to grow in Baker's mind. It had always been his aim to travel further south from Gondokoro. If he now went off at the first opportunity, leaving Petherick to follow on as best he might, the honour of succouring the two explorers could be his. He had long harboured this dream.

Any imaginings Baker may have harboured of dashing off alone at the head of his rescue column, with all flags flying, crumbled one day when he tried to marshal his escort on the river bank. He knew they were mingling with men in the camps of the traders and braced himself for trouble as several of them asked for permission to make a cattle raid. He refused, at which the ringleader began to abuse him in front of all his colleagues. Enraged, Baker ordered that the man should be given twenty-five strokes of the whip. At once, sticks were picked up and the ringleader rushed at Baker. 'To stop his blow, and to knock him into the middle of the crowd, was not difficult . . .' Immediately, Baker found his theories about exerting physical authority put to a severe test, because forty men surrounded him.

Help came from a quarter Baker scarcely could have expected. Ill with fever, Florence had been watching the scene from the cabin of the sailing boat. She ran out, calling for help from the least mutinous of the men, and pushed her way into the middle of the crowd. Her sudden appearance made Baker's attackers pause – a chance of which he took advantage by telling the drummer-boy to beat a tattoo. Then he shouted at the top of his voice, 'Fall in!' Half of the men did so, the rest stood in a menacing group. Florence then appealed to Sam to forgive the ringleader of the mutiny if he would beg for pardon. This seeming compromise won the day; the men were dismissed from a parade that had so narrowly escaped calamity.

The diary entries are brief and terse for this period, but Baker later admitted knowing from this moment that his expedition was 'fated'. He did not accept failure, but saw how his earlier confidence was utterly misplaced. All his escort were Arabs, now his proven enemies. He could only trust Saat, a mere boy, and Richarn, another black with a mission background.

In this plight, relief of a sort came from the Circassian slaver,

Khurshid Aga. He had followed closely in the wake of Baker's vessels, and was now encamped some distance off. He agreed to sell three oxen to Baker; these were immediately slaughtered to give the mutineers a feast, in the hope of winning back their loyalty. It was a show of weakness rather than strength, but as the strips of meat were laid across the embers of their fires the men said they were ready to march wherever they were told. Even the ringleader swore he would stand in front of Baker if arrows were flying, so that his body would receive them first.

Franz Morlang was by now also in Gondokoro, taking a last look at the unkempt remains of the mission building there before turning around and letting his boat be carried by the current down to Khartoum. In his jaundiced frame of mind, the setback Baker had received could have come as no surprise.

Two more days dragged by. Sam filled the time by exercising the horses in the countryside near the camp, visiting villages and sketching. The people were undeniably hostile to what the traders were doing. While Baker was walking through the camp he heard chains rattling in the storehouse of a Copt whose father was the consular agent of the United States in Khartoum. On looking closer, he saw the depot was full of slaves. When the Copt had arrived in Gondokoro the American flag was flying from his mast: at a time when the Civil War was at its height, the irony was inescapable.

The oppressive waiting came to a noisy end in the early morning of 15 February, when a rattle of gunfire was heard in the south. This was the traditional style in which a caravan heralded its approach – probably the long-awaited force of ivory hunters in the pay of De Bono had appeared at last.

It was the ubiquitous young Saat who came running to Baker's boat with the exciting news. De Bono's men certainly had arrived – and accompanying them were Speke and Grant. The two explorers were at the moment being entertained by Khurshid Aga, whose camp was on the southern side of Gondokoro. But soon they would be coming on again, in this direction, proclaimed Saat ecstatically.

At these words, Sam leapt to his feet, sprang ashore and began striding along the river bank. He was elated, his head full of patriotic fervour: 'Hurrah for Old England!' A passage had at last been forced through the centre of Africa from the southern hemisphere to the north, and Britons had done it.

He hurried on in the morning sun, until at last he could see the two Englishmen in the distance. From a hundred yards away Baker could recognize the fair-haired Speke, at the head of a large group of people. He came steadily nearer, between the line of vessels moored to the river bank and the brick built remains of the Austrian mission house. Baker began to shout greetings and wave his cap in the air. Whatever else might befall, he knew that good fortune had borne him to the fore on an historic occasion. He ran with all his might.

Speke was no less overwhelmed. 'What a joy it was I can scarcely tell,' he was to recount, upon recognizing his 'old friend Baker, famed for his sports in Ceylon'.

After an exuberant handshake, Speke introduced his colleague Grant. Until Baker was quite close, both explorers had assumed his lone figure was that of Petherick, who had a large bushy beard much like the one which Baker was sporting; it was almost ten years since Speke and Baker had last seen one another, and in those earlier days Sam was still clean-shaven.

The two newcomers were at once invited back to the *dahabiah*, while Baker's men surrounded them with the smoke and noise of musket fire. Following along the bank were a score of black men and women, the tired survivors of the hundred-strong expedition which Speke had led inland from the East African coast more than two years before. It had plainly been a terrible journey – both white men bore every sign of total exhaustion.

But their spirits were now soaring. 'We could not talk fast enough,' said Speke later. Baker said jovially that they had arrived too soon – he had hoped to find them 'on the equator in some terrible fix', so that he could have helped them out of it. It was true enough, he heard, that the explorers had been held virtually as prisoners in the two biggest African kingdoms on their route. But at last, after skirting the great Lake Victoria and seeing the place where the Nile flowed from it, they had abandoned the river route and travelled due north overland until finally reaching De Bono's outpost. From there they were escorted on the last stretch of one hundred and fifty miles to Gondokoro.

But where was Petherick? This was one of Speke's first questions. For month after month, he and Grant had expected the consul to appear from the north and help them. Why had he failed them? The explorers had already put this query to Khurshid Aga, but not speaking either Arabic or French they were unable to make any sense of his reply. It was baffling to the overwrought Speke that his own countryman had not been waiting to meet them in Gondokoro, many months after the date agreed for their rendezvous. Still less had he come on towards the lakes. Baker explained that Petherick was even now on the far side of the river, where he had a trading encampment.

As they walked along and talked, Baker's men were still firing off their guns, one accidentally shooting a donkey: 'A melancholy sacrifice as an offering at the completion of this geographical discovery.'

Sam hurried his compatriots along to his boat, sat them down on the deck beneath a sun awning, and called for refreshments. Then came a moment of awkwardness as Florence was introduced. How it went off was recounted in a private letter some years later by Grant: 'Speke was utterly surprised to see a pretty woman with Baker, who had lost his *wife* a few years previously – and you can imagine that Speke made a blundering remark about this party – something to the effect that, "I thought your wife was dead." She was introduced to me as his *"chère amie"* . . .' If this was somewhat awkward for the three men, it must have been worse for Florence. All else apart, she was still feeling ill. Although Sam does not mention this in his diary, Franz Morlang was sufficiently concerned to write the following day: 'Mrs Baker continues feverish.' The Austrian played a part in entertaining the explorers, before taking leave of them three days later and sailing for Khartoum.

Speke had been anxious to hurry down the river as well, so that he could send a message to tell the world that 'the Nile was settled'. But he decided to wait so that he could make an observation by the moon to fix the longitude – for all his impetuosity, he was a stickler for scientific accuracy. His quarrels about geography with Richard Burton, companion of his former travels, made him especially careful. Moreover, Baker managed to persuade him that a modicum of rest was needed in Gondokoro: both the explorers looked thin and feverish; their clothes were dishevelled and Grant's bare knees were sticking through his much-patched trousers.

The two men spent hours pouring out the details of their experiences, in particular those at the court of the Bugandan despot, Mutesa. In many respects, Buganda showed a degree of organization rare in Africa, but it was barbaric in ways Speke could not start to justify – 'fond of the Negroes' though he confessed himself to be. Mutesa would order one of his many wives to be strangled for the most trifling offences. On ceremonial occasions, as when a king was crowned, scores of people would be done to death by burning. Mutesa was fascinated by guns, which he never knew of until the white men appeared. To prove their efficacy, a cow would be led into the royal presence every morning, for Speke to shoot it. By way of diversion, innocent bystanders were shot by courtiers.

The people of Buganda were described by Speke as being intelligent and handsome, especially the women. He told how they accosted him, eager to examine the strange white visitor minutely – and how he had walked arm in arm with Kariana, the pretty wife of an official of the court, as though they were 'strolling in Hyde Park'. He did not reveal quite everything about his relations with the opposite sex in Buganda: the accounts in his journal of an emotional relationship with a young girl named Meri, who shared his hut, were to be severely bowdlerized when Blackwoods of Edinburgh came to publish them. Speke certainly kept it a secret that he had fathered a child in Buganda . . .

As the travellers continued their story, they told how Mutesa at last let them go beyond Lake Victoria, northwards to a kingdom called Bunyoro, where they were harassed by its rapacious monarch, Kamrasi. Only after he stripped them of almost all their possessions were they able to make their way through uninhabited bushlands to De Bono's camp.

As Baker listened to these accounts, his mind was suffused with admiration, wonder and disappointment. Should he now simply go back to Khartoum? He asked Speke: 'Does not one leaf of the laurel remain for me?' It did: he could go and look for the lake called Luta N'zige ('Dead Locust'). It was known to exist, somewhere to the west of Lake Victoria, and Speke believed that the Nile flowed into it and out again. This was guesswork, however, since he and Grant had not followed the course of the river as they would have wished because of the obstacles put in their way by King Kamrasi. At their news, Baker's heart leapt. He handed Speke his own diary and made him write a three-page guide for finding the way to the mysterious inland sea; Grant, a skilled artist, drew a sketch-map, based largely on intuition and vague African reports.

Immediately, Baker's mind was made up. He would go to search for the Dead Locust Lake. His boats must return to Khartoum, because it was impossible to travel any further on the Nile – the rapids above Gondokoro ruled that out. Moreover, the tribes along the river beyond the rapids were reputed to be implacably hostile to the travellers; west of that section of the Nile were the Nyam-Nyams, notorious for their cannibalism. So the way south for Sam and Florence must be roughly over the terrain covered by Speke and Grant as they came up to Gondokoro, well to the east of the Nile's supposed course to the great lakes.

That route would lead to the river which Speke had named the Somerset Nile, after the English county where he was born and was intensely proud of. It ran, so Speke assumed, out of Lake Victoria (although he had not followed its course), flowing first north-west then more easterly towards the Luta N'zige which Baker hoped to discover. All this was, of course, not so much geography as speculation.

After crossing the Somerset Nile, Sam and Florence would be in the kingdom of Kamrasi – 'a sour, greedy African', warned Grant repeatedly. From him, permission must be wrung to travel on eastwards to the unknown lake. It would be a journey of several hundred miles, almost to the line of the equator. South from the lake there were rumoured to be some vast mountains, according to Speke and Grant.

Although Baker was some years older than his companions, they became, in those days at Gondokoro, closely linked. All were keen on hunting, and Grant – a normally undemonstrative Scot – shared Baker's enthusiasm for painting in watercolours.

So when Petherick suddenly appeared on 20 February, five days after Speke's arrival, there was little likelihood that he was going to be received on equal terms. By every yardstick he had shown himself to be a blunderer; but worse, he must now answer the suspicion that he had put self-interest before duty. Almost any other man but Speke would, in his own hour of triumph, have taken a generous view of Petherick's inept behaviour. That was not Speke's way however. He was pathologically vengeful.

Petherick's expedition had been through many tribulations. The false reports of its destruction might easily have come true. Yet Speke's greeting was sardonic, for although while they were together in London he had encouraged Petherick to go on with his trading while mounting a support operation, he now thought the consul's ideas of what mattered most were out of balance. To make matters worse, the young Scottish doctor, James Murie, was willing to speak out about what had happened during the march. When the expedition was *in extremis* Petherick had allowed his mutinous followers to go raiding for cattle; they seized two thousand animals from one tribe, although losing half of them while being ambushed by another. It also seemed that Petherick had turned a blind eye when some of his men took black girls as slaves. Perhaps the most sensational item was that Murie had, under instructions, boiled the severed heads of three Africans killed in a skirmish. The brains and skin were removed, so that the skulls could be sent home to be sold to the Royal College of Surgeons. This morsel was underlined for emphasis by Baker when he made notes in his diary of Murie's revelations.

The tragic figure in all this tale of failure and folly is Katherine Petherick. For her, the experience of a lifetime was about to end in calamity and tears. It had almost ended in death, for during the many times she was ill in those nightmare wanderings in the West Nile swamps, Murie once declared her beyond hope. When she reached Gondokoro she was so weak that her mind tended to wander; her clothes were in tatters, her skirt made from an old piece of red calico bought from an Arab. She wrote that when she looked in a mirror she hardly recognized herself.

Yet at the start she had been buxom and good-looking, with dark ringlets hanging down her cheeks. Kate Petherick was also a woman of varied talents: she could use a sextant, was well versed in natural history, and sketched with some skill. Although born in Malvern, Worcestershire, her father was a German, Sigismund Edelman. She was well into her thirties when Petherick led her to the altar, but the wait must have seemed worth it: before they left England her husband – because of his speeches on the Sudan and the public subscription for him to help Speke – became something of a celebrity. He had even been invited to Buckingham Palace to meet the Prince Consort. As for Kate, she was presented by Mr Holland, the Bond Street gunsmith, with the latest invention – a five-barrelled pistol.

Amid all the hostilities and cross-currents of those days in Gondokoro, she remained totally loyal to 'Peth', whatever his failings. In a series of piteous letters to her sister in Liverpool she chronicled what happened. The revenge taken by Speke for the consul's failure to meet him was simple and damning – he refused to accept aid of any kind from him, to make it appear that the money subscribed in England had served no useful purpose. Kate Petherick was quick to see the implications and went to Baker, pleading with him not to offer his boats to Speke for the journey to Khartoum. According to her account, Baker replied: 'Oh, Mrs Petherick, it will be a positive service to me if he goes to Khartoum in my boats, as the men are paid in advance and his will serve as escort and guard.' Weeping, she asked if her husband could give Speke and Grant some supplies, and Baker agreed. But when the goods were sent in baskets to the explorer, they were returned with a note: 'All the articles enumerated had been packed up by friend Baker.'

In an attempt to restore their position, the Pethericks invited Speke and Grant to dinner on their boat on Sunday evening, 22 February. Baker was also there, but whether Florence was among the guests is not clear. Kate Petherick recalled that she cooked a large ham brought out from England and during the meal tried to persuade Speke to accept her husband's aid. He replied, in a drawling voice: 'I do not wish to recognize the succour dodge.' She got up and left the table, knowing that her husband's reputation would be destroyed when Speke got back to England.

The role Baker played in all this is equivocal. During the days before Petherick appeared, he had poured all his own supplies on the impoverished travellers and offered them the use of his boats to go on down the Nile. He could well have withdrawn these offers after the arrival of the Pethericks, whose own *dahabiah* had been waiting for months at Gondokoro in charge of an Arab crew. He did not, presumably because it would have meant clashing with Speke, who had been implacably hostile to Petherick from the moment he reached Gondokoro and found the consul was not there to greet him. At the best of times, Speke found it difficult to pursue a logical argument – there was an element of instability in his family. Now he was in a mood of manic excitement. At the height of the quarrel in Gondokoro he found time to write a letter he would send off from Khartoum to Galton, the Royal Geographical Society official. In it he lashed out at Burton, saying he knew nothing of topography despite Speke's efforts to teach him: 'He gave up his lessons too soon.' He also declared that he would soon return to Africa and march across the continent from east to west: 'For unless I do it, it will not be done this century.'

Such arrogance made Speke impossible to argue with, and in the last analysis there was also an element of class pervading his row with Petherick. Yet even the relationship among the more gentlemanly companions was not without its difficulties. Speke and Grant had seen a great deal of Florence and were genuinely shocked that Sam intended to take her into the lands they had just traversed. She lacked even the indefinable protection of being a wife. As Grant was to put it: 'In talking over the matter with Speke I said, what a shame to have so delicate a creature with him. Speke thought so too and told Baker he really should marry her. Baker promised this when he would return to Alexandria.'

On his part, Sam extracted from both of them a promise that they would never mention Florence's existence when they got home. They more or less kept to their bond. Another person who would never mention the existence of Florence at Gondokoro was Kate Petherick. Many years later, in her published version of what had happened, there is not one word about the other white woman who was there. By then, Florence was famous and there was no need for secrecy, but her Victorian readers would have well understood the inference behind that silence.

Speke and Grant left Gondokoro ten days after arriving, using the boat in which Sam and Florence had been living. Everyone was there to see them off, even Kate Petherick. Well to the fore was Khurshid Aga, who had presented them with a case of wine and a box of cigars. They liked him – as did Baker, who thought he was a 'bold robber', much preferable to the run of 'toad-eating' Khartoumers.

The explorers gone, both Petherick and Baker weighed their tactics. The consul knew his one hope of recovering himself was to make some geographical discovery. He pondered the idea of pressing forward at once to the unknown lake, the Luta N'zige, by a route distinct from the one outlined by Speke. Baker likewise wanted to start immediately.

Both men soon found they were contending with every obstacle the slave traders could devise. They were not wanted further south, in the lands where such rich pickings were to be had, so every attempt to discipline their retinues provoked mutiny. It was Petherick who proposed that they might well combine forces to look for the Luta N'zige; Baker agreed, although he wrote in his diary that Petherick was too vacillating to trust.

As soon as the idea was mooted, the mutterings of rebellion were redoubled. Not one of Baker's men was willing to travel with the representative of Britain, the open enemy of the slave traders. If they could find a way, they would kill Petherick. The consul later admitted: 'The hue and cry was so bitter against me that, during our stay at Gondokoro, my life was certainly not a valuable one.' The Pethericks saw there was nothing left for them but to retreat to Khartoum, so a completely new proposition was put to Baker, for an elephant-shooting expedition in the north. He refused. 'To be beaten back is too much,' he wrote doggedly in his diary.

It was now obvious to him that his only way to break away from Gondokoro with at least some of his men was to join up with a trading party. He approached the leader of the group that had brought Speke northwards. Baker believed that once out of the chaotic country around Gondokoro and through to a place called Faloro, he could find his own way forwards. The leader agreed to have Baker's party, numbering little more than forty, attached to his own force, which was two hundred strong. This seemed an ideal solution, because his men could not pretend that they would be in danger of attack when in such powerful company.

But one morning, just before the agreed departure date, Sam returned to the tent after his usual inspection of the transport animals to find Florence looking pale and excited. She asked for the headman of the escort to be called and when he presented himself demanded whether the men were willing to march. The headman said they were. 'Then strike the tent, and load the animals,' she ordered. 'We start this moment.'

Sam listened in amazement, until she explained that the boy Saat had overheard the men plotting in the night and came to tell her at daybreak. They intended to desert with their arms and ammunition, to join the trading force. If Baker tried to stop them, they would shoot him. The leader of the force was a party to the plot: he was intending to set off two days early, to take Baker by surprise.

At this news, Baker ordered that a bedstead should be put outside the tent; upon it he laid five double-barrelled guns loaded with

95

buckshot, a revolver and a sharp sabre. He held a sixth gun and gave two more to Saat and Richarn. The camp drum was beaten and all the men were ordered to present themselves in marching order – with the locks of their guns tied up in the mackintosh wrappers that protected the powder from the rain.

Only fifteen men appeared and stood defiantly before Baker. Behind him stood Florence, who was watching for any man to remove the waterproof from his gun so that it could be fired. She would point him out, then Sam would shoot him immediately 'and take his chance with the rest'. After an ominous silence, Sam shouted in Arabic for the men to put down their guns. The men refused, at which he cocked his rifle. The men backed away and sat in groups of two or three under the trees. Taking advantage of their uncertainty, Sam sent Richarn to collect the guns, which were given up without argument. The fifteen men were dismissed, their papers scrawled with the word 'Mutineer' in English.

The net result of this alarmingly close shave was that Baker was left with little more than a score of men; they were the ones who had not come forward that morning when ordered, so there was scant reason to see them as any more reliable. In his predicament, he turned to Khurshid Aga – who always seemed a friend of sorts. Would he provide ten elephant hunters, with whom Sam and Florence could hunt in the regions around Gondokoro? Then he wanted Khurshid to hire for him, when back in Khartoum, a party of thirty trustworthy blacks – not Arabs – with whom he could set out for the Luta N'zige. This would mean waiting a year until the boats could come again to Gondokoro on the north wind, but at least it would avoid the shame of returning defeated to the capital. The Circassian agreed, and Baker slept happily, feeling he had found some way out of the impasse.

Next morning Khurshid returned. He had chosen the ten best men, told them the plan to which he had agreed – and been given a flat rejection. The men refused to serve with the Englishman, who they said was not only a spy but would lure them down to the south, where they would all be murdered. He was a madman. 'They would mutiny immediately,' explained Khurshid, 'if you were forced upon them.'

With the stubbornness of desperation, Baker said that in that case he would simply stay at Gondokoro. He had seeds to grow crops and supplies to last a year. There would be four of them: Florence, himself, Saat and Richarn. It would be fatal, warned the Circassian, because after the traders left in a few weeks they would be defenceless, an easy prey for the surrounding tribesmen.

After he left them they sat silently. Sam looked at Florence: 'I dared not think of her position in the event of my death amongst such savages as those around her. These thoughts were shared by her; but she, knowing that I had resolved to succeed, never once hinted an advice for retreat.' Another scheme whirled through his mind. He and Florence on horseback, together with Saat and Richarn on camels, would make a dash to the south, taking nothing but their guns and a supply of beads to buy food. This idea was abandoned when a Bari chief assured Sam that the distant tribes would never give food for beads. They wanted only cattle. 'You can do nothing here without plenty of men and guns,' the chief assured him.

Meanwhile, the remaining members of the escort were conspiring. Saat brought the news that they would agree to march, but only as a pretext for getting Baker into the territory of a slave trader called Chenooda. There they would turn upon him, and kill him if he tried to stop them making off with all the guns and ammunition.

That night screams in the distance awoke Sam as he was sleeping uneasily in the tent. He felt Florence, who was also awake, pull gently at his sleeve; she never made a sound on such occasions, even a whisper – she 'was not a *screamer*', he wrote proudly. Sam peered into the blackness and by the head of his bed saw a dark shape. 'Who is that?' he demanded, with his finger on the trigger of his pistol. He repeated the challenge, for the last time. 'Fadeela,' replied a woman's voice. Sam struck a match and in a corner of the tent saw one of the slave women employed to grind corn. She was covered in blood and had fled from some of the escort. Outside, the screams were continuing, and Sam hurried off to investigate. Two other slave women were being thrashed with whips of rhinoceros hide for being absent without permission, three men holding each of them down for their punishment. Sam snatched the whips and laid about him furiously.

While Sam and Florence faced these vexing tribulations over their escort, the Pethericks were also still in Gondokoro, grappling with similar troubles. Both were ill, and during a quarrel their headman had been shot dead by one of his own men. On 16 March, Baker wrote in his diary: 'Petherick, poor fellow, is regularly broken down in spirits and health owing to constant anxiety – Mrs Petherick also.' It betrays the strain he was likewise under that the following day the diary contains the same words, repeated exactly. Yet there was little real goodwill on either side and a week later a violent quarrel burst out. It revolved around the cattle-stealing incident during the consul's journey. James Murie did not try to hide the facts, although he was sorry for the man he accused. Baker lost his temper when 'Mrs P, in her usual polite manner' asserted that he would also allow cattle raids if sufficiently hard pressed. 'Verily these are dangerous people,' he wrote. 'A liberal abuse of Speke both by her and Petherick ended the conversation, which will be one of the last I intend to have . . .' Even so, he sent a series of official letters to Petherick, asking him in his official capacity to seek recompense from the Egyptian government for the mutiny of his men. The journey to Gondokoro had cost him £700, said Baker. Not surprisingly, the consul ignored these demands.

Three days after the quarrel, Baker decided on a stratagem that meant certain death if it failed. A party of Khurshid Aga's men was leaving for the south, and he would follow close behind with as many of his own escort as he could muster. He believed that he might be able to bribe them to help him through, partly because he was known to be friendly with their leader. Khurshid was not going on this march and after his previous failure stayed carefully neutral; but he did promise to care for the goods that Baker was forced to leave behind through being unable to hire porters.

Seventeen of the escort agreed to march, although their motives were suspect – one was a known leader of the mutineers. There were also rumours that Khurshid's men meant to provoke an attack on Baker's party by a tribe that had lately massacred a trading force more than a hundred strong. If that happened, hope of help from any quarter could be ruled out.

On 26 March, the firing of guns and beating of drums announced the deliberately sudden departure of Khurshid's men in the early afternoon. As they set off behind their blood-red Turkish ensign they sent Baker a message: they dared him to follow.

Hurriedly, the donkeys and camels were loaded with every ounce they could carry. Florence was mounted on a large hunter named Tetel, with several leather bags slung to the pommel. Sam rode a horse named Filfil. (He no longer had Priest, the animal bought at

St Croix, because it had to be shot after becoming paralysed in its hind legs.) In the early evening, by moonlight, they were ready to start. There was neither guide nor interpreter to help them, but Sam knew that the route lay to the east of a mountain named Belignan, whose bulk could be seen outlined against the sky in the distance. That way, he ordered. James Murie was there to see them go off: Sam and Florence leaned down to shake hands with him from the saddle.

After several hours they overtook Khurshid's men and made a camp on a patch of rising ground. The entry in the diary reads: 'No water, and nothing to eat as all were too tired to cook. Slept sound.' They were on their way, at last, to the Luta N'zige.

CHAPTER 7

Florence on the March

After the death of the Bavarian, Johann Schmidt, many of the jobs he would have done were shouldered by Florence. She had been Sam's companion for more than four years; he increasingly relied upon her common sense when decisions were made and knew that her calmness counterbalanced his weaknesses – impetuosity and a quick temper. Among the traits they shared was a boisterous sense of humour, for there was no room for feminine delicacy, as the Victorians interpreted it, in their day-to-day existence. Florence had long grown used to the noisome realities of camp life, the heat, stink and vermin, animals being slaughtered, skinned, eviscerated and cut up, malcontents being beaten. She found little scope for privacy.

When they were on the march, Florence now always dressed in loosely-cut breeches and kneelength gaiters. Unlike Sam, who left his massive arms bare almost to the shoulders, she wore a long-sleeved blouse, belted at the waist. Both of them were heavily tanned, which only made more striking their blue eyes and fair hair, a constant source of wonderment to African tribesmen. The villagers were acquainted with the Arabs – who because they were merely brown were called 'white men'. To prove that the colour of his face was deceptive, that he was a 'very white man', Sam would take off his shirt; it was a sporting gesture that evoked yells of amusement. He became known as 'Mlidju', the big-bearded one, she as 'Rijadnay', the white pearl, or 'Njinyeri', the morning star. At one village, where Sam was conferring under a tree with the headman, he suddenly heard a shout from the hut where he had left Florence and watched in alarm as the entire village raced towards it. 'For a moment I thought the hut was on fire, and I joined the crowd and arrived at the doorway, where I found a tremendous press to see some extraordinary sight. Everyone was squeezing for the best place; and, driving them to one side, I found the wonder that had excited their curiosity.' The hut being dark, Florence had gone to the doorway to do her hair – 'which, being very long and blonde, was suddenly noticed . . .' As Sam put it, a gorilla would not have made a greater stir in a London street.

Quite often, Florence in her breeches and gaiters was assumed to be Sam's young son. Once they were surrounded by a crowd of several hundred Africans who imagined they were 'Turks' looking for ivory or slaves. A hunchback who knew some Arabic acted as interpreter and began staring quizzically at Florence. Sam explained that she was his wife. 'Your wife! What a lie! He is a boy!' The more Sam insisted, the louder the hunchback responded, *'Katab!'* – 'What a lie!'

Despite this exchange, Sam hired the hunchback as a guide through several miles of a dangerous part of the journey south of Gondokoro. The expedition had been travelling fast for several days, despite ground that was rocky and scarred with ravines. Haste was vital, because if Khurshid's trading caravan took the lead it might set one of the tribes against them, provoking an ambush in which the small group, little more than twenty, would have scant prospects of survival. The presence of the heavily-laden baggage animals, carrying beads and presents with which Baker hoped to bribe his way to the unknown lake, made the party even more of a lure. Only if good progress could be maintained was there also a chance of getting beyond this region before the rains, which would turn the ravines into impassable, rushing torrents. But the delays in Gondokoro caused by the mutinies made the hope of achieving this fairly slim.

Searching for the best route, Sam and Florence rode ahead on horseback. They knew that smoother countryside awaited them beyond a mountain called Ellyria and it seemed that by forced marches they were keeping well in the lead of the traders. Even so, their advance was agonizingly slow. On every steep slope the camels would stumble and fall, so that their loads had to be taken off, manhandled to the next hilltop and there restored to their backs.

The donkeys were much better on rough ground, but when the troubles with the camels forced a halt they would sit down and refuse to get up again until beaten. Travelling by night to 'steal a march' on the traders meant further hazards: thorns tore open bags containing precious food, and in reconnoitring ahead for the path, Sam was cut all over his face and body by sharp-spiked bushes hanging from the rocks.

At last, they found their way through the worst of the ravine-country. For the moment, the rains were less of a hazard. Climbing a rocky slope on foot, and leading their horses by their bridles, Sam and Florence reached a small plateau that looked down upon the smooth plain they knew would soon bring relief to their men and animals. But the body of the expedition lay several miles behind, so Sam and Florence sat under a tree, to decide whether they should ride on alone to the chief of the district and try to win his favour.

As they sat there, they suddenly heard men's voices and were delighted that the camels and donkeys had travelled so swiftly. The noise grew louder, stones rattled in the ravine, and Sam got up to welcome his men. Then he saw, emerging from the dark trees fifty yards away, the waving ensign of the new arrivals. It was not his own Union Jack, but the red banner and crescent of the Turks. His own men had been overtaken, and were now somewhere well in the rear.

The trading party filed by, its size making Sam painfully aware of his own puny forces. There were a hundred and forty armed men – who totally ignored him – and twice as many African porters, carrying trade goods, ammunition and general impedimenta. He was possessed by rage, feeling that they were 'treating him with the contempt of a dog'; he longed for a fight, whatever the odds.

At the very end of the trading party was its leader, Ibrahim, riding on a donkey. Ibrahim was an olive-skinned Syrian, with glowering eyes, who acted as Khurshid Aga's main freebooter. He now stared fixedly ahead as his donkey trotted past the two infidels who had so rashly accepted his challenge at Gondokoro. Sam was too angry and proud to do anything, but Florence called out, asking Ibrahim to come and speak to them. Sam followed her example; the Arab got off his donkey and came over. Sam appealed to him to co-operate, said there was no reason why the tribesmen should be incited to destroy his expedition. After all, Ibrahim's employer, Khurshid, was friendly to Europeans and had welcomed Speke and Grant to Gondokoro. He mixed into this speech an element of menace, saying that if he and Florence were killed, the news would get back to Khartoum and Ibrahim would be hanged.

The Syrian replied that all his men believed that Baker was merely a consul in disguise, who would report back everything that they did. Florence then spoke her own piece, telling Ibrahim that they would not be driven back. Sam was an Englishman, she pointed out proudly, and the arm of Britain was long. She added a bait: if they were to discover countries rich in ivory, he would be the first to learn of it. Finally, Sam threw in the offer of money and a double-barrelled gun. Ibrahim yielded, pointed out a distant tree on the plain where they could safely make their camp, then got back on his donkey. He did not, he said, want his own men to know that the conversation had taken place.

The mixture of bribery and coercion was not a particularly dignified way of salvaging the expedition, but no other options existed. It meant that a curious, grudging alliance would grow up between the two parties. On the one side, Baker's people had the protection of the slave traders against the hostility of the local tribes – an hostility that was fuelled by the brutalities of the traders themselves. The traders eventually realized that Baker, with his cache of unusual, European-style goods, which he was willing to give to chiefs rather than use for barter, might manage to blaze a trail they could follow into lands of untapped wealth. The rank and file were also impressed by Ibrahim's new gun. However, they did not trust Baker, as an infidel and likely informer. For the first time, outsiders were watching a Khartoum trading caravan at work.

The darker side of this work was revealed when a base had been set up among the Latooka tribe, after a long march south and eastwards. Incited by one chief, the traders swept down on a district with which he was at war and seized more than two thousand head of cows and sheep. These they then began to use for buying ivory and young girls, whom they would sell for the equivalent of five English pounds each when they were back in Khartoum. Baker's own men watched the success of this raiding party with a gloomy envy; so did the local villagers among whom they were camped. One night, the villagers tried to break into the Arabs' camp to steal some of the cattle, and when one was spotted by a sentry there was a brief rattle of musket fire. Baker jumped up, and hurried from the tent, carrying a lantern that always stood beside his bed. The sentry had hit an intruder, who was lying on the ground with wounds in his chest; a shot had also struck him in the eye. The Arabs wanted for amusement to bayonet the dying man, but Baker held them off. When the man had died the Arabs cut off his hands at the wrists to get copper bracelets. 'The body was very considerately dragged to the entrance to my camp,' recorded Baker. In the morning he ordered it to be removed some distance, where buzzards, vultures, crows and marabou storks collected. Baker watched them stripping the bones and saw how one vulture was almost strong enough to turn the body over by pulling at the flesh on the arm at the opposite side to where it stood. 'In a few hours a well-picked skeleton was all that was left of the Latooka.' Having several times studied birds of prey eating bodies Baker noted that they always went first for the eyes, inner parts of the thighs, and beneath the arms, before moving to the coarser portions.

On a different occasion, the Turks found a man who had stolen into their camp to talk to his daughter, who was being held as a slave. The girl had her arms around her father's neck. The man was dragged away, tied to a tree and shot. After he was dead, one of the men fired into his body out of mere bloodthirstiness. One day, Sam and Florence saw a child of 'about two', not understanding its fate and quite contented, being marched along by the raiders in a party of child slaves, all tied together in a line with a long leather thong.

Yet some of Khurshid's men were less savage than others. Baker was genuinely sorry for one of them, who was killed in a skirmish: 'A very civil fellow,' he wrote in the diary, 'and altogether a pleasant fellow.' Another, whose home was in West Africa, delighted in telling Sam and Florence about his experiences in Europe, which he had visited while serving on a frigate in the Turkish navy. He recalled with great vividness attending a ball in Greenwich, beside the Thames, where he swore that several ladies fell instantly in love with him, under the impression that he was a pasha. This man was interested in botany and spent much of his spare time collecting plants for Baker's collection.

The traders were continually appealing for medicines to treat various ailments; yet they were not given any of the dwindling reserve of quinine, the only antidote to malaria.

The one activity in which Sam was always willing to engage, to entertain all comers, was sketching. He was good at making instant likenesses, and enjoyed letting his fancy run free. One day he drew a girl with three breasts – 'A regular screamer, as the Yankees would say.'

In his journal he made many drawings of shields, pipes and newly-found plants; he often speculated on the suitability of African trees for European climates. Also he carefully noted any scraps of information extracted from visitors to the camp about their final objective, the Luta N'zige lake. To reach it they must first travel two hundred miles or more due south, to a river that was presumably the Nile once more – but flowed mainly from east to west. Across this river was the kingdom of Kamrasi, the ruler who had so tormented Speke. But between them and Kamrasi, directly in the line of march, lay several lesser rivers, now said to be becoming impassable. The rains were beginning.

At first, Sam found a measure of relief in the downpours, because they lowered the temperature and reminded him of home. He would slosh about, not caring if his shoes were so full that the water came out over the backs of the heels, and make fun of his men for looking bedraggled. One night, he skinned a large puff-adder by flashes of tropical lightning that lit up the camp; staring at the countenance of the dead snake, he relished the gothic eeriness of the scene. Yet before long, he was to rue his welcome for the rains.

The Arab traders could not be hurried, inching forward from one tribe to the next and leaving behind depots full of slaves, cattle and ivory. Willynilly, Sam and Florence went slowly too, because the remnants of their escort claimed they dared not travel on alone through such unsettled areas. Ahead lay the rising rivers.

Sam did his best to reach a separate accord with the chiefs, for he and Florence might have to come back this way. Usually, when the chiefs came to see him, Florence would get out a dress and put it on, and he would wear a light silk jacket. To add ceremony to the occasion, a Persian carpet was laid out on the floor of the tent.

One day, Sam decided to try a different effect. He unpacked his Highland costume – the Atholl kilt, his sporran, socks and bonnet. When he had put it on, he stuck several ostrich feathers in the bonnet for good measure. Sam noted with satisfaction that the visiting chief, 'naked as he was born', looked completely dumb-founded. Then presents were handed out, mainly bead necklaces and handkerchiefs. The chief was delighted and said he would send his wives along to see Florence: it was an alarming prospect, since he had more wives than he could count on his fingers and each would expect gifts for herself and her children.

A compromise was reached: the chief should send his favourite wife. She gazed in amazement at the first white people she had ever seen, and Sam was pleased at being able to make a 'very correct likeness' of her in his sketchbook. Emboldened, the wife told Florence that her looks would be much improved if she knocked out her four front teeth in her lower jaw, in the Latooka manner, not to mention sticking an ornament in her lower lip. The favourite wife took out and showed Florence the piece of polished crystal, several inches long, which was stuck through her lip and held in place with a twist of wire. Having an inspiration, Sam took from his instrument box a glass thermometer that no longer worked; after breaking the glass stem into three neat pieces, he handed them over as lip ornaments.

Afterwards, he pondered on why the White Nile tribes knocked out the lower front teeth. 'Were the meat of the country tender, the loss of teeth might be a trifle; but I have usually found that even a good set of grinders are sometimes puzzled to go through the oper-ation needful to a Latooka beefsteak.'

Further south, among the Obbo tribe, good relations were estab-lished with an old chief called Katchiba. He was a splendid musician and played for the newcomers during his first visit to them upon an eight-stringed guitar. They thought it the sweetest singing they had heard anywhere in Africa. Katchiba was a humorist as well and despite his years would dance and perform a variety of antics at the least provocation. He was also renowned as a rainmaker and because the rains seemed to be stopping and the land drying up was at that moment being pressed by his people to bring on a deluge.

Rather anxiously, Katchiba discussed the demand with Sam through an interpreter and eventually decided to blow four blasts on his rainmaking whistle. In search of supplementary magic, he asked pleadingly whether the white man used whistles. This gave Sam a chance to show off one of his talents: he put his fingers in his mouth and produced the ear-splitting sound that he used, when hunting in Scotland, to call his hounds. Luckily for both of them, there was a thunderstorm four days later.

Among the gifts which delighted Katchiba was the last of the expedition's teacups, a tin plate and a pair of green goggles. He was also entranced by a card covered in shirt buttons, to which Florence attached a string so that he might wear it around his neck. But there was one object in the tent that Katchiba coveted most of all – the chamberpot, which had survived so many vicissitudes. He explained that it would be a splendid receptacle for serving meals on important occasions. Sam replied that it was a 'sacred vessel' that had to accompany him everywhere – at which Katchiba politely withdrew his request.

The account of this incident in the diary has an amiable postscript: 'He is really not a bad old fellow for a native.' After all, the idea of using a chamberpot for bringing in the stew was not so outlandish: Sam had seen one being used for just such a purpose in Khartoum and had gone to the trouble of drawing it, complete with a straw cover like a Chinaman's hat to keep the food warm.

After a while, Sam developed so much confidence in the chief that he decided to leave Florence behind with him while making a reconnaissance towards the south, to examine the level of the rivers between the Obbo country and Kamrasi. Katchiba promised to put a spell on the hut in which she was living, so that nothing untoward could happen in Sam's absence. It was the first time they had been separated since two years earlier, when Baker had made several hunting trips on his own near the Abyssinian borders. This time he took only three men with him and would sleep in the open, lying on an oxhide and covering himself with a plaid blanket.

Once more there were chances to hunt, for he spotted huge herds of elephants. But he resisted the urge, having more pressing business, until one morning he came across twelve bulls and followed them on horseback until he could get a shot at one. When he fired, the horse reared and threw him, while the elephant turned and charged towards the spot from where the bullet had come. Baker had to run for it, leaving his rifle behind in the tall grass. Luckily, the elephant decided to chase the horse, which was only recovered several days later by an African search-party. Baker found his rifle after a long hunt in the grass, and furiously reproached himself for the 'indiscretion' of trying to hunt while on the march.

Back with Chief Katchiba, after learning that the rivers were indeed too high to ford, he found Florence well cared for and in good health.

Since it was impossible to renew the march, Sam looked for ways to make life more tolerable. He decided to resurrect the skills acquired ten years before, when he founded his own brewery in the mountains of Ceylon. This time, he would make wine, using the wild black grapes that were ripening. They were not very juicy, but more than two hundred pounds were collected and pressed in the iron bath; the thick extract was then allowed to ferment. Sam was forced to concede that the product did not taste much like wine, but it was drunk with every effort at enjoyment. Far more successful was the whisky distillery he was to construct later, using two large jars, one inverted into the other, and a kettle in a pan of cold water, at the end of a long bamboo, to condense the spirit. He was so proud of his design that he sketched it in the diary and recorded that he was turning out a quart a day. 'My whisky is really first rate,' he exulted. The raw material was sweet potatoes, of which there was no lack. Sometimes the man put in charge of production would be found lying asleep on his back, with the fire out, but there were always volunteers ready to take over his job. Sam decided the whisky had a 'marvellous effect' after two years of almost total abstinence.

On and off, while waiting for the rivers to subside, he and Florence spent months with Katchiba, and once when elephants were ravaging the gardens around his village, Sam volunteered to try and shoot some. It was impossible to follow them into their hiding places by day, because the grass was too high, so he decided to dig a grave-like trench in the gardens and wait there with his most massive gun, the 'Baby'.

In the middle of the night, he could hear from the trench the huge herd rampaging in the gardens, but everything was too indistinct for a shot. He held his fire, until one of the elephants came lumbering within twelve paces of the hole. Baker picked up his gun, then whistled so that the animal would turn and give him a chance to shoot at the shoulder. He fired, the gun flashed and roared in the night and the elephant was heard to fall. But was it dead? Sam sensed his position was too dangerous to make a move, so he felt he must wait until dawn.

As the light began to grow and the first birds sang, he saw Florence coming down the path from the village, leading men armed with axes and knives. She had heard the gun and was bringing a party to cut up the anticipated carcass. But the elephant was not yet quite dead – it had got to its feet and was standing among the tall grass. As its human adversaries moved towards it there was a thud; it had crumpled heavily to the ground and died. Before allowing it to be cut up, Sam sent for his tape measure. The bull was 10' 6½" from foot to shoulder, and one of the tusks was 6' 6" long.

Sometimes, if the game was in open country, Florence would come out as a helper. When Sam dismounted to approach his quarry on foot, she would wait among the trees, but still in the saddle. At the sound of a shot she would ride at full gallop, leading his own horse by the bridle, so that he could jump on to its back and race in pursuit if the animal were only wounded and might get away.

Such interludes became rare as the weeks and months dragged by, for the rains had made the countryside a sodden morass. Both Sam and Florence began to suffer from bouts of fever that weakened and dispirited them. Once when they came back to Katchiba's village they were so ill that gloomy reports went to the chief: the white people were dying. He hurried down and found them both prostrate in a hut, quite unable to help each other. Katchiba brought his magic into play, filling his mouth with water and spouting it around the hut, then taking a branch and waving it above their heads. At that he left, assuring them that they would live – and they soon began to get better.

But white ants and rats infested their hut. At night, the rats chased across their beds, until Sam put down arsenic for them. The smell of the dead rodents in their holes was only slightly preferable to the scampering of the live ones. Sam wrote miserably: 'Altogether I am thoroughly sick of this expedition. I shall plod along with dogged obstinacy, but God only knows the end. I shall be grateful if the day ever arrives once more to see Old England . . . white ants and rats, robbers and smallpox, these are my companions and neighbours.' He knew that Speke and Grant must long since have arrived home, to revel in their success, while he felt painfully stalemated.

As the rains continued, his horses and the transport animals started to die, one by one. Their main enemy was the tsetse fly, and once the deaths began there was no halt to them. The last to go were the donkeys, their eyes and noses streaming, their coats standing out stiffly. Unless riding oxen could be bought along the way, the rest of the journey must be on foot.

Supplies that were not vital, but made life more tolerable in the wilds, were abandoned, because what they took with them must be borne by porters, either on their heads or slung between poles. The armed escort, which had numbered more than forty when recruited in Khartoum a year before, was now reduced to a dozen. Even that sullen remnant was something to be grateful for, because Baker only narrowly overcame a second mutiny. Once more he trusted to his fists and knocked Bellal, the ringleader, on to his back. Bellal and two others then deserted with their guns and ammunition, to join a trading group operating some miles away. 'May the vultures pick their bones,' said Baker.

Some time later two of the three were killed in a fight and their guns, covered in blood but recognizable by the numbers on their stocks, were brought back to the camp. Baker took grim pleasure in the knowledge that the Arabs, both his own men and those in Khurshid's caravan, believed his remark about the vultures had proved a potent curse.

Yet he also felt there must be a curse on him. The bouts of malaria he and Florence were suffering became more frequent. It was a struggle to do the most simple jobs around the camp – mending the tent or their clothes, boiling down fat to make soap, or 'tinkering', to make rings and bracelets that could be used as presents. On 17 October 1863, there is a long, obsessive account in the diary in a shaky handwriting of the best treatment for malaria, setting out the doses of quinine and tartar emetic to be taken at the various stages of an attack. It is not hard to imagine the lowering effect, both psychologically and physically, of repeated vomiting caused by the emetic to 'cleanse the stomach of bile'.

The rains continued, and despite blazing fires all the goods in the camp were covered in mildew. By November, Baker was hardly able to keep up his diary, but managed to compose a letter to be sent back to England 'making certain requests' in case of his death; the diary does not reveal what these were.

With brief interludes, the end of the year passed by in a haze of recurrent malaria. Sam was in worse condition than Florence; on 27 December he wrote 'I have fever again', and against each of the four next days there is just a one-word entry: 'Fever.'

But with the start of 1864 came the chance to move south and Sam took one of the last doses of quinine in the medicine chest so that he would be strong enough to mount one of two riding oxen they had acquired. Originally there were three, given the names 'Beef', 'Steak' and 'Suet'. But Beef became ill, and his name was changed to 'Bones' before he died. The two remaining oxen proved difficult beasts: one fled and was never caught, while Suet threw Florence to the ground by suddenly kicking and plunging. A more docile ox was gallantly offered to Florence by Ibrahim, the Arab trader, but Sam had to walk eighteen miles in one day. It taxed him severely, although he thought it would have been 'a pleasant stroll' if he were in good health.

Soon the expedition was at a latitude well beyond any point reached before by Europeans coming from the north. The only people who had preceded them were a few bands of Arab marauders, making tentative probes towards Kamrasi's kingdom, about which they knew no more than the rumours picked up from local Africans. Sam and Florence were on a different route from that followed by Speke and Grant on their journey towards Gondokoro from the south. They were also going in the opposite direction. But Speke had warned them that whatever the route, a stretch of uninhabited land must be crossed by forced marches lasting several days.

Recovering himself in a fresher climate, Baker began making diligent notes of altitudes, latitudes and longitudes. Yet the travelling was not always unhindered. One day a marsh had to be crossed and the goods were carried over it on a bedstead to keep them dry. Sam suggested that Florence should be transported in the same way, but after a trial she was declared to be 'too heavy'. At this, Sam said he would carry her across on his back, and set off confidently. Halfway over, his feet sank into the bottom of the swamp and Florence, after trying to swim in the foetid, mosquito-infested water, was dragged by the Arabs to firm ground. It proved much harder to pull Sam from his position. Although the incident seemed humorous at the time, another bout of fever came on shortly afterwards.

In the middle of January 1864, all the porters deserted, through fear of going into unknown country, and Baker was forced to abandon his 'emblem of civilization', the big tin bathtub, along with many other goods; through the difficulty of raising porters, the tent had already been left in the care of Chief Katchiba.

Ibrahim and a selected handful of his men were still keeping close to the apparently implacable white man, the tables having gradually turned as he led the way by compass across terrain into which they had never dared venture until now. Baker offered to take them to Kamrasi, whom he knew from Speke had tremendous stocks of ivory, as long as they promised not to engage in slave-trading or cattle-raiding. He felt, anyway, that they lacked the numbers to cause much trouble.

By combining forces, they were able to assemble enough porters to cover the last stage of the journey to the edge of Kamrasi's kingdom – to the river Speke had named the 'Somerset Nile', in honour of the English county where he was born. Baker writes proudly in his diary on 22 January: 'Marched 6 h. 40 m., reaching the Somerset river, or Victoria White Nile. I never made so tedious a journey, owing to the delays of grass, streams and deep swamps, but since we gained the forest these obstacles were not so numerous. Many tracks of elephants, rhinoceros and buffaloes; but we saw nothing. Halted eighty feet above the river; altitude above sea-level, by observation, 3864 ft.'

Beyond the opposite bank, now shrouded in mist, lay the capital of King Kamrasi, only a few marches distant. On him their fortunes rested, for somehow he must be bribed and flattered into letting them make the journey to the south-west, towards the Luta N'zige lake. But as Speke had repeatedly warned, Kamrasi was uniquely devious, almost impossible to deal with.

They must beguile Kamrasi – and unwrap the final mystery: how far was it to the lake? Everybody gave them a different answer. One man had told them confidently that the journey took six moons. If this were true, or even remotely so, Sam and Florence knew that by setting out to find it they would go to almost certain death. For they had, a few days before, used up their last doses of quinine.

CHAPTER 8

The Way to the Lake

King Kamrasi was a large man, whose protuberant eyes gave him a peculiar cast of features. The king also had, in Baker's view, quite peculiar ideas. Yes, the white man could go to look for the lake, but the white woman must stay behind. Kamrasi wanted her for his wife. He was ready, however, to hand over several wives of his own in exchange.

This proposition came at the end of several weeks in Kamrasi's clutches. From their dwindling reservoir of supplies, gifts had been yielded up to him one by one: a Persian carpet, fifteen feet square, a double-barrelled rifle, shoes, a Kashmir shawl, several pairs of socks, the yellow muslin handkerchief Florence wore on her head, then handful after handful of necklaces and bracelets . . . For his part, Kamrasi was a grudging host, keeping his visitors in muddy huts in a mosquito-ridden swamp outside his capital. Suspicious about their assurances that nothing for him was left, he made them unpack their portmanteaux – where what Sam bitterly called 'the family linen' was revealed as no more than a few ragged towels.

So now Kamrasi wanted Florence. At this, Sam took out a revolver, strode over to the startled king and put the gun two feet from his chest. Weak with fever, yet wild with rage, he told Kamrasi that he would shoot him there and then if the demand were repeated. Florence also jumped up and belaboured the king in Arabic (which he did not understand), with an expression Sam thought was about as amiable as Medusa's head. Finally, their woman interpreter, who spoke Kamrasi's language but came from a hostile tribe, added her voice to the altercation.

Realizing that he was stepping beyond the mark, Kamrasi switched to more mundane requests. He fancied the kilt which Sam had worn to impress him, and his compass; after all, Speke had given the king a chronometer, although it broke while he was showing his councillors how he thought it worked. He soon found that Baker would give him nothing else – relations between them were now distinctly icy.

Yet in asking for Florence the king was only reflecting a general reaction to the first European woman ever seen in Central Africa. News of her was to spread quickly into neighbouring tribes. When Mutesa, the ruler of Buganda, sent an envoy down to Zanzibar, he made various requests, for guns, an Indian cook – and a white girl. (His concupiscence was likewise unrequited.)

'I trust I have seen the last of Kamrasi,' wrote Baker angrily. 'A greater brute cannot exist.' Nevertheless, there was no questioning that the Bunyoro people, the subjects of the king, were culturally more advanced than the tribes living further north. For one thing, they wore clothes: the men dressed in gowns made of soft bark-cloth, the women left their breasts bare but wore short double petticoats. Several members of Speke's expedition had chosen to desert in Bunyoro; one, who had since been appointed a chief, was sent to interrogate Baker on his arrival in the country, to establish that he really was an English traveller, not merely some freebooting trader.

In every village there were teams of musicians, who played on harps and flutes. Sam found the dancing rather odd: 'The women wriggle their posteriors. This is supposed to be the charm of the dance.' As the continual fever undermined his powers, the fascination of such rituals was on the wane.

The journal, once so meticulous, was beginning to show signs of the fears now dominating Baker's thoughts. On arrival in the capital he had asked the king what remained in a medicine chest left behind by Speke. Nothing, was the reply – everything was swallowed. It seemed almost like a death-knell, for the last hope of obtaining any quinine for the final stage of the journey was now gone. Time was also slipping away so fast that there could be little chance, after reaching the lake, of forcing a way back to Gondokoro before the last trading boats of 1864 went down the Nile to Khartoum. That would mean waiting another whole year. 'After all my toil I am done. With quinine I could risk anything, another year in this hell . . .' But without it, death was a 'simple certainty'. As an afterthought he scrawled: 'My own men would burn my journals and steal my guns.'

To retreat when so close to grasping 'the leaf from the laurel' was unbearable, yet he trembled for Florence. On the way from the river to Mrooli, where Kamrasi lived, she was more ill than he had ever seen her before. Suffering desperately from gastric fever, she had to be carried on an *angarep* (wooden bedstead). He walked close alongside her in the heat, although one day the fever attacked him so fiercely that he was forced to call a halt and lie down under a tree beside a path for five hours. At the height of a bout of fever it was always a comfort to suck some acid wild fruit, but none could be found in Bunyoro; the staple diet of the country was the banana-like plantain.

Kamrasi was aware of the risks they would take by travelling to the Luta N'zige. 'Go if you like, but don't blame me if you can't get back,' he told them. 'It is twenty days, you may believe it as you like.'

So now they felt they knew how long it would take to make the trip, if they could survive it. Florence declared herself ready to go, and Sam resolved to look only at the northern end of the lake, where the Nile was said to enter and leave it again, and from there try to dash the three hundred miles northwards to Gondokoro, without trying to accompany any trading party. Of course such a tactic meant further risks, because the expedition now numbered only eighteen. The latest death from malaria was that of Fadeela, the slave woman hired in Khartoum who one night had sought sanctuary in their tent, to escape being whipped by the Arabs.

When the day came to start, with Kamrasi's grudging acceptance, their guides told them they must keep to the south bank of a river called the Kafa, until they came to a large swamp through which they must push their way. They had several riding oxen, and on the orders of Kamrasi an escort was to be drummed up to guard them against marauders from neighbouring tribes. The escort, three hundred strong, was assembling in a village a few miles along the route.

Baker was in the lead on his riding ox when the escort suddenly swooped down, shouting and waving spears and shields. The warriors were dressed for battle, painted and adorned to scare their foes. They wore the horns of antelopes on their heads, had cows' tails tied behind, and were cloaked in leopard and monkey skins. As they advanced, they danced and grimaced.

Baker's men imagined they were being attacked. 'It's a fight,' they shouted in alarm. 'Let's fire!' For a moment he was in doubt himself – Kamrasi was not a man to trust. Then he saw women and children were also running towards them with the warriors. It was, in an outlandish way, a parade-ground display. So the expedition moved on, its escort jumping frenetically around, the warriors making sham feints at the oxen, and engaging in mock fights with one another. Many of them wore false beards, made from the bushy ends of cows' tails. 'They were perfect illustrations of my childish ideas of devils – horns, tails and all,' wrote Baker. Not everything was make-believe, however: one man in the escort had in some undisclosed fashion annoyed the chief in charge, so he was beaten to the ground with sticks until he was covered in blood.

The seeming goodwill of Kamrasi in supplying half a regiment was viewed with suspicion by Florence. His declared wish to have her in his retinue of wives made her wonder: would they seize a suitable moment to ambush the expedition and carry her off?

Sam did not have such fears, but felt more dismayed at being surrounded by a force which plundered each village it came to. The warriors announced themselves in advance and the villagers fled before them. Everything was stripped, so that when the expedition wanted food, this had to be bought from the escort with beads. What was worse, Kamrasi's hand-picked men spent so much time dancing and roistering at night that they were never ready to start until the sun was high. This meant travelling in the intense heat, often more than a hundred degrees Fahrenheit, rather than starting at dawn and stopping early. One day Sam was so overcome by renewed fever that he fell off his ox.

He and Florence could make little contact with the escort, except by signs or through their woman interpreter. One day, the tall chief in charge of what Sam dubbed 'The Devil's Own Regiment' asked if he might hear a gun fired. This duty was given to Saat, the mission boy, who had a light rifle and found nothing more pleasing than a chance to fire it. So he put the gun close to the chief's ear, and pulled the trigger. In the roar and smoke the chief dashed off with his hands over his ears, and as a show of derision Saat fired his second barrel into the air. The significance was not lost on his master, who decided that firearms were so little known in these parts that a well-delivered charge of forty light balls from the massive 'Baby' – the Child of a

Cannon – could put the entire Bunyoro army to flight.

The expedition was now wending its way through humid lands never previously visited by outsiders, either Arab or European. Baker was careful to record, as far as his strength would allow, the geography and his position. By observations of the stars Canopus and Capella he made the latitude to be one degree twenty-three minutes north of the equator. When he reached any high ground from which he could survey the horizons he brought out the telescope Admiral Murray had given him four years before.

Once Sam found a delicious crimson fruit and managed to bring out his brushes to make a colour illustration of it in the journal. A different kind of delicacy that suddenly made its appearance was coffee; it was not grown locally, but imported from a tribe further south. Kamrasi's people did not grind the beans, but chewed them as a stimulant. When Sam and Florence made for themselves the first cups of coffee they had tasted for months there was general wonderment.

Another import, brought a thousand miles from Zanzibar over Africa's slow and uncertain trade routes, was copper and brass wire. The artistry with which the local blacksmiths made fine wire with their iron hammers drew admiration from Baker, who enjoyed metal-working himself.

When he studied the fine black earthenware of Bunyoro it led him to speculate about the way pottery could measure a people's level of civilization. At one end of the scale he placed the Chinese, who were already making porcelain while the British were still barbarous, whereas primitive races did no more than use gourds as bowls and bottles. The next stage, he decided, was to copy the gourds in pottery, and progress from nature could be judged by varying degrees of artistry; by this yardstick the Bunyoro people were well advanced.

Yet for all his ponderings, Baker found it hard to enter the minds of the people around him. They generally enraged him beyond bearing – and so strengthened his prejudices – but occasionally behaved in a way that compelled admiration. There was, for example, the case of the abandoned riding ox, which one morning became hopelessly stuck in one of the boggy valleys along the route. Baker had been riding it at the time, and when he saw the animal could not be freed decided to leave it until a strong force could go to drag it out: at the next village, where a halt was called, his guides sent back fifty men with ropes.

After dark, Baker was sitting outside his hut and smoking a pipe-
ful of local tobacco – it was a habit he had only recently acquired –
when singing sounded in the distance. As it came nearer he and
Florence wondered if the local populace was planning to entertain
them with dancing: it was not a prospect they relished, because both
were feeling weak and feverish. Then, Saat appeared with the
local headman, who explained that the ox had died in the swamp,
and that the body was being brought to him.

'What!' cried Baker. 'Brought his body, the entire ox, to me?' The
headman confirmed it: the ox was to be carried to his door. 'I could
not allow any of your property to be lost on the road,' said the headman. 'Otherwise, we might have been suspected of having stolen the
body.' Baker went to the entrance of the courtyard surrounding
the hut – and there lay the ox on a litter. It had been carried for
eight miles on long posts criss-crossed with bamboo.

When he offered the bearers the body to eat, they expressed shock,
saying they could not touch it – the ox had simply died rather than
been slaughtered. After some friendly exchanges, the men went off,
refusing to take any payment for their labours. That evening, Baker
observed genially in his diary: 'I must say nothing against these
niggers after this – they are annoying, but this covers many sins.'

The affair of the ox made Baker analyse the difference in eating
habits between the people he was now among and those further
north. In Bunyoro the crocodile was regarded as too disgusting to
taste, however hungry you might be, whereas across the Somerset
Nile the creature's musky flesh was sought after, being considered
an aphrodisiac. As the ox-bearers had demonstrated, any animal
that died, rather than being slaughtered, was thought unfit to eat;
yet near Gondokoro he had seen a group of tribesmen cooking a
boar's head which was alive with maggots – tapping the head as it
grew hot to encourage the inmates to rush out of the various orifices,
'like people escaping from the doors of a theatre on fire'.

But for all their fastidiousness, their neat clothes and fine earthenware, Kamrasi's people were poor farmers. Food was often hard to
buy, so that the expedition, hounded by fever, was further en-
feebled by hunger. Sam watched over the ailing Florence, wondering
how much longer her slight frame could endure the strain; all too
many of the villages where they halted were near marshes, giving off

'bad air' and clouds of mosquitoes.

One afternoon, after travelling through a·mimosa forest, the expedition found itself at a swamp more than half a mile wide. This proved to be so deep that the oxen were swimming and the porters up to their necks in the dank water. In no state to walk, Sam and Florence were taken across on *angareps*, twelve men holding each one. All at once, the chief guide, carrying his bundle of possessions on his head, walked into a hole so deep that he vanished below the surface, the bundle drifting away like a marker buoy. Warned by his watery experience the expedition was able to make a detour and reached the far side safely.

Day by day, the remnant of the expedition went doggedly on: Sam, Florence, followed by the two blacks, Saat and Richarn, next the two slave women, the interpreter and then the twelve remaining Arabs. The Arabs were by now totally sceptical about the lake and were almost resigned to being led to their deaths.

On a day in early March the travellers came to yet another swamp, its surface covered with a matted layer of water-grass and plants. This covering, about two feet thick, acted as a bridge, as long as you did not pause too long in any one spot. The porters ran swiftly across, sinking up to their ankles, and Sam began the journey, urging Florence to keep close behind him. The natural bridge was only eighty paces wide.

He was a quarter of the way over when he turned to see how Florence was coping. She had stopped, her face contorted and purple. Her legs were gradually sinking through the reeds. At the instant he saw her she began to double up and fall, 'as though shot dead'.

Sam strode back over the weeds, took hold of her seemingly lifeless body, then shouted for help. With several of his men he dragged her across the surface, keeping her head just over the water; if they had tried to carry her, despite the lightness of her weight, all would have sunk through the weeds and become trapped. When they were on solid ground, he picked her up and walked to the shade of a tree.

It seemed as though she might simply have fainted, and Sam bathed her forehead with water. Yet it was something more – her hands were tightly clenched, and so were her teeth, but her eyes were wide and staring. She was in the throes of a seizure, caused by the sun and exhaustion.

Most of the porters were now further ahead on the path, so Sam ordered Saat to run forward and find an *angarep* on which she might be carried to the next village. Saat was also told to bring back a bag with clothes, because Florence had become soaked from head to foot while being dragged through the water. While he waited, Sam put his hand inside her shirt and massaged her heart; the slave women rubbed her feet. Nothing would make her respond. She lay like a corpse.

When Saat returned, Sam put new clothes on her and she was lifted on to the *angarep*. Then the procession moved forwards with funereal slowness. As they walked, he put his hand under her head and held it high, for the sounds in her throat showed that she might choke. There was nothing more to be done until they reached a village, and there Florence was set down in a dark hut. Sam forced open her jaws and pushed a small piece of wood between her teeth. He saw that her tongue was completely dry, so he put a rag into her mouth and dripped water on to it to moisten her mouth. All through the night, she never moved.

Outside in the village, the fiendish escort was dancing and singing, the noise throbbing into the hut. Before the dawn, Baker went out and called to the tall chief in charge. Tersely, he said the warriors were no longer wanted and should go back to Kamrasi. The chief demurred: his orders were to keep with the expedition until it reached the lake. Baker said that he needed only the guides: if by dawn the escort was still there he would take out his guns and fire into it.

By morning the escort had melted away. But Florence was unchanged. Sam counted her breathing, faint but regular, about five times a minute. In his diary he wrote: 'F. seems to have congestion of the brain.'

There was no food in the village, so he knew it was impossible to stay there. Florence was placed once again on the *angarep* and the procession wound on to the next village. Sam walked by her side, up the hills, through small streams, amid fields of ripening sugar cane, across tree-dotted meadows and among the papyrus of the marshes. The high papyrus seemed to wave above the expedition like the plumes over a hearse.

They reached a small village where there was little to eat, so Sam went out and shot some guinea-fowl, before returning to his vigil. Florence still did not move, as she lay in the light of candles made from balls of fat and pieces of rag. It was now more than five years

120

that he and Florence had been together, but at the moment when their love was about to culminate in triumph, it seemed as though her death would snatch everything away. He wrote bitterly: 'Is so terrible a sacrifice to be the result of my selfish exile?'

Once more the dawn broke and the march was renewed. Sam walked mechanically with the litter, watching for any change in Florence's condition. He had not slept, but was past feeling fatigue. The countryside was unchanging and the lake – which now seemed so unimportant – was by all accounts some long distance away. As the night came on, Sam prepared himself again, dropping water into her mouth. But Florence lay still. In the hut was the flickering light; outside there was no sound, except the crying of night-birds.

Suddenly he heard the sound of hyenas, the scavengers of Africa. If Florence were to be buried here, her grave would not be untroubled . . . These thoughts drifted through his fevered mind as he placed wet cloths on Florence's forehead. As the dawn broke red he went to the entrance of the hut to breathe in the morning air. While he stood there he suddenly heard a voice behind him. She murmured softly: '*Mein Gott*.'

Sam rushed over to look at her. She was conscious, but delirious. Florence was to remain in that state for several days, often having violent convulsions. But the expedition could not halt, because it was on the extreme borders of Buganda and King Mutesa's soldiers had plundered the villages, most of which stood deserted. There was no food. As they travelled through the forests, searches were made for honey. Sam walked on dazedly and feverish, while Florence groaned and cried on the *angarep*. One evening, when they came to a village, it seemed certain that she would die in her delirium. Sam told his men to put a new handle on the pickaxe and to look for a place to dig the grave. Then he fell down on to a mat and went to sleep, at the last point of exhaustion. There was nothing to be done.

In later years, Florence would relate how she returned to consciousness to hear the sound of hoes and mattocks, as the men worked on her grave. As Sam awoke, to see the sunlight coming through the door of the hut, he jumped up in alarm, feeling sure that she must have died while he slept, and he had not been with her. A first glance seemed to confirm his fears, because she lay with a look of serenity on her features; they seemed like marble. But then

he saw her breast rising and falling steadily – the agonized movements of recent days were gone. At that moment her eyes opened
briefly and she stared up at Sam with a clear calmness he never
thought to see again.

For two days the expedition halted. There was almost nothing to
be bought except eggs, and from these Sam made a soup that
Florence was able to swallow, although still perilously weak. She
was entirely unaware of how long she had been unconscious since
collapsing in the swamp, but her mind was fully restored. As she
recovered, she expressed no thoughts of turning back.

Although later Sam was to recount fully the story of Florence's
escape from death, his diary entries at the time were terse and
factual. For 4 March 1864, the day when the crisis passed, he only
wrote: 'Marched, five hours forty minutes due west. Country much
wooded, thick and thorny. F. woke up from her delirium.'

When Florence was well enough to be carried, the cavalcade moved
on again. It was travelling along the top of a ridge, beside a swamp
nearly sixteen miles wide. Far away to the west were the outlines
of high mountains and it seemed that these would have to be
crossed before the Luta N'zige lake was reached. This was a daunting
thought, for they were now at a height of almost 4000 feet, and the
mountains seemed decidedly more than that. Perhaps the stories
that the lake was six months' journey away were true after all:
Kamrasi had said twenty days, but nothing from him could be
relied upon. It was impossible to gain precise information from the
guides, who made a fetish of secrecy.

Although the current knowledge of Central African geography
was flimsy, Baker knew that somewhere in this region of great lakes
were the fabled Mountains of the Moon, said to be the ultimate
sources of the Nile. They were near to the equator, according to
Speke, beyond a country named Ruanda. If possible, Speke had
suggested, the expedition should go down there from the Luta
N'zige, to investigate reports that Ruanda contained large supplies
of copper. Baker knew this was out of the question: it was now a
matter of just seeing the Luta N'zige and extricating themselves
alive. Yet he suspected that they were travelling towards the centre
of the lake, far to the south of where the Nile reputedly flowed into
it – and further from Gondokoro than he wished.

One day they reached a village which the exhausted Sam understood to be called Parkani. The local people now insisted that the lake was near at hand, although Baker could barely hide his mistrust, for the tall mountains still lay ahead. Then his guide revealed that the mountains were on the *far* side of the lake: if they started early in the morning, they could wash in the lake before midday. (In fact, Parkani was not the name of the village – it is a word meaning 'very close'.)

That night, Baker could scarcely sleep for excitement, and he aroused the whole expedition before dawn. The guide was promised two handfuls of beads if they were truly going to stand beside the lake that day and he responded by taking the lead at a swinging pace. Florence was still being borne on an *angarep* while Baker, fighting back his fever, was astride the last riding ox. Their followers struggled along in the rear.

After the sun had risen they climbed a hill – and a quarter of a mile below them was the lake. 'The glory of our prize burst suddenly upon me! There, like a sea of quicksilver, lay far beneath the grand expanse of water . . .' It seemed to be stretching endlessly away to the south and west and was up to fifty miles wide. The mountains rose high from the opposite shore and through his telescope Baker could see waterfalls cascading down them. He had planned that if ever they should reach the Luta N'zige he should lead his men in three hearty cheers 'in the tradition of Old England', but when it came to it, he could not.

Sam and Florence just stood and stared. Their followers, clustered around them, poured out excited comments. Two of the Arabs who had been to Alexandria and seen the Mediterranean – now more than three thousand miles away – said the lake was 'just like the sea'.

The path to the water was steep and twisting. It could only be tackled on foot, so Florence took a large stick in one hand and rested the other on Sam's shoulder. Every twenty paces she was forced to halt and recover her strength, until after two hours they were beneath the rocky granite face and came to a wide sandy plain. It was still more than a mile through trees and shrubs, over rough grass, to the lake's edge.

Florence followed Sam, who in the exultation of the moment was striding ahead to where the wavelets broke on the shore. She had prepared in her own way for this moment: that morning she had put a ribbon in her hair, a ribbon with the red, white and green colours of Hungary. Now she took it off and tied it to the branch of a bush near the water's edge. The symbol of the country to which she would never return fluttered in the breeze of the lake.

Sam was far in front, silhouetted at the lakeside, its expanse sparkling in the morning sun. He later recalled: 'I rushed into the lake, and thirsty with heat and fatigue, with a heart full of gratitude, I drank deeply from the Sources of the Nile.' He knew that at last, at the age of forty-two, he was something more than just a sporting gentleman and after-dinner raconteur. His name as an African explorer would now stand alongside those of Livingstone, Speke, Grant and Burton.

CHAPTER 9

Tarnished Heroes

Even while Baker gazed enraptured at the Luta N'zige in March 1864, the Royal Geographical Society was deciding that in him lay the best hope of salvation from a painful dilemma. Nobody knew where he was; some reports said he was dead; and it was certainly going to be many months before the news of his discovery got to London. Moreover, the RGS had shown little confidence in him when he first set off on his travels. But the whole prospect for African exploration was in such fearful disarray, with so many reputations in tatters, that Sir Roderick Murchison and his fellow-geographers were now relying upon him to emerge triumphant from the Sources of the Nile. If he did not, the standing of the society, which had persuaded the Queen and the Prince of Wales to be its patrons, must crumble away. For the prestige of the RGS depended almost entirely upon African discovery, whose grip on the public imagination far surpassed explorations in Asia or the polar regions.

In mid-Victorian times, the possibility of reaching the Mountains of the Moon and filling in the 'blank spaces' on the map of Africa stirred the blood just as, in a different age, would the idea of exploring space and conquering quite another lunar landscape. Passions grew so inflamed about the facts of African geography that in the course of correspondence in the weekly *Athenaeum* the German traveller, Heinrich Barth, accused a British savant, William Cooley, of 'barefaced sophistry and malignant perversion'.

Yet a measure of invective did little harm in itself. It might even serve its turn by keeping interest keen. What dismayed Murchison was the sudden fall from esteem of the very men who were the standard-bearers of the society – not to say, even of Britain itself – in the Dark Continent.

The greatest débâcle was of David Livingstone. At the moment of Baker's discovery, he was slipping unhappily away from the coast of East Africa, taking a circuitous route home to a reception he knew would be bleak and critical. His Zambezi expedition, in which Baker had so much wanted to be involved at the start of 1858, had proved a tortured, expensive failure. The lives of many missionaries were sacrificed to malaria – Livingstone's wife was among the victims – and there was intense disenchantment in the British government, which had supported the expedition with more than £50,000. The affair did not endear the prim and long-serving Foreign Secretary, Lord John Russell, to Africa in general or the RGS in particular. This was especially unsettling for the socially ambitious Murchison, Livingstone's close friend and a fellow Scot.

An editorial in *The Times* voiced perfectly the general judgement on Livingstone's performance. After pointing out, with an echo of his famous exhortation about spreading 'commerce and Christianity', that the expedition had won neither trade nor converts, it ended: 'In a word, the thousands subscribed by the Universities and contributed by the Government have been productive only of the most fatal results.' So much, incidentally, for Livingstone's claim to have found a cure that made malaria 'not a whit more dangerous than the common cold'. His pill, consisting of jalop, calomel, rhubarb and quinine, was urged by the Admiralty on the captains of all Her Majesty's ships in tropical waters, on the orders of the trusting Lord Russell himself. But it did not work better than any other concoctions.

Even more bewildering was the precipitate fall from grace of John Speke, who in the middle of 1863 had brought interest in African exploration to its zenith. On the day he and Grant first addressed the RGS about their travels there was such a crush of enthusiasts trying to get in that a window was broken. The clamour was so great that an extra meeting was held the next evening, and the Prince of Wales attended with the Comte de Paris.

Speke's ebullient telegram from Egypt – 'The Nile is settled' – had prompted Murchison to call this 'a feat by far more wonderful than anything which has been accomplished in my life'. The newspapers took the cue and by the time the two men arrived home they were national heroes. At Southampton they were greeted by a band and the mayor, who invited them to a banquet (it was declined in the haste to get to London); their baggage was passed through customs without inspection on the personal orders of Russell.

The first signs that the splendour would turn sour came with Speke's public attacks on Petherick: not only were these directed at the consul's failure to meet him in Gondokoro, but they also implied that he was just a dubious Nile trader with unclean hands. If true, how could it be that the RGS had mounted a public subscription for him and underwritten his application for the consulship? Speke was relentless from the first opportunity. In Alexandria he and Grant were entertained by Colquhoun, to whom they talked freely on many matters (including Sam Baker's companion); but most of all, they unburdened themselves about Petherick. On 4 June 1863, Colquhoun sent a despatch to Austen Layard, permanent under-secretary at the Foreign Office: 'The state of Khartoum – our consular establishment there will require some attention, perhaps a total reforming – if we are to have a consulate where the consul should be above the reach of anything approaching to a suspicion of tampering in scenes such as Captain Speke describes, as subsisting in those far-away countries.' The seed was sown, and soon afterwards Colquhoun was writing to Murchison about the Sudan in a way that obliquely attacked Petherick: 'The slave-trading demoralizes everyone apparently who sets foot in it.'

Speke fired the opening shot in public when he told the crowded Burlington House meeting in Piccadilly: 'Mr Petherick was in perfect health and excellent spirits, and trading energetically, when I last heard of him.' Well aware of what Speke had in store for him, Petherick had written a long letter home, giving his account of what happened at Gondokoro; after Speke's first attack, this was passed to the *Athenaeum*, which closely followed African matters. The magazine published it on 29 August, with an editorial note, saying that although some misunderstandings seem to have marred the 'joyous meeting' at Gondokoro, all mention of these was being omitted, in the hope that they were forgotten. The omissions were made through pressure by Murchison.

What remained of Petherick's *apologia* told how he had spent £4000 or £5000 on equipping his expedition, so that he was heavily out of pocket despite the funds given him by the RGS. He told how his 'darling Kate' was his inspiration during all his troubles. Then he ended: 'Much, you may suppose, to my annoyance, Speke had made over the exploration of the second lake to Mr Baker, whose boats he accepted, but, not to be outdone, I determined to proceed to it from a different direction.' Petherick went on to explain how that scheme had to be abandoned, because the hue and cry against him made it impossible to organize an expedition.

This version did nothing to mollify Speke, whose closest friends were now growing dismayed by his over-excited arrogance. Nor did it lessen the anxieties in the Foreign Office stirred up by Colquhoun's suggestions that Petherick was active in the slave trade. At the end of September, Russell sent a private message to Speke saying that 'reports have reached H.M.'s government connecting Mr Consul Petherick with the slave trade on the White Nile'. Russell continued that he would be 'much obliged to Captain Speke if he could name some trustworthy person who would be willing to undertake the journey to Egypt for the purpose of suspending Consul Petherick . . .' There is no trace of Speke's reply, but twelve days later Russell minuted that Petherick should be dismissed. At the end of October a peremptory despatch went to Khartoum, giving three months' notice to close down the consulate entirely.

When this draconian move became known, the battle was joined between Speke on one side – with less strident support from Grant – and Petherick's family and friends on the other. At first, Murchison put about the rumour that Petherick was to be tried for slave-dealing, but soon afterwards began seeking to spread balm on the wounds. Kate Petherick had written a 3000 word letter to the RGS, recounting her tribulations; Murchison rightly called it 'a very touching narrative', and praised her courage and devotion.

By November, the Petherick-Speke controversy was finding its way into the columns of *The Times*. The consul, in a letter sent off before learning of his dismissal, rejected any idea that he was in 'perfect health and trading energetically'. He said Speke's allusion was 'calculated to mislead', because he never did any trading on the journey to Gondokoro and was now very ill with an infestation of guinea worms.

About this time another figure, long out of sight, prepared to renew his own battle with Speke: from the West African island of Fernando Po, where he was the consul, Captain Richard Burton began levelling charges of geographical incompetence. Writing to his malicious friend Lord Houghton – who could be relied upon to

Stiffly posed for an 1857 photograph: Sam Baker, elephant hunter, author and well-to-do man of leisure. At 36, he concealed behind his high spirits a mounting sense of frustration.

The sisters of Sam Baker. Seated right is Min, who brought up her
brother's children after he became a widower. She and Annie wear the
tartan of the Duke of Atholl, with whom the family was friendly. Centre is
Ellen, the eldest, married to a clergyman.

Maharajah Duleep Singh in his
Indian finery in 1858.

Baker (in cap) working on the
Romanian railway – the job he
took in order to stay with
Florence.

Dressed for Africa. Designed by Sam, stitched by Florence, this outfit was
dyed with the juice of wild fruits.

Crossing the desert; the engraving is based upon one of Sam's sketches.
Later in their travels Florence adopted male attire.

Galla slave girls waiting to be transported down the Nile. Baker called
them the "Venuses of Abyssinia" and said they made good wives.

Guillaume Lejean, the Bakers'
French companion

Explorer Alexine Tinné, killed
in the Sahara

John Petherick, British consul in Khartoum.

John Speke and James Grant (seated). In 1860-63, these two young British
army officers travelled from Zanzibar, through the heart of Africa, to the
Upper Nile. For Speke, their triumph would have a bitter ending.

Florence serves tea at Gondokoro to Speke and Grant. They were shocked
to learn that Sam intended taking her to seek the Source of the Nile; but
this Victorian engraving treats the historic moment in purely romantic
terms.

Gondokoro, the slave-traders' paradise. Guns were fired off to greet new
arrivals – a custom which often was a pretext for settling old rivalries.

Charged by an elephant. This scene is reproduced from one of the scores of watercolours – many in humorous vein – which Baker painted of his African adventures.

Life in camp. Sam conveys the spirit of the five years he and Florence spent in Africa. In the foreground is their pet monkey, Wallady.

Sam and Florence are welcomed with an African dance. This engraving,
from the French magazine *Le Tour du Monde*, is a racy interpretation of
one of Sam's paintings.

Storm on Lake Albert. "Everyone was at work baling with all their might; I
had no idea that the canoe could live."

Florence in 1865. This earliest surviving picture of her was taken in Paris
when she was twenty-four. Within a few weeks, "Baker's woman" (as
Livingstone called her) would be introduced to London society and
become world-famous.

Florence with Sam and his
youngest brother James (left).
During the family quarrels,
James would side with the
newly-weds.

The Duke of Sutherland,
wealthy and dissipated friend of
the Bakers.

The young Prince of Wales.
This is a photograph he gave to
Sam.

The Prince and Princess of Wales in Egypt, 1869. Sir Samuel is on the steps (right). Sitting left is a lady-in-waiting, the Hon. Mrs. Grey.

Florence in Alexandria, just before the start of the second African expedition.

His Excellency Sir Samuel Baker Pasha, in the service of the Egyptian government.

Fighting in Masindi, capital of Bunyoro, in 1872. It was the moment of
Baker's greatest miscalculation.

APOSTLES OF LIBERTY.

Wilberforce to Sir S. Baker. RECEIVE A NATION'S THANKS, WITH MINE, FOR FIGHTING FREEDOM'S CAUSE.

Cartoon in the magazine *Judy* (9 July, 1873) expressing British emotions
over the fight against slavery.

Colonel Valentine Baker, friend of royalty and man-about-town. This photograph was taken when he was forty-seven, before his disgrace.

Sam and Florence at their home in Devon, in the early 1890s. Shortly
before his death, Sam was planning to go back to Africa on a lion-hunting
expedition.

spread barbed words around – Burton said that Speke 'would be pronounced a failure' and had 'claimed too much' by declaring himself the discoverer of the Nile sources.

Well before the end of the year, Murchison himself was to turn fiercely against Speke, in whose success he at first took such delight. This was nothing to do with the Petherick furore, but sprang from the explorer's brutal snub to the RGS. Despite having been sponsored by the society for his journey, Speke refused to write anything for its journal. Instead, he decided to keep his diaries a close secret and tell everything in his forthcoming book; for this, he had signed a rewarding contract with the Edinburgh publisher, William Blackwood. To Murchison, it seemed like ingratitude bordering on treachery: the man who only recently was awarded the society's gold medal for his first African journey, who was hinting to Murchison that he would like to be put forward for a knighthood, now would not write a scientific paper for fear of its damaging his own profit.

The book was, without question, a prodigious feat by both Speke and his publisher. Brought out less than six months after his return, it ran to 650 pages and had nearly seventy engravings. But the text was not without anxieties for Blackwood, who insisted on toning down some blatant passages about Speke's sexual doings in Uganda. His persuasions also reduced the malicious paragraphs on Petherick. 'I have read all your remarks about Petherick and have corrected my proofs as best I can,' said Speke brusquely. 'I wish to God I never had met the beast, for both he and his wife are writing against me in the most blackguard style.'

The book appeared a fortnight before Christmas, which Speke spent at home in Somerset. There were noisy celebrations there to acclaim the local hero, and at a banquet in Taunton he declared: 'You may depend upon it, gentlemen, it was the pride both of my county and my country that carried me through my undertaking.' But the best-selling *Journal of the Discovery of the Source of the Nile* fanned the flames of acrimony. More and more bitter correspondence filled the newspapers. Petherick's relations even ordered a pamphlet to be printed, setting out their censure on Speke; they distributed this to public figures and newspapers up and down the land.

By the spring, the tide was running fast against Speke. The coolness of the RGS towards him was such that Murchison only narrowly managed to stop him resigning his membership, which would have provoked more public controversy. Yet for all his hopes of keeping up a smooth façade, Murchison was so dismayed by the sketchy, slipshod paper on the Upper Nile which Speke eventually handed him that he published it in the RGS journal with a preamble openly criticizing its feebleness.

There was also an alarmed feeling that Speke might have put both the Foreign Office and the RGS into an awkward corner by persuading them that Petherick was a slave trader. Although slow and cumbersome, Petherick was dogged: back in Khartoum, he had dragooned several of his counterparts into writing letters exonerating him from any guilt. Even Georges Thibaut, whose son-in-law had been put in irons by the consul, wrote a suave note saying that the accusations of 'illicit trading' astonished him. The Belgian consul in the Sudan, E. de Pruyssenaere, sent a long letter to the *Athenaeum*, praising Petherick and urging that the consulate should be re-opened. 'It is an ever-lasting scandal to civilized Europe thus to authorize, by her silence, the infamous piracy which has stained the White Nile with blood; and for anti-slavery England, who, instead of declaring herself impotent by abolishing her consulate in Khartoum, should have surrounded it with all the prestige possible, authorized severe measures, and extended a hand to enforce their execution.'

De Pruyssenaere's letter was published on 9 April, and on 28 April Murchison was writing to Russell urging that the consulate should be reopened. He spoke sympathetically about Petherick's 'long and severe illness' – in direct contradiction of the earlier jibe by Speke about the consul's perfect health. It seemed that Colquhoun was also taking fright: he was now writing to London in support of Petherick, the man whom he had so effectively denounced nine months earlier, on the advice of Speke.

At the moment when Murchison was declaring his *volte-face* to Russell, the erstwhile idol was in Paris, damaging his own position still further. Speke was seeing the Empress Eugénie and the French Geographical Society, to promote his schemes for a trans-African journey in which the British and French would co-operate. He wanted France to put up the money. This possessed diplomatic niceties to which he was blithely indifferent; in a letter to a friend he seemed more interested in relating how the empress 'thought he was a great muff for refusing Mutesa's offer of a thousand women'. While across the Channel, he sent Murchison telegrams attacking Petherick and said he was planning to start a 'Central African Association'. That sounded suspiciously like a rival to the RGS.

On 12 June, Lord Russell wrote an internal Foreign Office minute: 'The Geographical Society are anxious to break off all relations with Captain Speke, and I am desirous of acting with them in Central Africa.' At the end of the month, Murchison was telling Layard, Russell's deputy, that he deeply regretted Speke's 'aberrations', and harked back to the explorer's visit to Paris: 'What "liaison" he may have with the Empress of France I know not, except that he proposed to that potentate an interior expedition to the Gaboon . . .' In a letter to Grant, the RGS president complained of Speke's 'wild and impracticable scheme of regimenting niggers and proselytizing Africa on a new plan . . .'

Yet at this moment, Murchison contrived an event that was destined to bring Speke back into the centre of public attention – albeit in a tragic and shattering way. He arranged a public debate between Speke and his old adversary, Richard Burton, about the Sources of the Nile. Was this simply in the interests of African geography? Given Murchison's anger with Speke, and his close knowledge of the capabilities of the contestants, his motives must have been far more complicated. Burton was recognized as having one of the cleverest minds of his generation. He was a practised and elegant public performer. Against the brilliant Burton would be pitted the mentally far slower Speke, who had been bluntly described by the *Spectator* as so inarticulate that he was brave even to try addressing an audience. When he was nervous, Speke sometimes tried to hide the fact by adopting a singsong Anglo-Indian style he had picked up during his army service in the East. If that were not handicap enough, he was partially deaf, because during his explorations a beetle had crawled into one of his ears, died there and set up an infection. So Speke would have to strain to hear Burton's argument and any questions from the body of the hall.

The confrontation was planned for the meeting of the British Association in Bath in September. It was a pleasing prospect for Burton who did not forget the way in which Speke had snatched the *kudos* for their joint expedition six years earlier. He knew Speke

131

could not, as an officer and a gentleman, refuse this challenge.

Burton arrived back in England a month before the appointment in Bath. He resolved to push his arguments about the Nile still further in book form, in co-operation with one of Speke's most persistent critics, James McQueen. It was an odd alliance, because McQueen was aged eighty-five and had been involving himself in African history and geography since long before either Burton or Speke were born: as a plantation manager in the West Indies he had diligently questioned slaves about their homelands. After coming home, and editing a newspaper in his native Glasgow, he settled in London and made his name as a reviewer, essayist and author. Old age did not weaken his literary rhetoric. In the Speke-Petherick quarrel he sided strongly with the ex-consul, saying that 'his character as a merchant and a public servant' had been 'blasted in the eyes of his countrymen and the civilized world'.

The joint book, *The Nile Basin*, begins with a scholarly presentation of his theories by Burton. Then comes McQueen's contribution – a torrent of ferocious invective. One theme he returns to again and again: Speke's sexual behaviour in Uganda. He was not, of course, the only one to have been struck by Speke's frankness about his amorous diversions. As soon as his book appeared at the end of 1863, a reviewer in the *Athenaeum* remarked pointedly that 'a young, unmarried man' must have found himself in an 'awkward position' by having two pretty virgins in his hut.

McQueen went much further. Referring ironically to Speke as the 'great prince', he asked whether he would find, on his return to Uganda, more people there than formerly who were 'half black and half white'. Would there be 'hair like Speke's' on one Ugandan head? Such forthrightness, given the age when it was written, must have been based upon some reckless remarks by Speke – who certainly tended to be indiscreet – that McQueen had picked up from fellow Africanists. McQueen went on to argue that the RGS should not send to Africa 'men, if such there be, who "kiss and tell", then boast that they do so'. In an ironic cut at Speke's theory that the Ugandans were descended from the Israelites, he said that 'surely Captain Speke could have felt no degradation in marrying a lineal descendant of the great Jewish king David'.

Yet Speke was never to read these jibes. Before the book appeared he was dead. After a chance encounter with Burton in a Bath lecture hall, the day before they were to have their public debate – an encounter in which both stared at each other without speaking – he hurried away to the home of a relation outside the town. From there he went into the fields with a double-barrelled gun, to shoot partridges. Less than three hours after setting eyes on his adversary he was dead, shot through the chest by his own weapon. At the inquest, the verdict was 'Accidental Death', although in his lifetime of hunting there was no known instance of a gun in his possession having gone off unintentionally.

At the funeral in a Somerset village church, the only three mourners who were not members of Speke's family were Murchison, James Grant, the dead man's fellow explorer, and David Livingstone – just back in Britain after his calamitous Zambezi expedition.

So now, what bold spirit remained to whom the RGS might cleave, which man still upheld Britain's name in African exploration? Certainly not Burton; he was regarded by every respectable member of society with a kind of horrified fascination, because of what Livingstone castigated as his 'bestial immorality'. Nor was Grant, humourless and reserved, a figure to capture the public imagination; Livingstone had some hard words for him as well: 'The [Nile] sources led to his getting a good wife, £2000 a year, and a London house with her, though he never saw them.'

Of course, there was still Livingstone himself, but some time must pass before his reputation could be revived. On meeting Russell, a few weeks before the death of Speke, the doctor had found the Foreign Secretary 'very cold'. All other failings apart, Livingstone had provoked a great deal of diplomatic trouble by quarrelling with the Portuguese, while travelling through their colony of Mozambique.

So in searching for a new hero, Murchison realized there was just one man: Sam Baker, the lone traveller. His qualities were many – he was of private means, a renowned sportsman and author of two successful books on Ceylon, a person of intelligence and wit. His family included a brother who was the colonel of a fashionable cavalry regiment and was known to be close to the Prince of Wales. Another brother, John, was a Fellow of the RGS. The material sent back by Sam Baker from Khartoum, about his journeys along the eastern Nile tributaries, proved him an attentive and scientific traveller. There was only one slight personal question-mark: he might not be quite alone, and the company he was keeping seemed rather unusual. Even the reticent Grant had dropped a few hints, and these did not escape the ear of Livingstone – always receptive to gossip about a rival's weaknesses. But it seemed safe enough to Murchison that a gentleman of Baker's experience would know what to do about some little woman he had chosen to take along for solace.

The RGS and the Baker family were in regular touch. At first, the family was appealing for news of Sam, which the society was unable to provide. But on 24 February 1864 – only three weeks, as it happened, before he reached the Luta N'zige – there was a development that reveals very clearly the direction in which the minds of Murchison and his colleagues were turning. Francis Galton, the RGS secretary, wrote to John Baker saying that the society was planning an expedition to clear up 'many points left uncertain by Captain Speke's work'. It was considered that Sam was the man to lead it. 'Can you tell me where he probably is at this moment?' asked Galton. 'Had he the intention of returning to England when you last heard from him? And what direction was he then proceeding? and when?'

Flattering as it may have been to know that Sam was thought fitted to take over from Speke, the family had no means of enlightening Galton. The society kept its plan secret, but three months later, giving his anniversary address, Murchison was at pains to acclaim that 'undaunted, generous, and self-sacrificing explorer, Mr Samuel Baker'. These adjectives may have sounded a little premature to some of his listeners, for at that moment Baker was not known to have done anything especially remarkable; as Murchison confessed, there had been no tidings of him for a year.

But after the death of Speke, a unique new quality attached itself to Baker. He was known to have been on warm terms with the tragic captain – in his book, Speke had called him 'my old friend Baker'. With death, all Speke's failings were wiped away, his name was spoken with reverence and sorrow. So to honour Baker was in a sense to pay tribute to his departed friend, to show that the book was shut on all former animosities. In Murchison's mind an idea was germinating – that even in his absence Baker should be given the society's highest award, its gold medal.

Yet a gloomy possibility could not be ignored; Baker might be dead. Speke had expressed this anxiety in an unfinished letter, dated 14 September 1864, found on his desk. 'I have great fears about the fate of Baker,' he wrote. Why had his old friend not yet returned to Gondokoro or sent any message? In the last sentences he ever wrote before setting out on his ill-starred shooting trip, Speke conjectured that Baker had fallen a victim to foul play.

CHAPTER 10

Sailing the
Inland Sea

At the point where he had reached the lake, Baker was only fifty miles north-east of the Ruwenzoris, the Mountains of the Moon, with perpetually snow-capped peaks rising to almost 17,000 feet. He did not see them, perhaps because they are so often cloaked in mist and cloud; and it would be another twenty-five years before any European traveller made that ultimate African discovery.

If Sam and Florence had realized how near at hand was a second great prize, would they have dared go in search of it? Probably not. The mountains lay beyond the confines of Bunyoro, and a small, exhausted party with dwindling supplies could not hope to push its way through the neighbouring tribes. Even the challenge of the peaks nearest at hand could not be accepted, although Sam gazed longingly across the water at them. The Blue Mountains, as the local people called them, towered up for several thousand feet above the western shore. From a fishing village called Vacovia, where his expedition made its camp, it was only as far to the opposite shore as the width of the English Channel between Dover and Calais.

Every such temptation must be thrust away. All Baker could do was to learn as much as he could, from fishermen who occasionally made the crossing in their dugout canoes, about the tribes on the opposite side. He knew that the real challenge was to get back alive. 'I must not waste an hour,' he wrote in his diary.

Yet it was proving hard enough simply to leave Vacovia. His aim was to go by canoe along the eastern shore, up to the point where the Somerset or Victoria Nile was said to flow into the lake, and from there head back to Gondokoro by the shortest route. But canoes big enough to make the journey were not easily found, and Baker suspected that the villagers were deliberately inventing excuses to hold him up – 'delaying us purposely in the hope of extorting beads'.

Even if there were no cause for haste, this was not a place to linger, for like most African lakes, the Luta N'zige hid a variety of menace beneath its beauty. To walk knee-deep in the water was perilous, because the crocodiles were so hungry and numerous. The air of Vacovia, below the steep lakeside cliffs, was heavy and humid, so that the morning after their arrival everybody in the expedition was unable to stand. The place was a fever trap. It should be healthier on the lake – Baker reasoned – if only the voyage could be started.

'I would give much at this moment for a few bottles of sherry,' he scrawled in a weary hand. 'There is no stimulant to be obtained to relieve the extreme lassitude . . .' Sam studied Florence and the rest of the party and decided there was one thing they most resembled: scarecrows. In an effort to put some life into everyone, an ox had been slaughtered to celebrate the discovery. The huge feast of roast beef, and a cheering speech in which Baker promised his men that all their past failings were forgotten, momentarily raised the spirits of the expedition; but it was a tired, ragged band.

On 22 March 1864, two large canoes appeared; they were hollowed-out trees, the longer being thirty-two feet. Eight rowers were collected, to be divided up between the boats, two at the back and two at the front of each. Baker decided to put what remained of his escort in the larger canoe. He would travel in the smaller, with Florence, the slave women, the interpreter and his two mission-educated blacks, Saat and Richarn.

To give Florence some protection, a canopy was rigged up, using bamboo supports, straw and an ox-hide. It was not, Sam admitted to himself, as luxurious as the cabins in the Peninsular and Oriental Company's steamships, but should serve for a while against sun and rain. But it was exceedingly crowded if Sam also went underneath the canopy – 'we were like two tortoises in one shell'.

As the hour to set off came near, excitement was so high that even fever was, for the moment, forgotten. Goods were wrapped and stowed away, dried fish and live fowls were taken on as provisions, and the local chief was given a handful of beads to work his magic on the denizens of the lake. He threw the beads into the waves, so that no hippopotamus would wish to overturn the canoes.

The sky was cloudy but the lake was calm, as the paddlers rhythmically drove the boats along, beside steep cliffs with evergreens clinging into the crevices. Where rivulets cascaded down the rocks of granite and red porphyry, they were shaded by date palms. Sometimes the cliffs rose sheer from the water, at others they retreated to give way to white beaches. These were scenes Europeans had never set eyes on before, and Baker felt proudly that he was victorious where so many others had failed – since the days when Julius Caesar had sent his legionaries to the Sudan. Never before had an explorer from the north, travelling against the flow of the Nile, reached those legends of history, the great African lakes.

The hippopotami were everywhere around the canoes, sporting and rolling. They were easy targets, but if one were shot the paddlers would insist upon stopping to cut up the body. This might take a whole day, and the delay could not be borne. There were elephants as well, bathing in the lake: one was seen standing with only his head and trunk above the surface; when the canoes came near he lowered himself in the water until only the tip of his trunk was showing, then rose and majestically strode off into the waterside jungle. Once twelve bull elephants were spotted, bathing in a shallow backwater. The rifle was ready, but the temptation resisted.

Only a single shot was fired during the lake journey, to test whether spray was putting the rifles out of action. The dugout paddlers knew nothing of guns and were so alarmed by this seeming witchcraft that they could hardly be persuaded to take the canoes to where a large crocodile had vanished from sight, after being hit behind the eye. The animal, about sixteen feet long, was seen to be lying on the bottom of the lake, apparently dead. The water was not deep, so Baker borrowed a lance from one of the paddlers and drove it hard downwards, to force the barbs through the scales at the back of the neck. The crocodile was gently hauled up. A rope with a slip-knot was waiting, and when this had been drawn tight around the jaws the creature was towed to the bank. It was not as dead as it looked, because just before being decapitated it snapped furiously at a bamboo thrust down its throat by Baker. To the Arabs in the party the flesh was a *bonne-bouche* and they hacked off the tastiest pieces for their evening meal. The local Africans watched this with horror, for to them the crocodile was unclean and inedible. Baker thought

138

likewise: 'Nothing can be more disgusting. I have tasted crocodile, but could never succeed in swallowing it.'

While the sun shone, the lake journey was a delight, although the dugouts were cramped and clumsy, but when rain began to deluge down the passengers shivered and grew feverish once more. It was not always possible to stop at night at a lakeside village, so the canoes would be drawn up on an empty beach and everyone would retreat under their ox-hides. By morning, the party was drenched, as well as exhausted by a night spent fending off clouds of mosquitoes.

But if the whining insects could be relied upon to make their appearance every night, the paddlers were less trustworthy by day. No villager wanted to make a journey right up the lake, and one morning Baker looked around to discover that all the canoeists had vanished during the darkness. The inhabitants of a nearby village were also gone, to avoid being pressed to act as substitutes. An order sent to the lakeside villages by Kamrasi that the expedition should be helped with manpower seemed to carry little weight.

Baker decided to push on alone, although he and his men found it impossible to control the primitive craft when they tried to use the paddles. The expedition began travelling in circles on the surface of the Luta N'zige, and by the end of the day stopped exhausted on a lonely beach after making only a few miles. Beneath his ox-hide, Baker wondered hard what to do, for he realized that his men were again discouraged, thinking themselves 'sacrifices to geography'. By the morning he felt sure the solution was to fit up the canoes with rudders, by attaching a paddle to the stern.

He set to work on the smaller canoe with his hunting knife and an auger, a sharp carpenter's tool that was still fortunately in the baggage. He then lashed the paddle on with a strip of hide – his men watching him gloomily from where they lay on the ground. When he was finished, he tossed the auger to them, and announced that he was setting off at once in his boat. He said they could stay or follow as they chose – knowing that they dare not lose sight of him.

Before pushing off, Baker fixed up a primitive mast and yard, to which he attached a Highland plaid. For the rest of the journey the canoe was to astonish everyone who saw it, because this was the first time that a sail had ever been used on the Luta N'zige. With the aid of the breeze, coming from the south-west along the direction of the lake, Baker's own boat was able to make four miles an hour, while the escort wallowed in his wake. Sailing in Central Africa seemed easy – although this verdict would soon be proved far too optimistic.

After rounding a promontory, Sam and Florence found themselves in a long, shallow bay. In the distance was another headland, but discretion made them steer towards land in the middle of the bay, rather than risk a journey well out from the coast. It was to prove a fortunate choice, not least because at a village they sailed past a group of men could be seen waving paddles – a sign that they were offering their services. A brief stop was made, the paddlers were taken aboard, and the local headman was asked to assist the second canoe. By early afternoon the rest of the day's journey was almost over: all that remained was to reach the headland sighted in the morning, and the canoeists were boldly taking the shortest route, well out from the shore. But there was an ominous hint in the weather, for storm clouds were gathering on the far side of the lake and a heavy swell had developed. If this heralded a gale, the going might be dangerous on the open water; so through the woman interpreter the paddlers were urged to make all speed.

The weather began to change with dramatic suddenness, and as the wind strengthened Baker saw that the gale he feared was chasing up behind his boat. Everyone on board joined in the paddling, and looked yearningly at the distant cliffs. When the storm hit them, the headland was only a mile and a half away. But white-crested waves began breaking over the sides of the canoe, tropical lightning hurtled through the sky like cricket-balls, the rain fell in torrents, and the western shore was lost in flying mist. There were no alternatives but to run before the storm and to bale out the canoe as fast as possible as it laboured through the waves. Nothing could be seen through the storm except the high cliffs shrouded in rain. 'We went along at a grand rate, as the arched cover of the canoe acted somewhat as a sail; and it was an exciting moment when we at length neared the shore, and approached the foaming breakers that were rolling wildly upon (happily) a sandy beach beneath the cliffs.'

As the canoe rushed up the beach, with the paddlers working away until the last moment, a heavy wave came in hot pursuit, rolling over everyone. As the bottom of the dugout grated across the sand, Florence crawled from beneath the canopy – 'like a caddis worm from its nest' – and jumped into the water. The expedition had survived the furies of the lake, although everything was sodden.

Only the gunpowder, in sealed canisters, was undamaged. That evening, Sam and Florence sat in a lakeside hut, beside a flaming fire. They were dressed only in two Highland blankets, from which they had wrung as much water as possible; their wet clothes, and all their other ragged possessions, were drying off. There was chicken stew for dinner, made of the birds that were travelling live in wicker cages in the canoe but had been drowned during the storm. Contentment at having survived the lake's fickle mood was heightened by the safe arrival of the second canoe, which made its landfall close by.

Next day the lake was still too rough for the party to go on, so Baker explored the surrounding district. The cliffs were more than a thousand feet high and a large waterfall cascaded down. Mushrooms waited to be gathered nearby; they were the common European variety, which made them taste even more delectable to the two nostalgic leaders of the expedition. Another delicacy, reminding them of salmon, was a huge lake fish, the *baggera*; half of one was found floating in the water, the marks on it showing that a crocodile had bitten it in two – and even the abandoned portion weighed fifty pounds.

After thirteen days of voyaging, the appearance of the Luta N'zige changed decisively. The western shore was closer and the watersides were fringed with matted layers, often half a mile wide, of reeds and water hyacinths. To the north, the lake narrowed and ended in a forest of reeds. The water flowed in that direction. They now seemed to be at the place where the Nile entered and left the huge reservoir on which they were sailing. Downstream, beyond the reed forest, the river must take an unknown route northwards, until it reached the rapids above Gondokoro. In the other direction, to the east, it seemed to come from where the expedition had crossed it at the start of the year, and further on still from Lake Victoria.

There was, however, a basic conundrum, centred on the altitudes of the two lakes. According to Speke's figures, derived from the boiling point of water, the Victoria was 3700 feet above sea level; but beside the Luta N'zige, Baker's thermometer read 207.8 degrees Fahrenheit, giving an altitude of 2388 feet. Even allowing for a gradual fall from Lake Victoria to Baker's crossing-point into Bunyoro, more than a thousand feet were unexplained.

Unless there was some total confusion about the river flowing from Lake Victoria – that it was not the Nile at all – there must be a large waterfall near the point the expedition had now reached. Baker decided to look for it, even though this would put paid to his last hopes of returning to Gondokoro in time to get down the river in 1864. He put the dilemma to Florence, who at the time was helpless with a renewed attack of malaria. 'Seeing is believing,' she said. Her idea was that the river should be followed to the presumed waterfall, and as far beyond as needed to be sure where it came from. Then they should come downstream again to the Luta N'zige and try to sail northwards on the river all the way to Gondokoro. It was a magnificent concept, but as events would soon show, it was far more than their strength could contend with.

At least, they must make a journey to the waterfall. Its existence was confirmed by the chief of Magungo, the town at the head of the lake. The chief, with whom they talked through their woman interpreter, was a valuable source of geographical morsels, saying that in former days boats had brought cowrie shells and copper to Magungo from far to the south. He also introduced a group of visitors from the far side of the lake, people of Mallegga, who wore cloaks of finely-sewn antelope skins and spoke in a language quite unlike that of Bunyoro.

The journey to the waterfall was made by canoe, eastwards up the river; it narrowed in about ten miles from more than a quarter of a mile wide to less than half that. On either side, the banks of weeds began giving way to high cliffs; the water was now clear and deep. At dawn, a heavy fog would lie over the river, and one morning, above the noise of the paddles, the sound of roaring water could be heard. At first it seemed like thunder.

As the river grew narrower, the expedition came to a deserted fishing village, around which were clustered scores of gigantic crocodiles. Never during their travels had Sam and Florence seen so many – on one small bank they counted twenty-seven.

The river became still more confined between tall cliffs. Then at a turn in the river Sam and Florence set eyes upon their second great discovery: the biggest waterfall on the Nile, Africa's longest river. The puzzle was solved – this was the reason for the higher altitude of Lake Victoria. The water crashed down in a single leap between vertical walls of rock. The intense green of the palms and plantains hanging upon the cliffs contrasted with the glittering foam at the foot of the cascade. As Baker encouraged the paddlers to go as near as they could, his show of bravado might have brought the expedition to disaster. He fired at one of a school of crocodiles that was sliding off a sandbank only twenty yards away. The first sound of the rifle terrified the paddlers, and the second, to finish off the animal, made them crouch in the bottom of the canoe. One of the men let go of his paddle, and the boat began to spin around in the eddying water. Hardly was the canoe brought under control, close to a bank of weeds, when a big bull hippopotamus attacked it and pushed it half out of the water. Around the mêlée, nearly a score of crocodiles waited with their snouts above the surface. 'Fine fun it would have been for these monsters,' wrote Baker afterwards, 'had the bull hippo been successful in his attempt to capsize us.'

But when the paddlers had regained their nerve, they were persuaded to keep the craft steady with the waterfall in full view. Baker brought out a sketching pad, to capture the scene.

The sight of the waterfall marked the end, for Sam and Florence, of their exploration in Africa, and the start of a long torment. The one need was to get back and tell the tale. Yet they were stranded in the very heart of the continent, 150 miles north of the equator. To get to Gondokoro, they must somehow try to retrace the overland route by which they had come south; there was no chance of following the unknown section of the Nile northwards from the Luta N'zige, because nobody would have gone with them in dugout canoes, at the mercy of the tribes along the river banks.

A few days earlier, Baker had decided that he could have 'lain down to sleep in contentment in this spot, with the consolation that, if the body had been vanquished, we died with the prize in our grasp'. Now there was a double cause for contentment – but they were to hover for months on end between life and death, between hope and utter resignation.

In the aimless wanderings that lay ahead, Baker was always on the rack of malaria. Sometimes he was unconscious, often he could not walk, and in those times when he could his knees trembled beneath him. He was able to write up his journal only by the most exhausting efforts of will. He lost count of the date, could scarcely keep track of the days of the week. The entries show that at times his mind was beginning to wander. He dreamt constantly of his mother and father, and of the wife who had died nearly ten years before.

'I am so ill and weak that I can hardly stand and I cannot get any

strength,' says one entry. Then follows a simple admission, from a
man who normally reckoned himself able to tackle any problem: 'I
do not know what to do.' A week later, he is brooding on the possibility of death, and says that every day he is growing weaker. The
diary is fragmentary. After four months of fever, during which he
could not get up for weeks on end, he begins taking vapour baths
impregnated by castor oil leaves. But they do him little good.

There was one immediate chance of help, and Baker's refusal to
take it only made the predicament greater. Kamrasi sent a message
to ask for his men, with their guns, to join in a war against an enemy
chief, and when Baker turned down this request the king decided to
starve out the expedition. He hoped that hunger would induce a
change of mind.

Every day, as they lay on their *angareps*, Sam and Florence would
talk of Europe and the things they would most like to have. Sam
decided that he wanted nothing in the world more than an English
beefsteak and a bottle of pale ale. But where they were camped, in a
ruined village just above the great waterfall, they could get no food,
except for occasional discoveries of mildewed grain hidden beneath
the remnants of huts. This diet was enlivened by a kind of wild
spinach. The only drink was tea made from wild thyme.

Sam and Florence discussed what would happen if one of them
died. Both felt that only will-power was keeping them alive, so that
if one went the other would quickly follow. Florence declared that
if she were left alive, on her own, she would shoot herself, rather
than risk falling into the hands of Kamrasi. 'We both looked upon
death rather as a pleasure, as affording *rest*,' wrote Sam. 'There
would be no more suffering; no fever; no long journey before us, that
in our weak state was an infliction; the only wish was to lay down
the burthen.' He told the headman of the escort that the one responsibility he had was to get the journals and the maps back to
Khartoum, so they might be sent to England.

After two months, in this lingering feebleness, Baker sent a message
to Kamrasi, saying that if he wanted to have discussions, he must
send fifty men and a supply of food. Then they would come to meet
him at his court. The fifty men were duly sent, so after a journey in
litters to the king's capital, Kisoona, the negotiations began.
Although Baker would not join in any attack, he did agree to help in
defence, if need be – for this was not a simple tribal war. The Nile

traders were now spilling over into Bunyoro, fostering bloodshed between the chiefs.

Ironically, they had arrived because white men had blazed the trail: brigands belonging to the Maltese trader de Bono were now filtering down from the advance camp where Speke and Grant had arrived from Bunyoro; they were allying themselves with Kamrasi's enemies. But Khurshid Aga's men, who had followed Baker, were supporting the king. This was the final mockery of Livingstone's call for the opening up of Africa through 'commerce and Christianity'. Englishmen were certainly making a path – but for the slave trade and Islam.

The meat and milk supplied by Kamrasi began to put new life into the travellers. His hopes of survival rising again, Baker persuaded the king not to flee so cravenly from his enemies. As a show of strength, a Union Jack was run up a flagpole in the compound of the expedition, and even the Highland costume was unpacked and as far as possible restored to its former splendour. Sam wore this out-fit when talking to Kamrasi.

As a masterstroke, Baker told emissaries from de Bono's private army that they must retire from Bunyoro within twelve hours, otherwise he would report them in Khartoum for having attacked a country which was under the protection of the British flag. If he did that, the leader of the 'Turkish invaders' would certainly be hanged. This piece of bluster succeeded, earning Baker new respect and authority in Bunyoro. But months were to drift by before there was a chance to escape from the king's clutches, while wars dragged on with rebellious chiefs.

There were, nonetheless, moments of happiness. In September, 1864, a parcel actually arrived from the outside world, passed down from the White Nile along the network of traders. 'We have received the *post*,' wrote Baker exultantly, for in the parcel was a number of letters from England. All were two years old, but poring over the handwriting gave him keen pleasure. The packet also contained some comparatively recent copies of the *Illustrated London News*, with pictures of women wearing the Paris fashions for the year before. After thoughtfully studying these, Florence cut them out with a pair of scissors and sent them to the king. Perhaps she intended them as a form of consolation prize.

Yet the realities of life in Africa crowded in. Prisoners taken in

battles were summarily executed in front of Kamrasi, until one day
Baker was so sickened by the sight of an elderly chief lying with his
leg fastened to a log of wood that he pleaded for the man's life. The
king promised to free him as soon as his people had sent a hundred
cattle as a ransom. Baker did not believe this, and his expectations
proved well founded: a few days later, Kamrasi personally shot the
old man.

Next, a headman was killed for having supplied elephant tusks to
the traders who were helping the enemies of Kamrasi. The 'execution'
was performed by Khurshid's men, who were establishing themselves as the king's appointed trading partners; they hung the
body on a tamarind tree by the neck, then drove all the slave women
and their children to the spot. 'This is what will happen to you if you
try to escape,' was the threat shouted at the terrified audience. The
incident reminded Baker of public executions in Britain; he considered the only difference was that there, women did not have to
be driven to attend, but went through morbid curiosity.

As the end of 1864 neared, Sam and Florence knew that the time
was nigh at last for them to get away. The boats would soon be
arriving once again at Gondokoro – and even the king found little
further use for his white guests, after having cajoled from them
almost all their last few possessions. The traders were also ready to
head north, with so much ivory that seven hundred porters were
needed to transport the tusks.

The traders had slaves, bought from Kamrasi, to take along as
well. Sam wrote angrily that the brutal way the Arabs examined the
women and children before buying them 'made him want to pitch
into them left and right'. But even so, he knew that for safety's
sake his small party must leave Bunyoro with the traders' caravan.

The journey to Gondokoro was slow, but with its every step the
decision Baker must now face came nearer. Was he going to take
Florence back with him to England? They had been together for
almost six years, through many dangers, comforting each other at
the point of death, closely wedded by isolation; they had slept side
by side in their tent, in rat-infested huts, on the open ground. Yet
they were not wedded in the eyes of the law or the Church. The
long-evaded choice must at last be taken. Even in his private
journals, it is apparent that Baker was still holding the options open –
to keep Florence or to part from her. To the casual reader, her

existence might hardly be noticed in the entries, because she was never mentioned by name, only by the initial 'F'. To someone not knowing the code, this might even be taken to mean Fadeela, the slave woman. The smokescreen is made denser by Baker's habit of calling the small Fletcher 24 rifle – which Florence often used – the 'F rifle'. These are not the actions of a man whose mind was made up. Such secrecy implies that he still viewed the liaison as one about which any permanent record must be avoided.

On Christmas Day, on the march back to Gondokoro, the diary lapsed into the classic Victorian manner: 'No beef nor plum pudding and all those most dear far, far away, but my heart is with them and full of gratitude to God for his protection and guidance throughout the past year . . . My heart is light, my limbs are strong . . . May I soon meet all those who will rejoice in my race being won.' He knew that if the rest of the journey went smoothly, he could be back with his family during the coming summer, soon after his forty-fourth birthday. If he should decide to break with Florence somewhere in Egypt or southern Europe, very few people would be the wiser. With her beauty and self-possession, she might soon find herself a husband closer in age to herself – someone not twenty years her senior. Most fortunately, during all their years together, she had never had a child.

Yet on the way to Gondokoro, they shared for several weeks the nearest they had ever come to a family life. Florence temporarily adopted a small slave boy, less than two years old, named Abbai. His mother had tried five times to escape, carrying him in her arms, and finally she was given 144 strokes with a hippopotamus whip and sold off to a separate group of Turkish traders. Abbai was left alone, so Florence fed him and let him sleep under her chair in the evenings, until he would be carried off and put on his mat for the night.

Every morning she would wash Abbai, smear him with red ochre and grease, then give him a gourd-shell of hot milk for breakfast. There were five other small children in the caravan being taken into slavery, who were fed and washed by Florence. Some of them were kept amused by Sam: 'I made bows and arrows for my boys, and taught them how to shoot at a mark, a large pumpkin being carved into a man's head to excite their aim.'

At Gondokoro, which they reached on 15 March 1865, there was a sad parting from these children. 'Poor little Abbai,' wrote Sam. 'I often wonder what will be his fate, and whether in his dreams he recalls the few months of happiness that brightened his earliest days of slavery.'

Little news from the outside world awaited them at the hated Gondokoro, and no letters. It seemed that in England, Sam's friends and relations had given up hope. This silence was equally a blow to Florence: nobody would be writing to her, so the vicarious pleasure of Sam's family was all she could look forward to.

But if they must wait longer to hear of England, the tidings from Khartoum were horrifying. Plague was raging there and half of the thirty thousand population was dead. Several of the boats which had reached Gondokoro were effectively plague-ships, most of their crews having succumbed on the journeys. On the only boat Baker could hire for the trip downstream, several victims had died during the journey from Khartoum, so he ordered it to be scrubbed out with boiling water and sand, then fumigated by the burning of tobacco. It was no use staying where they were; to get back to civilization they must take their chance with the plague.

The journey was made in extremes of heat and humidity, which brought on attacks of fever. Much more ominous, several men showed symptoms of the plague, a fatal sign being violent bleeding from the nose. After two weeks on the river, the deaths began, one victim being Saat, the mission boy who had fled into the consulate in Khartoum nearly three years before. In his final days he was tended by Florence, who bathed his face and moistened his tongue with water mixed with sugar bought from the traders at Gondokoro. Saat grew delirious, howled all night like an animal, then died when he seemed at the moment of recovery. He was buried near a clump of mimosas, and as the boat sailed on, Baker recalled how the expedition had begun with a death not very far from there – that of the Bavarian, Johann Schmidt.

On 1 April, there is a brief diary entry: 'Val's birthday, fever better.' The next day 'F fever. Foul wind.' A week later, Baker records rowing all night with his men, to hurry the journey along. Then on 15 April, the boat reached a new government station, garrisoned by a thousand men. Sam and Florence went ashore to dine with the local Turkish governor – 'to whom our thanks are due for the first civilized reception after years of savagedom'. That reception may be part of the reason for the next day's entry in the diary, because it was a forcible reminder of the nearness of Khartoum, now only a fortnight away.

For the first time, in a chronicle spanning four years of travelling, Baker named his companion. The entry reads: 'Bad cold – evenings hot and sultry, but a cold north wind blows at about 2 a.m. till sunrise giving dangerous chills. The fever is so dangerous here, and life so uncertain, that I have given Florence B. Finnian two cheques for £300 and £200 upon the Bank of Egypt Cairo Branch – this is in addition to moneys and effects left her by my will made in Khartoum previous to my departure – I have drawn on S. Baker and Co. London in favour of Bank of Egypt for £500* to cover the two cheques of £300 and £200. I have made this arrangement as one is utterly helpless should the fever attack one, and then I would be incapable of action in business matters – and she would be in great trouble in Egypt and Khartoum in case of my death.'

Writing down her name did not seem an easy matter. At first, he put only 'Florence', then inserted 'B. Finnian' afterwards. The whole passage is written in a curiously stilted, awkward style. What was its purpose?

It seems improbable that Baker really anticipated dying, at the very end of the expedition. The previous night he was well enough to go ashore to dinner. Many times on the journey he was in infinitely more desperate straits – although, it is true, cheques on the Bank of Egypt might have been little use to Florence when deep in the African wilds. But if his premonitions of death were not genuine, and merely a pretext for mentioning the cheques, some other motive must be sought.

This can only be related to his awareness that in a few months he would be home, to fame, to the welcome of aristocratic friends, to the applause of audiences at the Royal Geographical Society. The decision about Florence could not be much longer delayed. If he were already resolved to make her his wife at the first possible moment – the entry has no suggestion of that – it was pointless to give her two substantial cheques in her maiden name.

As they drew nearer to Khartoum the future must have been always in both their minds. The years of wandering, living for the moment, half-idyll, half-nightmare, were over. Baker's diary entry

* In the region of £10,000 ($20,000) at current values.

is surely the preparation for a parting, the talk of dying no more than a camouflage to cover his conscience as he wrote the cheques, and the letter he would send from Khartoum to the family firm to ensure they would be honoured. The compulsion of the moment to explain – or to excuse – his action, in the stiff little entry about 'Florence B. Finnian', could always be obliterated later, with a pair of scissors.

As they approached Khartoum, he was endlessly busy drafting the start of the book he would publish about the journey. (It is noteworthy that in the first sixty pages, a few brief references to Florence look suspiciously like later insertions.) There were also many letters to be written to family and friends, for sending off by the first boat to Egypt. One he addressed to Colquhoun in Alexandria, knowing that the consul-general would at once telegraph to London about the discoveries – the lake and the waterfall. The lake he would call after Prince Albert, the Queen's consort, who had died three years before. Nothing could be more fitting, that the two great reservoirs of the Nile, both found by Englishmen, should be named after Victoria and Albert. The waterfall he bestowed upon Sir Roderick Murchison, the RGS president, from whom a long-delayed letter had reached him while he was still in Bunyoro.

Writing now to Murchison, he explained: 'Your appreciation of my researches among the various Nile tributaries in 1861 gave me great pleasure, and was a timely stimulus at a moment when I was ill and broken down with fever.' Had he but known it, the naming of the Murchison Falls was a perfect *quid pro quo*, because a month before the news reached London, Sir Roderick Murchison announced that the long-lost traveller was to be awarded the society's Victoria Gold Medal.

The letter to Murchison contained a long and sober account of the journey, with much geographical grist. To his brother Valentine, his sister Min, and his four daughters, he was far more ebullient. He knew that, finally, he had matched their expectations. Yet in none of the letters was there a hint of Florence's existence: every account of his adventures was entirely in the first person singular. Writing to Lord Wharncliffe, he began: 'For "auld lang syne" I trust you will rejoice in my success.' The ending, after several high-spirited pages, said: 'I leave this [Khartoum] in a few days for Suakin, taking the Red Sea route to Suez instead of the tedious old Nile of which I have seen enough.'

Only in his letter to Colquhoun, who he knew would be wondering about the fate of Florence, was there the most guarded reference to her. After a summary of his discoveries, exclusively using 'I', he ended: 'However, thank God, here we are all right, having worked hard and won.' When the letter appeared in *The Times* (7 July 1865), the last sentence was altered: 'However, thank God, here I am, all right, having worked hard and won.'

Sam and Florence were in Khartoum for two months, from late April until 30 June. On 10 May, the letter to Wharncliffe talked confidently of departure 'in a few days', but six weeks later, Sam wrote to Colquhoun that he would be leaving in 'two or three days'. That stretched to more than a week, although there was no lack of boats going down the Nile and the water was high enough for navigating the sixth cataract, between Khartoum and Berber. At a time when there was every incentive to hurry on, to announce his discoveries in person, Baker marked time.

The explanation can only be his uncertainty about Florence – it must have been in Khartoum, that town 'of dust and misery' where plague had lately killed all but five hundred men in the garrison of 4000, that he came to recognize the truth: he could not part from Florence. Whatever the difficulties that might follow, he was taking her home. For all that, he was still maintaining the fiction that the victory was his alone, and his second letter to Colquhoun ended with this peroration: 'For the past three years I have not had one day of enjoyment – nothing but anxiety, difficulties, fatigue and fever. Having, thank God, succeeded, I do not regret the past if I have earned the good opinion of my own friends and countrymen. I should not have been contented to see a foreigner share the honour of the Nile sources with Speke and Grant . . .'

At the back of his diary are the names of people to whom he wrote before leaving Khartoum. Two of them were dead, although he could not know that: the sixth Duke of Atholl, and Admiral Henry Murray, the 'Skipper' of Piccadilly. A third was someone Baker might not have seemed likely to bother with, since they had parted on bleak terms more than six years earlier – the Maharajah, Duleep Singh. The letter is lost, but it seems probable that Baker was asking the maharajah to show gentlemanly discretion about the events on the Danube.

While they prepared for the journey to Suez, there was time for

Sam and Florence to learn about the people they knew when last in Khartoum. In particular, they heard much of the Tinnes, the 'Dutch ladies' who had waved them farewell from their steamer. Only the daughter, Alexine, was still alive, living in Arab style in Cairo. Her mother, her aunt, and two young maids had all died in the Sudan from malaria; so had a German botanist, Hermann Steudner, who was accompanying them on their calamitous last journey.

There was much news as well of the Pethericks, who after returning from Gondokoro spent many hapless months in Khartoum before going home. The governor-general, Musa Pasha, hounded the ex-consul so relentlessly that he sought refuge with the Austrian consulate. This produced such repercussions, including frightened resignations by most of the Sudanese working for the consulate, that the protection was withdrawn. At once, the Welshman showed his usual capacity for stirring up ill feeling on all sides by going around Khartoum – 'from house to house', as the Austrian consul bitterly remarked – saying that he was being victimized. The protection was restored, then taken away again on orders from Vienna, issued by the Duke of Rechberg-Rothenlowen, the Foreign Minister. It was scarcely to be wondered at that the Austrians wished to distance themselves from Petherick, for he was now planning an action for damages against the Egyptian ruler, Khedive Ismail, for having verbally accused him of slave-trading. This intention caused such a stir in Cairo, where the Pethericks established themselves for six months in the American mission, that the harassed Colquhoun urged them to go back to England and press the claim from there. The Pethericks had finally left Egypt just as Sam and Florence arrived in Khartoum.

The route Baker had chosen for the return to Europe was not directly to Cairo by way of the Nile, but across the desert to the Red Sea, then by steamer to Suez. He and Florence reached Suez early in September – so missing by only a week an encounter with a tireless and obsessive old man, on his way to a martyr's death. David Livingstone had just passed through Egypt on the route to India. From there he would go back to Africa, in the hope of regaining his reputation as the greatest explorer of all.

After Khartoum, Baker no longer kept a diary, but in the book he was preparing, his feelings on arrival in Suez are used as a vivid finale. 'Landing from the steamer, I once more found myself in an English hotel. The spacious inner court was arranged as an open conservatory; in this was a bar for refreshments, with "Allsopp's Pale Ale" on draught, with an ice accompaniment. What an Elysium! The beds had *sheets* and *pillow-cases*! neither of which I had possessed for years. The hotel was thronged with passengers to India, with rosy, blooming English ladies, and crowds of my own countrymen. I felt inclined to talk to everyone. Never was I so in love with my own countrymen and women . . .'

Then it was on to Cairo, and from there by train to Alexandria. 'Had I really come from the Nile Sources? It was no dream. A witness sat before me; a face still young, but bronzed like an Arab with years of exposure to a burning sun; haggard and worn with toil and sickness and shaded with cares, happily now passed; the devoted companion of my pilgrimage to whom I owed success and life – my wife.'

Well, not quite a wife. But Sam had sent off a telegram, to arrange a meeting in Paris which he hoped would put that right.

CHAPTER II

The Ideal
Englishman

Waiting in Paris to meet the express from Marseilles was Captain
James Baker, youngest of the four brothers. The telegram to him
from Egypt had not come as a complete surprise: by now, some
members of the family knew that Sam's triumphant homecoming
would not be without complications. Sam might have preferred
Valentine to be the first of the family to welcome Florence, but he
was in Ireland, leading the Tenth Hussars in a campaign against the
Fenian terrorists. Even so, James could be relied upon to be helpful –
he was an intelligent, open-minded man who after joining the Royal
Navy at fifteen had become a cavalry officer at twenty-five, then
taken a degree at Cambridge while in his thirties.

The brothers were together only briefly. Sam explained that he
and Florence would be married in London. Discreetly, but in London,
and at the earliest possible moment. He wanted James to hurry back
and make the arrangements. Perhaps James wondered why they had
not been married a little earlier – in Cairo, for instance; one must
wonder with him. Was it a lingering uncertainty?

Before they parted, the trio called at a Parisian photographic
salon. The resulting picture shows the brothers standing stiffly,
with Florence seated between them; James has kept on his bowler
hat, which is pulled down over his eyes. The photographer was
plainly concerned to adjust his exposure time to make the most of
Florence: the result, in the earliest surviving photograph of her,
catches a quality that was soon to be overlaid by English gentility.

She is dressed quite fashionably, in clothes probably bought in
Cairo or Alexandria. Her toque hat has a heavy veil, commonly

worn by European women of that time, when in hot climates, as protection against sun and insects. Now her veil is thrown back, to reveal that remarkable expression: defiant, almost mocking. The rest of her clothes are conventionally *à la mode* – close-fitting striped blouse, ear-rings, embroidered summer gloves. Over her dark skirt, which like the suits of the men did not fit the exposure that would record their countenances, she has thrown a chenille shawl.

Yet it is to her expression that one returns. About the set of her chin there is a toughness of someone who has endured a great deal. Florence also has an air that Victorian ladies might consider slightly *louche*. After all, she had been a mistress since the age of seventeen. If she was afraid of the next step, of the difficulties which Sam must have told her lay ahead, the photograph does not show the fact.

After a fortnight, Sam and Florence made their way to England, very quietly, one weekend. They took the train to Calais and crossed to Dover, where they stayed overnight in a boarding house close to the ferry quay. It was all quite different from the tumultuous home-coming of Speke, the man Baker considered his *alter ego* as an explorer – and whose strange death he had been so shocked to learn about. The only newspaper to record their arrival was the *Dover Chronicle and Sussex Advertiser*. In a list of passengers from the latest ferry, for Saturday, 14 October 1865, it records 'Mr and Mrs Baker, at 8 Esplanade'.

From Dover they went up to London through the autumnal orchards of Kent. For Florence, at the age of twenty-four, there must have been a sense of deep relief in seeing through the train window the country about which she had heard so much and was now to be her home. She had survived, and at last she had arrived. But Sam's daughters still did not even know of her existence – winning acceptance as a member of the family, entering into a way of life so remote from the nomadic African existence that was all she knew – how could she manage it? She could speak English, in a strong German accent, but there had never been any occasion for her to write it.

Her introduction to foggy, gaslit London was little other than furtive. Sam was resolved that both he and Florence must shun publicity in the newspapers until they were married. The ceremony was to be by special licence, which meant that the advance reading of banns in a church would be avoided. Yet the speed for getting it over with was governed by the law of the land: a marriage by special licence demanded residence for at least fifteen days in the parish where the wedding would take place. There was a further complication because Florence was a foreigner – the licence must be issued by the office of the Archbishop of Canterbury. All this meant that they must live, until the beginning of November, somewhere near a suitable church.

The solution was bold, yet effective. Sam and Florence went to a lodging house run by one Stephen Collins at 13 Arlington Street, Mayfair. It was a perfectly fashionable address, just off Piccadilly between St James's Street and Green Park. This was a part of London that Sam knew well, for across in St James's Square was his club, the Windham, whose splendid dinners he had recalled so wistfully while in the heart of Africa.

Despite the need for secrecy, he called at the Windham during the first week back in town. In the minutes of the management committee meeting for Tuesday, 24 October, between an item about a member's complaint that a pheasant served up for dinner was too tough to eat, and the record of a decision to dismiss a recalcitrant messenger boy, is a humdrum little note: 'Mr S. W. Baker has returned to England and paid his subscription.' It is a comment on the journalistic capabilities of the period that almost a fortnight elapsed before any London newspaper reported that the eagerly-awaited explorer was in London. Nor was there to be a line of coverage on the wedding itself, even though it was held in the centre of the capital.

Arlington Street is in the parish of St James's, the big neo-classic church built by Christopher Wren in 1682. In those days, the church was in the heart of 'clubland' – so much so that the rector often complained of the noxious fumes wafting across to his pulpit from the kitchen chimneys of those lusty institutions. On the north side, the church is in Piccadilly, almost opposite Albany, where the lamented Admiral Murray had entertained his sporting clique. To reach the church on their wedding day, Sam and Florence would need only take a discreet stroll along Jermyn Street, to its south entrance.

Of course, there was a possibility that in the interim Baker might be recognized when he left the lodgings and went about the town. Yet he had been long years away and his face was hidden behind that massive beard, grown in Africa. The people he deliberately made his presence known to, such as Sir Roderick Murchison, presumably bound themselves to keep quiet.

There was also a happening, two days after Sam and Florence arrived in London, that greatly took up the attentions of the newspapers. Lord Palmerston, whose doughty, gouty patriotism seemed to stand for all that was most British, died at eighty. He was prime minister to the end, and after his long supremacy at Westminster, the country was awestruck. On 27 October, the streets of London were lined to watch his funeral procession, carried through in the Victorian grand manner, with every civil honour.

In the days before the wedding, arranged for Saturday, 4 November, Florence made a first friend of her own sex, someone whose steadfastness was going to help her through the months ahead. Louisa, the wife of James Baker, admired Florence and at once set about helping her to feel at home in a strange city. James Baker was working at the War Office; fortunately, he and Louisa were living in Mayfair, close to Arlington Street.

It was an awkward time, because Sam made many journeys down to a big house in Richmond, on the western fringes of London, to see his four daughters. He had decided to tell them nothing about the wedding, until it was all over – or even about Florence's existence. So many years had passed since they had seen him that he must have been anxious to make them feel his affections were undivided, that they were not sharing with somebody else the father who for so long had been only a memory.

The youngest girl, Ethel, was little more than a baby when Sam had gone away. She was now ten. Then there were Constance, aged twelve, Agnes, fourteen, and Edith, almost eighteen. It might be most difficult to persuade Edith to accept as her stepmother a young woman only a few years more than her own age.

Five days before the wedding, Baker wrote to Edith, apologizing for being unable to see her. Although he did not explain why, he said he must go to see her aunt – his eldest sister. She lived across England, in Warwickshire, and was married to a country vicar: he knew that winning her tacit support for the marriage was likely to tax all his persuasive abilities. He also must see his youngest sister, Ann, married to a country squire in Worcestershire. 'I shall return on Saturday,' the letter promised, 'and run down to you some time on that day for an hour or two, but I must return to town, as I must dine with Sir Roderick Murchison.' (He forbore to mention that he would have even more important business to attend to on that particular Saturday.) The rather frantically scribbled note ended: 'Best love to Aunt Min and the chicks . . .'

If Sam had misgivings as to how his daughters might react to Florence, he must have more keenly worried about Min. Now in her early thirties, and still a spinster, she had looked after the girls ever since their mother died, from those far-off days in Lochgarry House. The girls were everything to her. As soon as he could, out of earshot of the girls, he gave Min the news about Florence, and of how he wanted to set up a home after the wedding: for himself, his daughters and their stepmother. Min did not react at once.

Sam did not take Florence with him to Warwickshire, where several of his relations were assembled to meet him: it seems that she went to stay with James and Louisa Baker. On the day before the wedding, he was back in London to collect the special licence from the office of the archbishop. The union was to be between 'Samuel White Baker Esquire, of the parish of St James, Westminster', and 'Florence Barbara Marie Finnian of the same parish, spinster'.

The ceremony itself was conducted by the curate, the Reverend John Oakley – a strange occasion, in a church that could hold a congregation of 2000. Beneath the tunnel-vaulted nave, as Sam and Florence walked to the altar, the only witnesses were James and Louisa. Theirs was the only wedding at St James's that day and was probably held unobtrusively in the small side chapel on the right of the nave.

When it came to signing the register, the girl who had so often watched scenes brutal enough to make most Victorian women faint clean away found that her nerves could not meet the test. She wrote nonsense – 'Forence Bavaba', followed by another clumsy try at 'Florence'. It was all crossed out, then she managed to put down, with a tense hand, 'Florence B. Finnian'.

She was now, at last, Florence Baker.

While Florence was struggling to write her name, Min was engaging in some far more fluent penmanship. She was opening her heart to her sister Ann – one of those relations whom Sam had met during the trip out of town. After saying how relieved she was to talk about the subject that filled her heart and thoughts, because Ann had now heard of Florence from 'Sam's frank, affectionate self', she plunged in headlong. 'Indeed it *is* a romance; of course, he ought to marry her at once, and we must all receive her with kindness and affection, which will not be difficult after her marvellous devotion; but as to future arrangements, I feel there would be something to sadden all concerned, in any case; my view of it is this, the children must know and love her, but Sam must not place her in a mother's position towards them.

'He must make up his mind to have a separate establishment for her in London and be contented to divide himself between the two homes.'

Min explained that she had come to this solution after much thinking and praying. She said that otherwise, the children would be slighted and looked at coldly – 'which they would be in this harsh world'. That might later make Sam and Florence full of remorse. 'If Sam brings her to head his children's house, I fear it will wrong them sadly, however angelic and good she may be . . .' She went on to suggest that in a few years, 'when all is blown over', Sam could unite his two homes.

'I hope, darling you will not fancy from what I have said that I feel hardly towards the poor girl, for indeed God forbid that I should do so; I pity, and love her, for all her tender devotion and do not even blame her. She was so young and unprotected.' (This remark provokes speculation as to exactly what the family was told about Florence's origins; from the conflicting tales passed around in later years, Sam was deliberately vague and merely let it be known that he had saved her, an orphan, from a fate worse than death. One family tale had it that Florence was the natural daughter of the Austrian emperor, Franz-Josef; hardly likely, since he would have been eleven at the time of her conception.)

As Min went on with her long *cri de cœur*, she told her sister that a letter had just arrived from their brother James. It revealed that even while she was writing, Sam and Florence were being married; plainly, there had been no eagerness to give Min enough advance warning of the exact time of the ceremony to give her a chance to attend. The letter also said 'that when Sam comes today he will break it to the children, poor little darlings'.

In the family strife now looming, James and his wife were to take the side of Florence, as Min already recognized: 'Louisa has done all in the way of affection and attention alone. She and Jem admire her so much that they argue blindly, foolishly and in a most one-sided way, I think.'

If there was tumult behind the scenes among his brothers and sisters, Baker felt no cross-currents when on the evening of their wedding day he and Florence went out to the dinner engagement he had spoken of to his eldest daughter. Sir Roderick Murchison was in no mood to cavil at the private life of his new hero. On the contrary, he was almost swooning with satisfaction at the thought of being immortalized in that magnificent cascade at the heart of Africa. A complaint in the *Athenaeum* magazine that it was improper to name a great natural feature after 'a private English gentleman' did not bother him a bit. Already the RGS was in the process of commissioning an oil painting eight feet tall of the Murchison Falls: it was to be done by Thomas Baines, who had, on a more modest scale, depicted the Victoria Falls, discovered ten years earlier by Livingstone on the Zambezi River. Not for nothing was the tall, domineering Murchison – whose impending baronetcy was being hurried along with a measure of bribery – called by one contemporary 'the very incarnation of all jobbing'. The older he grew (and he was now in his seventies) the more he saw his RGS presidency as a means of self-aggrandizement. In naming the Murchison Falls, Baker had judged his man well.

Hardly surprisingly, Sir Roderick was captivated by Florence's blonde and suntanned beauty, and he enthused ungrammatically in a letter about Baker: 'His little blue-eyed Hungarian wife who he picked up when abroad has accompanied him during all his five years in Africa and is still only 23 years of age. We all like her very much . . .' Perhaps 'picked up' might have been better expressed, but Florence clearly had one busy admirer in Establishment circles.

In the middle of the following week, every London paper announced that Baker would address a forthcoming meeting of the RGS in Burlington House, Piccadilly. With his usual sense of theatre, Murchison invited a good scattering of celebrities – the Comte de Paris, the Duke of Wellington, plenty of earls and some of the more important members of Parliament. He also arranged that Baker would display around the hall the sketches and watercolours he had done during his travels.

It was, as all reports agreed, a most successful evening. Baker spoke in a colourful and witty fashion, several times praised his wife, and threw in a dash of patriotism by telling how he raised the Union Jack over Bunyoro and put it under British protection. Only one of the dailies, the *Morning Herald*, attempted a pen portrait: 'He is a gentleman apparently a little over thirty years of age, of medium size, with a well-knit, but seemingly not unusually powerful frame, and with a face presenting regular features, and marked by a dark brown beard . . .' (At forty-four Baker must have relished the paper's estimate of his age.)

Murchison's words from the chair were everywhere quoted, especially his praise of Florence for accompanying the speaker on his arduous and perilous travels, thus showing 'what the wife of a gallant explorer can accomplish in duty to her husband'. The audience cheered Florence heartily.

Did any of the guests wonder why so few of Sam's lively, untutored paintings – most of which had been done while he was still in Africa – were of scenes involving Florence?

Of course, there was uninformed gossip, and guesswork about where and when the two celebrities became man and wife. One of the guests at the meeting was Lady Franklin, elderly widow of the Arctic explorer who had died searching for the North-West Passage. Shortly after listening to Baker she caught a steamer for India, arriving there in time for the New Year. In Bombay she met Livingstone, who was making his final plans for going back to Africa. On 1 January 1866, Livingstone wrote to his former travelling companion, William Cotton Oswell, a letter full of barbed gossip – including the following: 'Baker married his mistress at Cairo and from all accounts she deserved it after going through all she did for him. I heard about his woman, but it was not made public and if she turns out well, better it never should.'

The triumph of the Bakers was also being followed from afar (and with an equally jaundiced eye) by another African traveller: James Grant, who had been with Speke at the historic meeting with Sam and Florence at Gondokoro. By this time, Grant was back with his regiment in the Punjab, and there he received a series of letters describing the reception at Burlington House. One was from Murchison, praising Baker's 'nice little Hungarian *wife*'; in that artful Victorian way, Murchison underlined 'wife', and went on to say that Sam had announced her everywhere as Mrs Baker. She was being 'received as such by all his family'. The tone of the letter implies that Murchison was doubtful even yet that the Bakers were married; he certainly seemed totally unaware of the ceremony in St James's Church.

A more forthright correspondent was Colonel Christopher Rigby, the former British consul in Zanzibar. He was at this time in London, and gave Grant a vivid account of Baker's speech. He remarked upon the various mentions of Florence in the speech, adding drily that many members of the audience 'could not understand what Mrs Baker he referred to'. In his next letter, Rigby told Grant that Baker was 'putting his wife forward'. He then commented: 'Baker has certainly blown his own trumpet rather loudly and is not one to hide his own light under a bushel.'

Rigby also makes a sarcastic – and revealing – reference to Florence as 'the Wallachian lady'. It is plain that he and Grant had at some time talked about Florence together and had clues about her background; now an integral part of Romania, the Wallachian principality was in the 1860s regarded as a primitive region of the Balkans, with the bulk of its populace being ignorant peasants. To identify somebody as a Wallachian was not to pay them a compliment.

Such backbiting was only between friends. Soon after his Burlington House address, Baker was writing confidently to Lord Wharncliffe, to pick up the threads of their old friendship. He was at pains to explain about Florence, saying how she was receiving 'a warm welcome from all the family'. Anticipating what must have been in Wharncliffe's mind, he said: 'I never mentioned my marriage to any of my people by letter as I thought it much better to introduce her to my children as *"un fait accompli"* instead of harassing them by letter on such a subject from a distance.'

Writing again a little later, Baker mentioned how, in the heart of Africa, he used to tell Florence of the elephant-hunting exploits he and Wharncliffe shared in Ceylon. From among the trophies of his travels, Baker sent Lady Wharncliffe a plume of feathers from the marabou stork and a monkey-skin – 'unknown in England' – just like the ones he was presenting to the Queen and the Princess of Wales. In the New Year, when the Wharncliffes came to London from their seat in Yorkshire, they would dine with the Bakers; their willingness to do so reflected the universal acceptance of Florence.

For her part, she seems to have made the transition from African camp life – all she had ever known in adulthood – to the niceties of English high society with extraordinary aplomb.

While writing to Windsor Castle about the presentation of a monkey-skin muff to Victoria, the discoverer of Lake Albert grasped the chance to declare his loyalty, with all that verbal extravagance which the period found palatable. Far from civilization, said Baker, in a land of savages, he had learnt of the Queen's great affliction, the loss of her consort; perhaps, he ventured, in such surroundings one sympathized with the royal sorrow even more than did the multitudes at home.

When he came to tell of the lake itself his prose soared to the empyrean: 'I named it the Albert, as a companion to the "Victoria" lake, thinking that the many blessings bestowed by those royal hands were exemplified in the fertility spread by the Nile among foreign deserts.' Small wonder that he would in due course be allowed to dedicate to the Queen the book he was now sending, chapter after chapter, to the printers.

By the turn of the year, the book was becoming of overriding significance. Baker knew that he must catch the public imagination quickly, which meant being in the bookshops before the dog days of summer. He had the advantage of being able to draw upon his diaries, and there were his many sketches in hand from which professional artists were making engravings. But the biggest advantage of all was Baker's accomplishment as a writer. His two books about Ceylon and his many contributions to *The Field* were things of the past – of his pre-African life – but they gave him the assurance to dash off *The Albert Nyanza, Great Basin of the Nile* in a style both vivid and relaxed.

It was conversational narrative at its best: witty, opinionated, only rarely pompous. All his memories were fresh, so that the cryptic references to Florence could be filled out and many incidents he felt unable to put down at the time they happened were inserted into the narrative. Where he quoted from his diaries he felt no inhibitions about adding sentences here and there, or about removing passages that made him seem ever to despair of winning through in the end. After all, even though discovering Lake Albert had not been so easy that the unspoken maxim of the British upper classes – 'one should succeed without appearing to try' – quite fitted the case, the age nonetheless had rigid standards of manliness. Heroism meant a stiff upper lip.

Yet there was something else: he had taken a woman with him. In the literature of African exploration, it was a unique asset. As Rigby rightly said, Sam was 'putting his wife forward', and the increasing extent to which she is brought into the narrative as the book progresses shows how he grew to appreciate her dramatic worth. If he had cut her out of his life before returning to Britain, she could never have been mentioned in the book; how much the readers would have been denied – that vision of married love in hot and savage surroundings. The publisher likewise knew he was on to a good thing. He offered £4500 and half of all profits from the book, or £2500 and two-thirds of all profits. With characteristic self-confidence, Sam chose the latter.

In his depiction of Florence, he hit upon an artifice almost as dashing as being married in St James's Church: he would say that she was English. Without overdoing it, he fitted enough phrases implying this into the text to allow his readers of the 'tender sex', as he called them, to identify with her. 'Should anything offend the sensitive mind,' he urged, 'I must beseech my fair readers to reflect that the pilgrim's wife followed him, weary and footsore, through all his difficulties, led not by choice, but by devotion . . .' He also declared that despite his implorings for her to stay 'in the luxuries of home', she stuck to her pledge like Ruth in the Old Testament. He did not say outright that he and Florence were married before the journey began; there was no need, for his readers would never have dreamt otherwise.

If any stimulus were needed for these literary efforts, it came early in February with Baker's election to membership of the Athenaeum Club, the most august of all such London institutions (and in no way linked to the somewhat waspish magazine of the same name). Twelve candidates were put forward, but not more than three could be admitted. At the top of the list came Baker, who had been proposed by Murchison; following him were the pre-Raphaelite artist John Millais and an eminent mathematician named Thomas Hist.

Such recognition was only marred by the quarrels within the family. As the weeks went by, Florence began to find the attitude of Min more and more intolerable. Sam flatly rejected the idea of maintaining two homes, and was insistent upon having his daughters with him. He was prepared to let matters rest for a few months – he was, after all, intent on finishing his book – but Min now knew what the end must be. During January, an opening shot was fired when Florence asked for one of the children to accompany Sam and herself on a weekend trip: 'Of course, I could not refuse, so Connie will go,' wrote Min glumly to her sister.

By this time, the Arlington Street lodgings were abandoned in favour of a suite in Almond's Hotel, a handsome, chandeliered establishment at the end of Savile Row. From there, Florence began establishing links with Edith, who was seventeen. The first surviving letter from Florence is dated 24 March 1866, and written in her in-accurate but expressive German. 'Meine Liebe Edith', she begins, then goes into a long discussion about hiring housemaids and a lady's maid; she had already interviewed five. She then tells Edith to come up from Richmond one day later in the week, to stay a night in the hotel, then go off early the next day to somewhere in the country. The letter ends with 'much love and kisses'. Perhaps significantly, Sam also wrote to Edith, telling her to be sure to catch an early train. His coaxing had to build a bridge between Florence and his primly-reared daughters.

As the summer approached, Sam rented an imposing terrace house overlooking Regent's Park. He was openly quarrelling with Min about his determination to have the children there. Once more, Min poured out her woes in a letter to her sister Ann: 'All this is Florence's doing. Oh! Nannie dear, it is all so dreadful, she is vulgar-minded, not at all a lady, and therefore one cannot talk to her about the children and other subjects; the only way is to be silent.' Min accuses her brother James and his wife Louisa of 'treachery' – they and Florence have been 'calumnating her'.

The ripples spread outwards to France, where another brother, John, was living. He was married to the twin sister of Sam's first wife, and was plainly under pressure to take a hostile view of the new Mrs Samuel Baker. Writing to Ann – whose allegiance seems by now to have been with Florence – he says angrily that he has burnt a letter she had sent him. 'Dear Min has acted a noble part in all that she has done and I have such confidence in her good and unselfish conduct.' After much more in like tones, he adds a postscript, announcing that his opinions – and his wife's – are unchangeable.

Although in later years the rifts in the family about Florence would reveal themselves again, she and Sam easily won their battle. (Min then showed her resilience by quickly getting married, being widowed, and marrying again.)

In any case, the discord was soon drowned by the acclaim for *The Albert Nyanza*. It came out in two volumes at the end of May, and was praised everywhere. The reviews ran through the weekly magazines and newspapers column upon column. 'The best parts of the English character have rarely been more admirably exemplified than by Mr Baker in his manifold trials, perplexities and privations,' said the *Quarterly Review*. Long articles praised the unflagging spirit of the writing, the contributions to ethnology and natural history – and the humour. One magazine compared Baker to Herodotus. The *Pall Mall Gazette* saw him as the model Anglo-Saxon man, the concrete realization of the Englishman's opinion of himself in his very best idealized aspect – including his pluck in 'knocking down niggers, but knocking them down in the cause of virtue'. In short, proclaimed the *Gazette*, Baker was a fine fellow who had written the most delightful book in the world.

But the headiest tributes were paid to Florence, and the *Morning Advertiser* thought that many a fair bosom would palpitate with pride and many a bright eye grow moist with emotion. It drew attention to her picture facing the title-page of the first volume; she wears a serene and thoughtful expression, with one hand gently resting upon her chin.

If Sam was in doubt over carrying off his ruse about Florence's origins, the *Daily News* would have reassured him: 'A refined English lady, and her husband, an accomplished English gentleman, traced their way to the solution of the great world problem which from the beginning of time has baffled the curiosity of mankind.'

Several of the reviewers drew attention to the author's strong emotions about slavery, although at the same time he was noted to be uncompromisingly scathing about the blacks. Indeed, one entry in the index to his book neatly sums up Baker's racial opinions:

'NEGRO, a curious anomaly, 208; a creature of impulse, *ib*; absurd to condemn him *in toto*, as it is preposterous to compare his intellectual capacity with that of the white man, *ib*; cunning and a liar by nature, 209; in no instance has he evinced other than a retro-

gression when once freed from restraint, 211; why he was first introduced into our own colonies, and to America, 212; in a state of
slavery compelled to work, *ib*; when freed refuses to work, *ib*; for an
example of the results, look at St Domingo, 213; his first act when
emancipated to procure a slave for himself, *ib*.'

It was not only in literary circles that Baker was attracting attention. There was a mounting belief in Westminster that he
deserved some added recognition. Gladstone wrote to Murchison
saying that the explorer had done the nation a great honour in a
distant and barbarous land – and what was more, without costing
the State a penny. The last twenty pages of *The Albert Nyanza* impressed Gladstone as being a 'masterpiece', and it seemed that an
award was called for. That letter was dated 23 July 1866. Almost
simultaneously, the Foreign Secretary, Lord Stanley, was writing
to Disraeli, the Chancellor, in more specific terms: 'Baker is a man of
some private fortune, and I am told he does not want money. I
would knight him.' Who had told Stanley that the explorer did not
want money was undoubtedly none other than Lord Wharncliffe, a
close friend of both of them.

The gift of knighthood lay with the Prime Minister, Lord Derby.
He happened to be Lord Stanley's father, such was the cosy world of
politics in those days. On 28 July, Stanley composed a letter to his
father, and after suggesting a lesser honour for James Grant, returned
to his principal theme: 'Baker is a man, though not very wealthy,
of independent means: he went out at his own cost, which is an
additional claim to some reward: I should suggest a knighthood for
him.'

A fortnight later, the knighthood was announced. Three months
after that, Baker went to Buckingham Palace, to be dubbed 'Sir
Samuel' by the Queen, in time-honoured style. It was a splendid
step up for him, as the senior member of a family which looked back
nostalgically to its titles of former generations. It was even more a
step up for Florence, progressing in one year from a decidedly dubious
status to being Lady Baker. In spite of the censoriousness of the
age, there were people who knew something of her past but nonetheless thought she well deserved the title. Cotton Oswell, to whom
Livingstone had written so harshly about the Bakers, went to have
lunch with them. Afterwards he wrote to Livingstone's daughter,
calling Florence 'a trump' and praising her good looks.

Certainly, to the country at large she was becoming a heroine. A fortnight after going to the Palace, Sam took her up to Nottingham where he was addressing a large meeting, and she was repeatedly cheered at every mention of her name. Eventually, the Speaker of the House of Commons, who was presiding at the occasion, went down into the audience where she was sitting, and led her to the platform. There Florence stood and bowed, while the applause grew even louder. As for Sam, he was in his element. In the course of an extensive report, the *Nottingham Guardian* described his performance: 'Sir Samuel's address was entirely extemporaneous; it was delivered with a graphic freedom of style, a felicity of diction and an impressive earnestness which riveted the unflagging attention of an audience of 1400 persons for nearly two hours.'

But one person was far from amused when news of the knighthood reached him. That erstwhile explorer, now an Indian army officer once more, James Grant, sent off a frenzied letter to his publisher friend, John Blackwood.

After arguing that he and Speke were the real discoverers, that Baker was being knighted just for telling his story well and putting in some sensational stories, he explodes: 'By God! I never heard of anything more disgusting to us! The information about his woman too is not fair, for you know very well from poor Speke and myself the position she was in . . .' Grant ranted on, recalling that three years before Colquhoun told him and Speke how he believed that Florence 'had been in the position of barmaid in a continental town where Baker spent a year or two'. It was all, Grant declared, 'a rotten job'.

Blackwood hastily wrote back, and tried rather unconvincingly to persuade Grant that his own award – being made a Commander of the Bath – was better than a knighthood. Then he pleaded: 'I strongly advise you not to enter into any correspondence and above all not to let out anything about Mrs Baker's position. Whatever she may have been before, she went through a fiery baptism in Africa, sufficient to wash out the memory of any previous spots.'

It would seem that, after some heated exchanges with Baker by letter, Grant cooled off and took Blackwood's advice to keep quiet about Florence. But the talk, here and there, was to have its dire consequence.

Early in 1867, the Bakers went to stay with the Wharncliffes in Yorkshire. In the warm glow evoked by success, good fare and vintage port, Baker made a suggestion to his friend: perhaps Lady Wharncliffe could at a suitable moment ask the Palace if she might present Lady Baker, since they had never met.

The Bakers moved on to stay with Lord Halifax in Doncaster, for they were now celebrities, invited everywhere. In February, the Wharncliffes came up to their London house in Curzon Street and put the innocent-seeming request to the Palace. The response was a sharp refusal.

Although the source of her information is a mystery, the Queen knew about Lady Baker. To receive her was out of the question. Immorality was immorality, whether it happened in Mayfair or in a tent in the middle of Africa.

As the Queen was to write a few years later about her refusal to receive anyone having the slightest taint of impropriety: 'The *rule* has always been adhered to.' (Curiously enough, she was explaining in this case her refusal to see Mrs Millais, the wife of the artist elected to the Athenaeum Club at the same time as Baker. The offence of Mrs Millais was in having left her first husband, the critic John Ruskin, who was impotent: during the annulment proceedings she was declared to be *virgo intacta* despite several years of marriage. But even when these details were explained to the Queen, she was unrelenting, and instructed her Mistress of the Robes: 'You should advise Mrs Millais in her own interest to say no more about it.')

Since the moral severity of the widowed Victoria was well enough known – lauded, indeed, as the standard her subjects should aspire to – Baker could have had no inkling that the secrets of his private life were in her possession. Otherwise, he would not have dared put the proposition to Lady Wharncliffe. So it was a double shock when Wharncliffe (who had himself been completely unaware of the truth) asked him to come to Curzon Street and there broke the news.

Baker went back to the Athenaeum, and poured out his dismay in a long letter to Wharncliffe, asking his forgiveness for having caused such embarrassment. He could only say that he personally did not attach the least importance to the forms of marriage in various countries. If the mere registration before a magistrate in London were valid, 'what form shall be adopted where one party is Roman Catholic and the other Protestant, when in a wild country like Hungary and Turkey?'

He went on to say that as soon as they were back in England, he and Florence had been married, and even though their behaviour might be wrong in the eyes of the Queen, it was not so in the eyes of God. 'This refusal of the Queen is a poor reward for all the love and devotion through trials impossible to describe that Florence has shown me . . . Should I find that the world follows the example of the Queen, I shall give up my country and go elsewhere. For years I have been happy without the world, when we have been together with a poor hut or a shady tree for home, and thus with her I can be happy again and lay the world down at will . . . Forgive me, my dear Wharncliffe, for writing all this, but I know your sincere friendship and you know mine for you.'

The letter was certainly eloquent, even though it contained an element of sophistry; Wharncliffe must have written a reassuring answer, for on the next day, Baker was expressing his relief that he would not lose the affections of his old friend. Then he explained how his feeling towards Florence was 'perhaps more intense than is often bestowed upon women by their husbands', and that he was determined she would always remain in ignorance of what had happened. 'The Queen has the right to impose the pain as she chooses, therefore I will take good care never to place poor Florence in this position again . . .'

As if to ease the rebuff, Baker mentioned that he had told Murchison how he wanted to go back to Africa, in command of an Anglo-Egyptian expedition to explore all the Nile lakes, with steamers and a military force provided by the Khedive of Egypt. 'I know that my dear and faithful companion would travel in my path as before – and whatever the trials may be, none could approach the bitterness of the present.'

CHAPTER 12

Friend of the Prince

With his usual resilience, Baker soon threw off the dejection caused by Victoria's disapproval. A month later, he and Florence crossed the Channel to be honoured by the French Geographical Society. They now enjoyed the publicity which had been so carefully avoided during their previous visit to Paris, eighteen months before.

After being presented with a gold medal by the society's president, le Marquis de Chasseloup-Laubat, the explorer won the hearts of the onlookers by turning to Florence, standing beside him, and giving the medal to her. He then declared that, after his own compatriots, there was no nation he admired more than the French. With them, the British had marched side by side in the smoke of the battlefield, and were doing the same on the roads of geographical discovery.

Such sentiments were well suited to his audience – and as the magazine *Le Tour du Monde* explained, there was a particular cause for pleasure: '*Mais ce qui a surtout provoqué les applaudissements chaleureaux de l'auditoire, c'est la présence de Mme Baker, la belle et courageuse compagne du voyageur . . .*'

For their part, the Bakers were delighted to meet once more their friend from Khartoum days, Guillaume Lejean. He was also in the limelight that day, and gave a lecture to the assembly about his recent travels in the remoter parts of Kashmir.

It was undoubtedly intriguing for Sam to see what *Le Tour du Monde* was doing with its serialization of his book, for while the text was treated with respect, the large engravings upon which the magazine prided itself took remarkable liberties with the British

171

originals. The changes were all, quite simply, concerned with nakedness – because *Le Tour du Monde* took utmost advantage of what might be done in the name of geography. *The Albert Nyanza* became an orgy of voluptuous black breasts and bottoms. It is true that *Le Tour du Monde* was not alone in exploiting the potential of African exploration: British magazines of the time liked to depict the horrors of slavery by showing dusky nude maidens being tied to posts and whipped; but the French artists went at their task with an extra *panache*.

Perhaps what Baker saw in Paris explains the qualities that permeate his second African book, which he was then working on. The pictures are the acme of respectability, but the text gives rein to that animal vigour which he had earlier confined to his diaries. The descriptions of Abyssinian slave girls have a memorable liveliness. *The Nile Tributaries of Abyssinia* tells of the year he and Florence spent before reaching Khartoum (so that whereas it was coming out after *The Albert Nyanza* – which had already gone through several impressions – it described what was really a preliminary reconnaissance).

In search of a little extra prestige to help sales, Baker decided to ask the Prince of Wales if he would allow the book to be dedicated to him. The pretext was that the prince was the first member of the British royal family to have sailed on the Nile, during a visit to Cairo a few years before. The prince was perfectly willing, and at the end of October 1867, a first copy of the work was sent to him.

It is doubtful if Sam and Florence had met the heir-apparent by this time, although they were certainly moving in circles where he was familiar. They might well have encountered him during that autumn, if an attack of bronchitis had not stopped Baker going to Dunrobin Castle, the Scottish seat of the third Duke of Sutherland. The prince liked Dunrobin, with its spectacular architecture beside the Moray Firth, and habitually spent some weeks there during the stag-hunting season. The forty-year-old duke, handsome and supercilious, headed the most powerful family in the land: his grandfather had been called by the diarist Charles Greville 'a leviathan of wealth . . . I believe he is the richest man who ever died'. In London, the duke lived at Stafford House (now Lancaster House), at the top of the Mall close to Buckingham Palace. Although the Bakers had to forgo their visit to Dunrobin in 1867, it was not to be long before the duke would bring Sam and the prince together in a friendship that was to have extraordinary results.

In any case, one member of Sam's family was already much admired by the prince: Colonel Valentine Baker, commanding officer of the Tenth Hussars, the 'Prince of Wales Own'. It was common ground by the late 1860s that Valentine was easily the best cavalry officer the country possessed. He was dashing and inventive: many of his ideas, both in drill and military tactics, were being accepted as general practice. His writings on army matters were lucid and stylish. Nothing missed his attention – soon after taking over the Tenth he held exercises to find the best ways of transporting cavalry by train, and how quickest to get horses in and out of railway trucks. He elicited something close to adoration from his regiment and the prince much enjoyed going down to Aldershot as the honorary colonel, to join in manoeuvres. Valentine was often invited to dine at Marlborough House, the prince's London home just down the Mall from Stafford House.

Although he did have one frailty, many people in the army professed to see in Valentine the very reincarnation of Britain's greatest cavalry officer, the Marquess of Anglesey, second in command to Wellington at the battle of Waterloo – where he had lost a leg and ordered it to be ceremonially buried under a tree.

There was a natural speculation as to how far Valentine's great talents would carry him. In the meantime, Sam had his own ideas how they might be used. Writing to Wharncliffe a few days after the *Nile Tributaries* came out, he put forward his latest scheme for another expedition in Africa. He and Val would lead it together, to rescue a party of missionaries who were being held prisoner by Emperor Theodore, the ruler of Abyssinia. It seemed to Sam that his own experience in those parts, combined with his brother's military abilities, would make an unbeatable combination. All he needed was a thousand men, including 250 cavalry from the Tenth Hussars, to make a lightning advance into Ethiopia 'through my old friend Mek Nimmur's country'. At the time when he was writing this, the rescue of the missionaries was a *cause célèbre*. Baker told Wharncliffe: 'I am vain enough to think that in a few months I would either have Theodore as a living exhibition in the Zoological Gardens – or stuffed in a glass case at the British Museum.'

It was riling to Baker that the British government kept ignoring

173

his advice about rescuing the missionaries. In July, at the suggestion of Lord Derby, he sent a long memorandum to the Foreign Office, setting down in far more detail what he later outlined to Wharn-cliffe. But the army was thinking along different lines, and was to land a force more than forty thousand strong under General Robert Napier on the Red Sea coast of Abyssinia. Utter calamity was forecast by Baker for this plan (wrongly in the event); however, he wrote to Murchison on the subject: 'I feel rather disgusted that the Foreign Office has not offered me some post in the Abyssinia expedition, such as British Commissioner.' He also sent many letters to the newspapers arguing his ideas on how to overthrow the emperor, but by November 1867 it was clear that nothing was to come of it: the advance guard for Napier's elaborate and costly campaign was already going ashore.

Not wishing to waste his memorandum, Baker gave it to John Camden Hotten, a rather notorious publisher, for inclusion in a book describing Abyssinia, hurried out to catch the interest of the moment. In spite of the haste, Hotten was able to introduce a splendid innovation which even *Le Tour du Monde* would have envied: pictures of native nudes in colour.

Frustrated in one part of Africa, yet still yearning for an outlet for his energies – 'England is too tame!' he would complain – Baker turned to a mystery that was spasmodically bothering the Royal Geographical Society: the whereabouts of Dr Livingstone, by now almost sixty and thought to be wandering somewhere around the Nile sources. Reports reaching Zanzibar said at one stage that the old missionary was dead: Baker, among many others, thought this probably correct – although ex-consul Petherick, still hovering in the twilight of RGS affairs, rightly insisted that he was not. Throwing his cap into this new ring, Baker told Murchison: 'If the Egyptian Government would allow a steamer to be placed on the lakes, I would be delighted to go and meet my old friend Livingstone, if he lives. The inactivity of my present life is worse than an African fever.'

But nothing was to come of that, either. Livingstone would remain lost for many years longer – and at the start of 1868 the speculation over his whereabouts was quite forgotten for a time in the excitement about another missing man of God, also bearing a name strongly linked to Africa.

The Reverend Benjamin Speke had come up to London in the New Year from Somerset, to conduct the wedding of a friend, and completely vanished. The last that was known of him was when he bought a hat in Pimlico; his old hat was later found by a working man in Birdcage Walk. What could have happened? On account of his famous name, this country clergyman's fate filled the whole land with wild surmise.

It also filled columns in the newspapers, especially when the Speke family raised its reward for information from £100 to £500. On 5 February, *The Times* devoted a leader to the affair: 'The mystery of the day is the disappearance of Mr Speke.' It said that the 'more than extraordinary attention' was due to his station in life, and the celebrity his family name had acquired through the African adventures and sudden death of his brother. The leader tended to discount the idea of murder, rather knowingly advising that the police 'should not confine themselves to looking for a dead body'. But Baker took a gruesome view: in a letter to James Grant, on 6 February, he speculated that Ben Speke had been garotted and his body hidden.

The weeks went by and speculation was unabated. One writer, after a closely-printed column of conjecture, pronounced that the perpetrators of the crime were foreigners. Readers bombarded the newspapers with letters, recounting similar human mysteries; some persons of religious disposition saw in it all the hand of a Higher Being, or a lower one, as well as some arcane connection with the untimely departure from this world of the clergyman's brother.

Then on 25 February came the news: Benjamin Speke was found. The *Western Morning Star* gave the details: 'A man dressed as a bullock drover was arrested on Friday at Padstow with a large sum of money in his possession, and was remanded three days on suspicion of being a man named Ayre, who lately absconded from Hull. He was proved, however, not to be Ayre. Among his luggage various disguises were found. Being a man of superior deportment, further suspicion was aroused, and it was thought that his description corresponded to that of the Rev. Mr Speke. After great hesitation he admitted that he was that gentleman. He is now in the custody of the police at Bodmin.'

When it eventually came out, his explanation for causing so much fuss was simple enough: he wanted to escape from his existing mode of life and go to America, to preach the Gospel there. But the Cornish police, after pocketing the large reward, handed him back to his family, and friends let it be known that his aberration stemmed from an excessive study of the Bible and a morbid dread of marriage. The outcome gratified *The Times*, which had suspected all along that he was still alive somewhere, and was able pithily to observe: 'The question which everyone had asked himself was whether a strong man, in the vigour of life, could thus be made away with in the centre of London, whether our metropolis was infested with murderers of such skill that clergymen – and others – could have perished by their violence without trace.'

In an age when the Church still dominated rural life, and parsons viewed their calling with solemn pride, the ludicrous Speke affair caused embarrassment in rectories up and down the land. That is an added reason why Sam and Florence must have followed it closely – because Edith, eldest of Sam's daughters, had only two months earlier become married to a country rector. This match was the direct result of the Bakers' move out of London to Norfolk, where they leased a large rambling manor house, Hedenham Hall; the bridegroom was the rector of Hedenham village.

For Florence, the wedding was a landmark, in which she may have found some compensation for her own furtive ceremony two years before in St James's. She took upon herself the organizing of it all, for by now she had fully asserted her right to 'a mother's position'. Her photographs from this time indeed show that she was also beginning to look a trifle matronly: although she was still in her twenties so much good living in stately homes was having its effect on her once boyish figure. A letter written to Edith from Raby Castle in Yorkshire towards the end of 1867 gives a clear picture of the kind of life to which she was now accustomed: 'We have important company here, so many people we know: the Duke and Duchess of St Albans, Lord and Lady Halifax and Miss Wood, and Lord and Lady Taunton and two daughters. Lady Russell is also coming today . . .' She goes on to say how sorry she is to miss the birthday of one of the girls, and asks Edith to arrange 'a nice, big cake' and find out what book her sister would like as a present.

The letter is in German, but Florence was by now doggedly improving her English, with the help of her stepdaughters. The earliest surviving letter by her in English is undated, but must have been written in the spring of 1868. The language is so correct in every sense that she surely received help with it – but then, there was a particular reason in this instance why Florence would want to be word-perfect and ladylike. The letter was to the wife of Colquhoun, the erstwhile consul-general who knew so much about the old days. By now Colquhoun was knighted and retired in Scotland with a young wife, although he would shortly have a last moment of glory by representing the Queen at the opening of the Suez Canal. 'My dear Lady Colquhoun,' writes Florence, 'We are so sorry that you cannot come to us, especially as illness prevents you – it is no doubt this unseasonable weather that causes it, for it is certainly most trying. Here the east winds are dreadful . . .' She goes on to say that the Bakers were planning a stay in London, and would be at Almond's Hotel; since the Colquhouns were also going to be in town, there might be a chance to meet then. Finally, she thanks Sir Robert for his letter to her (which sadly does not survive). All things considered, Colquhoun must have been impressed.

The next known letter from Florence in English tells of life in quite the grandest castle that she and Sam had ever stayed in. At last they were at Dunrobin, with its palatial drawing-rooms and vast staircases. It was *de rigueur* for all gentlemen to wear the kilt, which would have pleased Sam. As though to make up for their absence the previous year, the Duke of Sutherland asked them to stay for more than a month. In the middle of September the Prince of Wales was coming with Princess Alexandra, to hunt and relax until well into the following month. The duke chose his guests for such occasions with care, for he and the prince understood each other well: neither could abide people who were dull. 'We shall have a very gay party the week after next,' Florence told Edith, 'as there will be two balls given for the Prince of Wales. It is so very kind of the Duchess to insist on our staying so long.' She told Edith how her father went deerstalking and had shot six stags. (Nowadays, he no longer killed his quarry by stabbing.)

Across the Highlands in Balmoral, somebody had been studying the guest list at Dunrobin and was not amused. She spoke to General Sir William Knollys, private secretary to the Prince of Wales, and he passed her message on, in writing. It demanded a reply.

So on 27 September 1868, Bertie sat down in his suite at Dunrobin to write to 'dear Mama'. At the start he occupied himself with some vague rumours that he had met with an accident, and dismissed them as 'a very bad joke'. Then he moved on to what was plainly the real purpose of the letter: 'Sir W. Knollys wrote to me that you had heard that Sir S. Baker and Lady Baker were here, and that you wished us to know that she had been on intimate terms with her husband before they were married.

'I had also heard the report; and spoke to the Duke about it, and he assures me that he and the Duchess had made enquiries into the matter and they had *no* doubt that there was *no* foundation for the story, and the Duchess is very particular about the ladies she asks and certainly would not have asked Lady Baker to meet Alix unless she felt certain that she was quite a fit person to know.

'She is one of the most quiet and ladylike persons one could see, and perfectly devoted and wrapt up in her husband – and I think it is very hard on both that this story should be believed, which must be most distressing to him, and very dreadful to her – and his name will always be known in history as the great discoverer . . .'

Having sent this bland rejoinder, he at once asked Baker to accompany him, at the end of the year, on a trip to Egypt. He wanted Sir Samuel to look after the arrangements in Cairo and plan some excursions. It was exactly ten years since Sam's meeting, also in Scotland, with the Maharajah Duleep Singh. As had happened then, the journey was to mark a turning point.

The Sutherlands were also going to Egypt, and in the vain hope of deflecting the Queen's criticism one sad exception had to be made to the party. As Sam told Wharncliffe: 'I have arranged to accompany the Prince to Egypt, but it was quite impossible for Lady Baker.'

It is a measure of the dismay Florence felt that she made Sam promise never to go abroad again without her after this. But there was a domestic consolation: her eldest stepdaughter, Edith, married to the Hedenham rector, had speedily produced a baby. It is symptomatic of her anxiety to be accepted as part of the family that she immediately began calling the child her grandson, although she was only twenty-seven. The parents invited her to become the godmother. On hearing the news, she wrote: '. . . I feel towards you all quite the love of your real mother . . .'

178

The birth came just in time for Baker to use it as the finale to his latest book, *Cast Up By the Sea*. This was an adventure story for boys, with many autobiographical overtones, ranging from Ceylon to Central Africa. In spite of some rather ponderous disquisitions about the slave trade, it was spirited enough to be reprinted many times, well into the twentieth century. Several of the main characters are easily identifiable – the handsome smuggler with 'herculean shoulders' is Sam, and his wife Polly is clearly based upon Florence. The junior heroine, a clergyman's daughter, is called Edith. The junior hero, Ned, has been brought up by the smuggler and his wife after being saved from a shipwreck in a storm (an echo of Sam's feat in Constanza). In the end, Ned proves to have come from a rich, aristocratic family and marries Edith – but only after exploring Africa and meeting a beautiful young black queen; she had wanted him as a husband, but died in his arms after being struck through the breast by an enemy arrow.

In the last paragraph of the book, Polly – 'who considered herself the grandmother' – is described gazing fondly at Edith's newborn child. In the closing sentence she speaks of the baby as 'a blessing from God to my childless home'. It is a poignant hint of how Sam and Florence must have felt at still being without any family of their own.

By the turn of the year, Baker was on his way to Egypt to do the groundwork before the arrival of the royal visitors, who were to travel as far south as Aswan. The prince wanted the minimum of formality, but the Egyptians were eager to set up a string of receptions and balls. Striking the right balance between these two needs was delicate work, so a heavy responsibility fell on Baker: he was the only member of the party experienced in dealing with the Egyptian authorities and could speak Arabic. By the time the prince and princess arrived off Alexandria at the start of February, everything was well in hand.

This is not to say that the trip was unmarred by acrid comment. A London satirical magazine, *Tomahawk*, seized the opportunity for a barely veiled attack on the prince's already notorious philandering. In a full-page cartoon, Britannia clings beseechingly to Bertie, and the British lion sobs into a handkerchief, while he strides towards an Egyptian temptress standing under palm trees with her hands upon her breasts. Far more pointed, however, was the letter

Victoria wrote to her son and heir as he set off. She protested that
for the sake of appearances, because his example would be quoted
for good or evil, he should have taken with him an older and 'more
sedate' person. 'The company of Sir S. Baker (and I am sorry to hear
also the Duke of Sutherland, whose style is not a good one in any
way) grieves me for these reasons. Sir S. Baker's principles are not
good, and I regret that he should be associated with you and dear
Alix. Travelling together leads to familiarity . . .'

After going on to tell him that it was all to be much deprecated,
and how anxious his papa always was on such matters, she ended:
'If you should ever become king you will find these friends *most*
dangerous and you will have to break with them all.'

From long experience of such diatribes, the prince replied coolly.
Sir Samuel was a grand sportsman and knew the country well –
'and whatever his principles may be he is unlikely to contaminate
us in any way – besides he will not be on the same boat with Alix and
me on the Nile'. In a later letter he even dared to return to the
subject, saying how glad he was that Baker was a member of the
party. Although he did not reveal that fact, he was also preparing to
speak the words that would do his 'unprincipled' friend and companion a tremendous favour.

A leisurely journey by steamer to Aswan and back, a distance of
nearly 1200 miles, was giving Baker ample chance to stir the royal
enthusiasm for the ambitious plan he was harbouring. He knew the
prince could be his most powerful advocate, to persuade the
Egyptians to give him command of a military expedition to the
great African lakes; this was broadly the scheme first mooted to
Murchison, fully two years before. When the river voyage was completed, there would be ten days of balls and banquets in Cairo,
offering occasions in plenty to talk of such matters to the Khedive
Ismail. If the Egyptian ruler, always eager to display his liberal
open-mindedness, could be cozened into giving Baker such an appointment, it would put an imprimatur of well-doing upon what
critics at home might otherwise consider merely a somewhat lavish
royal holiday: Baker explained clearly that the prime purpose of the
expedition would be to pacify an anarchic part of Africa and put
down slavery. As the Nile glided by, the prince became converted.

On hand to report the Nile journey was the august correspondent of *The Times*, William Howard Russell, famed for his coverage of the Crimean War. He described how the prince would stand beneath the awning on the steamer, gun in hand, on the watch for birds or other quarry. Around him his party lounged in easy chairs, gazing at the slowly changing panorama of fishing villages, sandy wastes and ruined temples. In the cabins on deck, the ladies of the entourage sat sketching or writing letters. The steamer, supplied by the Egyptians, contained so many ornate mirrors and gold-backed French armchairs that Baker had taken it upon himself to install some English carpets and furniture, on the grounds that the vessel looked too much like a floating boudoir.

Baker was constantly in the company of the prince, and Russell playfully related one of the misfortunes of their hunting expeditions: 'The Prince and Sir S. Baker had a stalk after a brace of fine crocodiles one day, but when they came within a shot of the place where they had marked their prey down, there was only a blank of sand indented by the scales and claws of the wary reptiles, which had subsided quietly into the Nile.' Sir Samuel's opposite number, the lady-in-waiting to Princess Alexandra, was the Honourable Mrs Grey, who kept a diary of the entire visit. She tells how one day a small boat in which some of the party was travelling became stuck on a mud bank. Baker and an equerry carried first the princess and then Mrs Grey to the bank by crossing their arms to form a chair and wading through the water. The diary conveys well the jauntiness of those weeks on the Nile, when any minor mishaps gave an agreeable sense of adventure, as well as something extra to write home about from the secure luxury of the steamer.

The business that really mattered took place in the more opulent atmosphere of Cairo. The khedive listened attentively to the Prince of Wales, with the Armenian-born Foreign Minister, Nubar Pasha, in close attendance. Baker's projects were nothing new to Nubar, because the Englishman had been writing to his ministry about them for months. To the khedive, the vision of bringing the entire African lakes region under Egyptian sovereignty was exhilarating, for it would vastly add to his domains and guarantee control of the Nile waters upon which everything in them depended.

Although he was only a few years from bankruptcy, and the peasants were already being ground down to pay the interest on his debts, Ismail was maintaining his style as a mixture of sybarite and nation-builder. He never stopped constructing bridges, railways, opera houses and palaces, so that even a bold campaign to annex a large segment of Africa down to the equator seemed well within his scope. There was, however, one fundamental obstacle in Baker's way: could the French-educated khedive be persuaded to give such an appointment to an Englishman? As William Howard Russell put it, Egypt was a country 'to which France generally lent ideas and agencies in every department of administration'.

The prince made it his business to resolve the matter; and perhaps Ismail was more easily persuaded because the Suez Canal, to be officially opened later in the year, was the brain-child of a Frenchman. It might seem an excellent moment to redress the balance. By the time the royal party left Alexandria at the end of March, it was common knowledge that Baker was to become Governor-General of the Equatorial Nile Basin, answerable only to the khedive himself, and with absolute and supreme authority. It was the highest post ever given to a European in the Egyptian administration.

Even the terms had been talked over by the prince. There seemed no reason to skimp on the cloth, when it came to such details as the budget for the expedition or its leader's salary, if you were dealing with a man reputed to have spent nearly £5,000,000 on his harem.

So eager was Sam to give Florence the glad tidings that he travelled from Alexandria to London, by way of Marseilles and Paris, in only a week. He knew himself to be at the pinnacle of his career: all else apart, after a few years as the servant of the khedive he would be a wealthy man for the rest of his life – if he could survive the term of office.

It was especially agreeable to be able to write to Wharncliffe, without wanting him to pull any more strings. There had been some embarrassment, a year before, when Baker had dared to ask him to sound out the possibility of a baronetcy and been told that it was beyond thinking of. That rebuff palled into nothingness now: 'The Viceroy gives me absolute and despotic command of the force . . . My pay is £10,000 a year, but should my services be required I must remain beyond the two years at the same rate . . . My dear little wife is full of determination to launch once more on the Albert Nyanza – this time we shall have a steamer of 130 tons and a little army instead of thirteen men . . .'

So after an interval of four years, the Bakers were on their way back to Central Africa. Sam was certainly glad to be escaping from the dull stuffiness of England; although in his late forties, he felt himself to be – as ever – a physical lion. Florence was twenty-eight and still game for adventure. She would also have been entitled to expect far more comfort and much less danger this time than there had been on their first expedition.

CHAPTER 13

A Ring of Spears

The time at last arrived when those well-remembered blue mountains along the western shore of the Albert Nyanza were again visible against the sky. Sam and Florence were once more in Bunyoro. The peaks, often hidden among clouds, were symbols of an ambition forever out of reach. It was in this setting, at a place called Masindi, that His Excellency Sir Samuel Baker Pasha, Major-General of the Ottoman Empire, would finally take the most painful decision of his life.

To have come to Masindi at all, into the very heart of Bunyoro, was a gambler's throw. It represented the last chance to fulfil the promise made two years before that he would become the master of half a million square miles of Africa, and annex all the Nile Basin right down to the equator. Now he and Florence were trapped, with one hundred soldiers and a few dozen servants. They were surrounded by an African army six thousand strong, armed with spears and muskets.

Florence was keeping a diary in English at the time, in a large copperplate hand, strikingly different from the style in which she wrote German. Her account traces, with only a few gaps, the whole course of the campaign.

'Thank God we are at last off,' had been her first words in the leather-bound journal on 8 February 1870. The expedition was then starting south from Khartoum with more than thirty boats and nearly half of the complement of 1400 men – 'like a fleet going to war', as Florence remarked. The plan was clear-cut: to set up a string of garrisoned stations on the White Nile, transport two small steamers in sections for assembly beyond the rapids at Gondokoro, sail to Lake Albert, then march far and wide with the Ottoman flag

184

in the khedive's name. For good measure they might even rescue Dr Livingstone, still wandering somewhere in those regions.

At the outset, the much-publicized expedition matched the hopes of its many well-wishers – that it would serve, in the words of Mr Gladstone, the interests of 'peace, commerce and freedom'. (The only disappointment was that Queen Victoria grimly refused to send a goodwill message.) Within a few weeks of leaving Khartoum, Baker intercepted and liberated several consignments of slaves. He was even able to catch the local Turkish governor red-handed in slave-dealing at Fashoda, the place where he and Florence had been given their 'first civilized reception' five years before on their way back from Lake Albert. Florence described two villagers coming on board at Fashoda: 'Sam asked these two poor fellows if the mudir (governor) had shot many of their men. They answered that he killed them like the grass, that they could not count how many were lying dead. It is really quite dreadful to hear their accounts of that horrid fellow of a mudir.' She watched a party of slaves having their leg-irons knocked off by the English mechanics who were with the expedition to assemble and maintain the steamers, and noted after interviewing two teenage girls: 'I never heard such dreadful accounts as these girls gave me of what goes on in these horrid zareebas of the traders, the brutality and cruelty in every way is disgusting. I am sure nobody could imagine what goes on in some parts of the world.'

Often the entries in Florence's diary are brief and homely: 'I am mending clothes today. We had a shower in the afternoon. Sam was not quite the thing today, he caught a cold.' Occasionally she found difficulty in spelling words – for example, interfere appears as 'intefear'. But it is constantly fascinating to see how the prim Victorian style acquired under the tutelage of her stepdaughters is applied to life in Africa: after praising a newly-made road she casually remarks that under it some men have been buried and the graves are too shallow – 'thus when one passes, the smell is rather strong, and unpleasant'. An Egyptian army officer goes on a journey with his harem, but two of the women become ill and die: 'I don't know how he ever expected to travel by land, with four wives.' Now and then she allows herself something close to a joke, usually at the expense of African behaviour. When a naked slave – 'rather a good-looking young man' – is freed and becomes a personal servant, Sam

gives him a long shirt for modesty's sake. 'Now one sees him sometimes with the shirt on and sometimes slung over his head and
nothing whatever to cover his body.'

A main duty for Florence was looking after food supplies, so she
always reported the results of sorties to shoot animals for meat.
When a hippo is killed she records: 'All the troops came running with
knives in their hands, and they looked quite happy to see such a
large beast lying before them. Sam shot him in the ear, with a shell
. . . one of his feet and a piece of his lip are going to be made into
soup, and also some roasted meat which we shall call roast beef, but
I am sorry to say he is not very young.' The chance to shoot hippos
was to be one of the few compensations for months of struggle to
hack a channel for the expedition's armada through a solid barrier
of waterborne plants, the unpredictable *sudd*, which in 1870 was at
its most dense for many years and blocked long stretches of the
White Nile.

Yet the impediments of plant-life were just a prelude to far more
serious human obstacles, for by the time Baker had established his
main garrison at Gondokoro he already knew that the people he
most expected to be his allies against slavery, the Africans, were
generally his enemies. By trying to end so suddenly a social and
economic system in which most chiefs had acquired a vested interest,
he was like a man who had upturned a beehive.

So when Gondokoro was renamed Ismailia after the khedive, and
Baker proclaimed that the surrounding country was Egyptian
territory, a war began. The main tribe, the Bari – 'these wretched
brutes, the Baris', as Florence described them – refused to submit
and were treated to punitive attacks. Among the 'lessons' dealt out
to them, the Bari were relieved of their corn and cattle to feed the
Ismailia garrison – the very plundering for which the slave traders
themselves were condemned. Fighting sometimes came right up to
the riverside and Florence watched it from the deck of a sailing ship.

Baker wrote to the Prince of Wales to tell him how he was getting
on; the prince sent the letter on to *The Times*. When it appeared,
the cheerfully warlike tones must have left Gladstone aghast, and
the seeds of later controversy were sown. But Baker went further
than telling how the Bari were being subdued, by revealing a mood
of mutiny among some of his own forces. 'My black troops are excellent. I wish I could say as much for the Egyptians, many of whom

are convicts transported to the Sudan for felonies.' He added, with an optimism events would soon belie: 'I have them tight in hand.'

The letter went on to say that most Egyptian officials were involved in the slave trade and were engaged in 'passive resistance' in order to wreck the expedition. All this was accurate enough, for Baker was, on a larger scale, struggling in that same web of forces which had destroyed Consul Petherick. It was perhaps a little tactless, however, for someone in the service of a foreign ruler to be expressing himself in such terms – and undiplomatic for the Prince of Wales to have passed the letter on for publication.

At the very moment when the readers of *The Times* were pondering the import of his news, Baker was starting his lunge towards Masindi. He had set off just before the arrival at Gondokoro of a despatch from the khedive himself, ordering that he should advance no further for the moment, but consolidate on the White Nile.

The advice was right. But Sam and Florence were at heart romantic adventurers, who wanted more than anything to go back again to the Sources of the Nile, to see not only 'their' lake, but the Victoria Nyanza as well. Then there was that other, very human, ambition – even though it was of scant concern to the khedive: 'We are very sorry as we cannot hear any news of poor Dr Livingstone,' wrote Florence in her diary, 'how delightful it would be if only we could find him!' They could not know, because of the utter lack of communication with the outside world, that seven hundred miles to the south, the missionary had recently been tracked down by a correspondent of the *New York Herald*, named Henry Stanley; their very ignorance of this was a factor in the decision to push on towards the great African lakes.

The entourage Baker was able to muster for the journey was scarcely adequate for his status and dignity as a 'Pasha of the first rank'. On leaving Egypt, he and Florence had two white personal servants, until the maidservant became pregnant and was sent home with the manservant – 'I shall be anything but sorry at their departure, as they think of nothing but love-making,' wrote Sam to one of his daughters. There was also no doctor, because the English surgeon attached to the expedition 'went quite out of his mind' from drink, as Florence had it, and died in Khartoum. All medical treatment, even simple tasks like extracting teeth, fell to Baker from then on. Finally, a large part of the military force had melted away, through sickness or discontent; after leaving a strong garrison at Gondokoro before heading south, Baker found himself with only a nucleus of loyal soldiers – and even this had to be augmented along the way with slave-trading mercenaries who volunteered to sign on for the Egyptian army. Most serious of all, his lack of troops and failure to raise porters from among the Bari meant that all hopes of assembling a steamer on the Nile above the cataracts must be given up: the still-unexplored stretch of river to Lake Albert could not be charted, and any advance to the equator might now be only by land.

As Baker marched south, he was obliged to set up several armed encampments along the route. Each one whittled down his strength a little more, until he entered Bunyoro with a mere hundred men. Even some of the armed slaving parties were bigger than that.

Yet Baker was immensely proud of his elite corps, consisting of black Sudanese Arabs; dressed in scarlet shirts and tarbooshes, they were nicknamed the 'Forty Thieves'. Some of this bodyguard had served in Mexico with the Egyptian division sent to help the ill-fated Emperor Maximilian, and its battle-hardened coolness was shortly to face its keenest test. At the head of the bodyguard was a tall Egyptian colonel, Abd-el-Kader, with whom Baker had a close rapport: although it was customary in that era for Englishmen to deride all Egyptians as effete and corrupt, Baker would never have anything but praise for the colonel. The Pasha had also taken along with him, as a senior member of the expedition, a naval lieutenant in his early twenties: Julian Baker, his own nephew. Although Julian was intelligent and energetic, becoming in due course a British admiral, a whiff of nepotism surrounded his appointment.

Then there was Florence – 'my little colonel', as Sam affectionately called her. She looked after the stores, supervised the kitchens, kept daily meteorological records, and collected botanical specimens. Unlike on the first expedition to Bunyoro, she now rarely wore male clothes, but rode on horseback in fashionable attire, her aim being to make a suitable impression on the chiefs and their womenfolk who would be met along the route. For such occasions, Baker himself generally put on a high-necked belted jacket and a pith helmet; but he also had a pasha's military uniform, consisting of tarboosh, embroidered frock coat with epaulettes, and a curved, jewelled sword. (We do not hear anything, this time, of his Highland kilt.)

One of his watercolours shows the meeting with a chief named Rot Jarma; this took place while the expedition was waiting on the northeast bank of the Victoria Nile in March 1872 for permission to cross into Bunyoro. He and Florence sit on chairs under an acacia tree, with Julian Baker a little apart. Standing beside them are two of the heavily-armed 'Forty Thieves' and an interpreter. The chief and his councillors, in leopard-skins, lounge against the bole of the tree. Framed by the jungly background is Baker's tent, of a square elegant design rather like the marquees commonly seen at garden parties.

Florence gives her version of the meeting in her diary: 'A great sheikh came to pay Sam a visit today – of course he immediately asked for a cow and some clothes, also beads, because he was an old friend of ours! Sam made him a present of a long blue shirt, and a tarboosh together with a beautiful piece of red cloth. The sheikh was delighted with himself when he was dressed, and we gave him a looking-glass to see himself. He began directly to dance.' She then comments bitterly on the ravages of the slave trade around Bunyoro since she left there six years earlier, and how formerly the villagers were dressed in spotless bark cloth – 'but now they are all dirty and uncared for'. One old chief, who had accompanied Sam and Florence to Lake Albert in 1864, looked 'very miserable' because the slavers had seized all his wives and children: he was cheered up with a gift of some clothes, and a cow from the diminishing herd being driven along with the expedition to supply food.

As the force paused beside the Victoria Nile, memories of the past crowded back into Florence's mind. 'I am sorry to say that this country reminds me of great misery. When I see all the old faces, then I cannot help thinking how we both suffered from illness and misery. The smell of the people makes me perfectly miserable, because I remember how I was carried by them, when dreadfully ill, and thrown down often, and often into the high grass and mud!'

Florence must have been glad to hear she would not have to confront Kamrasi, the Bunyoro king who once wanted her for his wife. He was now dead and his son, Kabba Rega, was ruling from a new capital named Masindi, ten days' journey from the Victoria Nile in the direction of Lake Albert. Although he was only about twenty, it was reported that Kabba Rega had fortified his personal position,

after murdering his brother, by having most of his relations slaughtered as well. In lordly fashion, Kabba Rega kept the newcomers
waiting for days before allowing them to cross the river; nor would
he help them with food or carriers for the march to his capital. It was
a slightly ominous beginning. By now, only two of more than twenty
horses with which the journey from Gondokoro had been started
were still alive, and Florence was reduced to riding an old nag she
nicknamed Rosinante, after Don Quixote's mount.

Baker was staking everything on a friendly reception in Masindi,
because the cattle were constantly dying and there had been no way
of carrying effective reserves of other food on the 400-mile journey
from Gondokoro; the baggage was limited to personal possessions,
presents for chiefs, beads for bartering, and ammunition.

At their first meeting with the young king in his large but unprepossessing mud-hut capital, Florence maintained an open
mind: 'He is a very clean-looking young man of about 18 or 19 years
old, he keeps the nails of his feet and hands beautifully clean and
wears a very nice bark cloth of a light brown colour, and a necklace
of pretty small different coloured beads. His skin is dark brown, his
eyes are large, but they always have a frightened look.'

At their reception for Kabba Rega, the members of Baker's bodyguard who could play musical instruments were formed up as the
band, which was listened to in wonderment by several thousand
people of the Masindi district. (Baker was always an enthusiast for
the power of music in Africa, declaring that all missionaries should
be able to play the bagpipes.) Before he left to go back to the royal
quarters, the king was given an array of presents, including a watch
and a snuff box that played a tune when the lid was opened. Dis-
satisfied, he also asked for a large Swiss musical box he had been
invited to listen to; but Baker was retaining it as a bait for the
future.

The tension at Masindi was to build up in spasms, with Baker often
telling himself that signs of hostility were being exaggerated by his
own imagination. Kabba Rega continued to visit him, asking for
more gifts and demanding that the soldiers should help him destroy
his greatest enemy Chief Rionga, who had taken refuge on an island
in the Nile. The first unmistakable warning of what was to come
occurred late one night, after Masindi had been wrapped for several
hours in total silence. Without any warning, the noise of a thousand

190

drums thundered in the darkness, and warriors could be heard shrieking all around. Horns were being blown, whistles and fifes added to the uproar, but in the moonlight there was nobody to be seen. Then the noise abruptly stopped. By this time, Baker's soldiers had assembled with their arms, but he decided to treat the affair as a practical joke: he ordered the band to play a few tunes, told the sentries to be on the alert, then went to bed.

Deciding that his only hope lay in an appearance of calm and normality, Baker began setting up a permanent station on a vacant patch of ground. The king was told that among its amenities would be a school for the local children. The land was soon cleared, huts built for the troops, gardens laid out and seeds planted. The centrepiece was a thatched building, twenty-eight feet long, declared to be 'Government House'; in it were set out samples of goods that Bunyoro would be able to buy if it opened up a regular trade with Egypt: tin plates, crockery, mirrors, knives, scissors, razors, watches, clocks, many kinds of cloth, spinning tops, tambourines and tin whistles. This display, in the spring of 1872, was the first 'trade fair' of European goods ever arranged in Central Africa.

The Bakers also built a house for themselves – and decorated it to impress Kabba Rega. They hung upon the walls two gold-framed mirrors, several sporting prints and coloured life-sized posters of beautiful women in evening dress, their jewels picked out in tinsel. At one end on a table a portrait of Queen Victoria was displayed and at the other a full-length photograph of Princess Alexandra.

When the buildings were complete, Kabba Rega was invited to pay a visit. He seemed dazzled by all the white man's novelties, and decided it was magic when he saw endlessly repeated reflections of himself in the facing wall mirrors. Julian Baker brought out an 'electric shock machine', with two handles attached to a galvanic battery; the king thought it hilarious and insisted that all his entourage should try the machine at maximum power, although declining to risk it himself. Then he inspected Florence's jewellery, and was given some of it – but his biggest disappointment was when she refused to hand over her seven-chambered Colt revolver.

She wrote in her diary, on 11 May: 'Kabba Rega came to pay me a visit after breakfast. He came with only a few people – we showed him my snug little house, and the large musical box which he asked for directly! In fact, he asked for everything we showed him. We gave him a beautiful bracelet and a necklace made of blue and white beads – He left us in about two hours, quite delighted with all his presents.' But she thought him 'cunning and lying'.

In the middle of May, there was a calculated show of confidence by Baker. He ran up the Ottoman flag outside his 'government house' and with the young king's seeming assent proclaimed that all of Bunyoro was now under the protection of the Khedive of Egypt. In material terms it meant nothing, since he knew himself – the khedive's representative – to be more at Kabba Rega's mercy with every day that went by. The high grass around the camp made it difficult to see much, but he realized that ranks of huts were being built on every side. Baker also knew that there were almost no women in Masindi any more: he was being surrounded by Kabba Rega's warriors. Contact with his nearest outpost, several weeks' journey away across the Victoria Nile, was impossible. Whatever happened, there could be no hope of reinforcements.

Why did the king want to destroy him? By now, it was plain that an unseen hand was manipulating events; the hand belonged to Abou Saood, a slave trader and ivory dealer whose employers, an Egyptian company, had been given monopoly rights over the White Nile trade. The motley collection of rival European and Levantine traders of the 1860s was gone, and Abou Saood had by terror tactics asserted such a mastery, right into Bunyoro, that Kabba Rega was his puppet. Abou Saood had ruled that Baker's force must be wiped out, said persistent rumours; so the king was now screwing up his courage to obey. There was no lack of irony: the agent of a company holding an Egyptian government concession was scheming for the destruction of a force led by the representative of the khedive.

The waiting went on. Florence's retinue of freed slave children diligently tended the gardens, in which all kinds of vegetables were already coming through the soil. The troops drilled each morning in an open space in the middle of Masindi, and when off duty bartered for food with beads. The distant blue mountains looked on: 'We are all longing to be off every day to travel on the lake again,' wrote Florence. But she knew in her heart that they never would. Everyone was watching for Kabba Rega to make his move.

It came on the last day of May, as the troops were parading. A war-drum suddenly began to throb its message from the king's compound. Baker and his nephew, and the Egyptian officers, ordered the men to form a square with the band in the centre and stand with their weapons at the ready. 'I was perfectly unarmed,' wrote Baker afterwards, 'as were the officers (excepting their side arms) and Lieutenant Baker.' As the drumming went on, five thousand warriors armed with shields and spears obeyed the call. They converged on the square, shouting their war-cries.

One person not on the scene was Florence. She had stayed in the camp, almost a quarter of a mile away, and was left with only a few guards, the sick, the camp servants, and the women and children. Sam knew that if a battle started, she was going to be overrun.

Florence had heard the war-drums and the tumult from the parade ground. 'Thus I ran down to the troops' camp and called every man out, sick or not, even down to the stable boys, and gave them each a gun, and posted them at different places around the whole camp.' From the ammunition store she snatched some military rockets, which could be used to set alight the thatched roofs of Masindi, and aimed them ready for firing. The moment any shooting was heard, the rockets would be loosed off. As she dashed about, setting up her frail defences, the warriors were running past in thousands towards the parade ground. The noise of drums and horns grew louder. Some of the men came towards her with their spears raised: 'Everybody was excited and anxious to have a fight . . . but they had not quite the courage to come closer.'

Across on the parade ground, Baker and his officers were looking for some way out of the trap, knowing that if fighting did begin, they would be destroyed by the weight of numbers; the soldiers carried only muzzle-loading muskets for drilling and after one volley would have no time to reload. At that moment, Baker spotted several senior chiefs of Bunyoro among the warriors, with an interpreter. He strolled casually over and called out: 'Well done! Let us all have a dance!' When this was translated, the chiefs looked momentarily bewildered, and Baker seized his chance. He told the band to strike up a lively tune, and announced that his men would perform a dance of their own. He asked for the crowd to stand away, then told his men to advance on every side with their bayonets. Baffled by these manoeuvres, the warriors fell back from the parade ground, and to Baker's relief one of the chiefs told them to sit. The band played on and the troops re-formed their square. With the initiative in his hands, Baker asked to see Kabba Rega, and after a delay while both sides watched one another warily, the king arrived. He was drunk, and could only reel to and fro waving his spear, until his chiefs urged him to leave.

For the moment, the fight had trickled out of the Bunyoro warriors and a senior chief named Kittakara turned shamefacedly to Baker and asked for the troops to be withdrawn. They could all dance, he explained, some other day when the sun was not so hot. So with Baker at their head, the troops filed back to the camp; as they did so, a small African boy ran from the crowd and took Baker by the hand to march along with him. It was Kittakara's own son, with whom Florence had made friends since the arrival in Masindi. That at least felt like a small victory.

The force had been extricated from the parade ground – but how was it to be got out of Bunyoro? There could now be no doubt that an attack would come: it was folly to imagine that bluff could work a second time. On 2 June, work began in the camp on a wooden-walled fortress, in which the gunpowder and ammunition could be stored. If need be, this would become the last redoubt. Within three days the main work on the fort was finished, the soldiers labouring in shifts to chop down trees and dig trenches. Now there was a new danger – supplies of food were running low and none could be bought in Masindi, creating the prospect of being starved out. Yet Kabba Rega's tactics were puzzling and contradictory, for every day he sent messengers with elephant tusks, to be exchanged for the merchandise laid out in Baker's 'government house'. If this was an attempt to lull his prey into a false sense of security, Florence at least was never impressed. In her quaint style, she wrote in her diary on 4 June: 'There is not a gentleman in the whole of Africa, I believe, unfortunate [sic] nobody knows what honour or good manners really are. They only think of lying and deceiving . . . The longer I am in this horrible country the more I abhor it, as the people are bad.' Nostalgic thoughts about England began to appear more often in her diary as the trap tightened.

A week after the parade-ground trial of nerves, Baker sent several messages to Kabba Rega, urging him to allow some food to be brought in. At the end of the day, porters arrived with two large packages of flour and seven jars of plantain cider; it looked like a peace offering. Most of the cider was sent off to the troops and the Bakers sat down to have their dinner, relieved that one more day had passed without trouble. They intended to have some of the cider themselves later. But as they were finishing their meal, an officer ran in to say that many of the soldiers seemed to be dying and others were rolling on the ground in agony.

Sam jumped from the table, seized his medicine box and raced towards the soldiers' quarters, telling Florence as he went to mix up large quantities of mustard and salt in water.

Several of the men were unconscious and thirty others hardly able to breathe. Some were delirious. The only hope was to make them all sick, so Sam began to force down their throats big doses of tartar emetic. Florence arrived with basins of brine and mustard, which the men were also made to swallow. Everyone began to vomit – 'The patients began to feel the symptoms of a rough passage across the British Channel,' wrote Sam with satisfaction afterwards. So the king's fatal gift was neutralized, without anyone having died.

Next morning, just after dawn, Sam and Florence were taking their usual stroll in the gravelled road that had been made in front of the 'government house'. Although there would be scant chance to celebrate, it was Sam's 51st birthday. As they walked, talking about the previous night's excitement, they waited for the return of Sam's favourite officer, Lieutenant Monsoor, and a corporal, from the house of a chief who had delivered the poisoned cider the previous evening. Monsoor had orders to ask the chief, who lived only two hundred yards away, if he could explain the poison. Perhaps, despite every likelihood to the contrary, it was an accident.

As Sam and Florence turned at the end of their walk, with a sergeant and a bugler nearby, a deafening shout came from somewhere beyond the tall grass surrounding the camp; then two shots were heard – which could only mean that Monsoor and his corporal had been attacked. At the same instant, spears and bullets began to fly, the bugler sounded the alarm, and Florence ran back to the house to fetch a rifle and ammunition belt. The sergeant fell dead, shot through the heart.

The real fighting had begun. The camp was encircled by unseen warriors, who showered the troops with spears, while sharp-shooters with muskets fired at intervals from the grass. Baker knew that if any hope for them remained at all, he must at once send a party to rescue Monsoor and the corporal. He also decided to set the town alight and drive the Bunyoro army away from the camp. Boys were sent out with torches, spreading fire throughout the town; all the while, spears continued to fly. But in little more than an hour, the fight was over, because the combination of flames and rifle fire was more than Kabba Rega's regiments could resist.

Baker returned to the camp, where the fatal casualties from the battle were laid out. Among them was Monsoor, with more than thirty spear-wounds. 'I could not help feeling his pulse, but there was no hope . . . I laid his arm gently by his side, and pressed his hand for the last time, for I loved Monsoor as a true friend . . . He was always kind to the boys, and would share even a scanty meal in hard times with either friend or stranger.'

While the men were being buried, Baker assessed his plight. The burning of Masindi had gained time for whatever lay ahead. But the expedition force could not long stay in the camp, with its food almost gone . . .

Until affairs became too desperate, Florence had made her own records in her diary, relating the daily incidents of camp life and reiterating her suspicions of 'Kabba Rega, the young cub'. They suddenly stop on the day the poisoned cider was delivered. It looks as though she had been writing up her account just as it became known that the men were taken ill: 'Ther. 6 a.m. 64 degrees, noon 70 degrees – Wind from the north-east – No work is going on today, as it is Friday – '. (Friday is the Islamic day of rest and worship.)

It would be many weeks before she could make another entry.

Several days drifted by in an uneasy truce. Africans wandered around the blackened ruins of Masindi, looking for possessions that had been buried under the huts. One morning, after he had tried to parley, a spear was hurled at Baker and thudded into the ground at his feet. Two soldiers then volunteered to go unarmed to Kabba Rega, bearing the large musical box for which he had so often asked, in the hope – however faint – that he would be charmed by it into friendship. With great misgivings, Baker saw them go. They never returned: the king took the musical box, then killed them.

It was decided that the troops must abandon their quarters, to concentrate all remaining forces around the powder magazine and the 'government house', over which the Ottoman flag still defiantly waved. On the night of 11 June, one section of the abandoned huts was set alight by warriors who had crept up to the camp in the darkness. Yells and shrieks sounded from beyond the flames. On the next night, more of the camp was set ablaze. The wooden fort became the last retreat. Sam built a bunker inside it for Florence with boxes and beds.

Next morning there was a general attack on the camp by warriors armed with guns, spears and poisoned arrows; although it was repulsed, Baker realized the bitter truth – there was nothing left but to try fighting a way out, back to the Victoria Nile.

There would be little the soldiers could carry, except guns and ammunition, for fighting was likely all the way. It was eighty miles to the river and there would be no guide.

The grass was more than head high all across the countryside, much of which was marshland: it was ideal terrain for ambuscades. Kabba Rega's regiments would be lying in wait everywhere as the retreating column groped for its route along a network of narrow, twisting paths, relying only on the compass and memory of the way it had come to Masindi many weeks before. Survival would depend upon courage, cool nerves and forced marches.

Baker gave his orders: the following morning the station was to be destroyed and everything that was not essential for the march would be left to burn. Then the retreat would begin. He told his troops that there would be an advance guard of fifteen men with rifles and a rearguard of the same strength. The rest of the soldiers would be spread along the line. Everyone who could use a weapon would be armed and if attacks were made on both flanks, alternate files would fire to left and right – aiming low because the warriors always crouched down after throwing their spears. Battle orders would be given by bugle calls. 'On no account must the column be broken up,' Baker told his men. 'If it is, we are lost.' Finally, he warned, there must be absolute silence on the march: the women and children must not say a word.

All through the night, Florence and the camp women packed the loads in boxes, everyone allocated as much as their strength made possible. There were three donkeys and two horses left, but nobody was going to ride, because the animals would be weighed down with baggage. For anyone who might be wounded or become sick, the prospects were grim. But the heaviest cloud hanging over Baker's plans for the retreat was the lack of food: how could the column march for a week or more on nothing? The provisions were almost gone.

At that moment, Florence revealed her secret. For several weeks, fearing some calamity, she had been hiding supplies of flour, and now she had six iron boxes full. 'Allah give her long life!' shouted the men. If carefully rationed, the hidden reserve would be enough to carry the expedition through to the Nile without the risk of starvation.

As the sun came up, Baker spread his tent over the merchandise in the 'government house'; on that he poured turpentine, ether, lamp oil and all the inflammable contents of his medicine chest – because he was coldly resolved to leave nothing for Kabba Rega. On the tent cloth he laid sixty rockets that could not be carried. In her 'snug little house', Florence sadly piled up her dresses and other possessions. It would be the task of the rearguard to spread the flames while the rest of the column waited on the edge of the camp.

A light rain was falling and the sky was grey.

The flames shot up, and Baker watched his Central African dreams vanish away. As Florence was to recall in a letter to one of her stepdaughters, her feelings were far more personal: 'I must say that my heart was very heavy to see all my beautiful things burn.'

Then the order was given: 'Forward!' As the flames climbed higher and the rockets exploded, the column wound its way down a narrow, winding route, hemmed in by grass. Florence was keeping extra ammunition for Sam's favourite rifle in the bosom of her dress and wore her Colt revolver in her belt. She also carried two bottles of brandy for anyone who was wounded, two cups, two umbrellas and 'many other little things'. Behind them walked two servants carrying loaded elephant rifles. The soldiers were heavily weighed down with luggage and carried their loaded rifles at the ready. The women and children, in the centre of the column, balanced on their heads as much as they could walk with.

Among the 'little things' Florence took with her on the march was a locket on a gold chain around her neck. She was extremely proud of that, because it was a gift from the Empress Eugénie of France and had reached her in Khartoum only shortly before the news came that Eugénie and her husband, Napoleon the Third, had been forced into exile. Somehow, the knowledge that it was one of Eugénie's last gifts as an empress made it more precious and Florence was longing to show it to Sam's daughters. But as she walked through the drenching grass, and waited for the spears, her hopes for that seemed faint and far away.

By the early afternoon of the first day, the preliminary assault was faced: the surprise element of the sudden departure from the camp had given only a brief respite. As the advance guard raked the undergrowth with bullets a lance hit a man named Howarti, walking a few steps ahead of Sam and Florence. With the spear sticking right through him, Howarti drew out a pistol from his belt and shot dead a warrior who had jumped from the ambush. Then he calmly pulled the spear out of his body. But a brief examination showed that the wound was fatal, because as he breathed the air rattled out of a gash in his stomach. After the attack was beaten off, Howarti was put on a stretcher and carried to a field, where a halt was called for the night. By morning, the wounded man was still alive, after being heavily dosed with laudanum and brandy; but he was to die during the day and his body was abandoned beside the path.

Lying awake, Baker realized that the entire Bunyoro army would be overtaking the column along parallel paths, so an all-out attack was certain. Only ten miles had been covered on the first day and seventy more miles lay ahead. He must go faster: more goods must be jettisoned.

A bonfire was started and a vast pile of possessions, all of which only the day before had been thought too precious or essential to abandon, were tossed into the flames. It was to be the first of several such fires on the march, as more and more articles were given up. Only the barest necessities for survival would be spared.

As the column wound its way on the second day into a hollow filled with a wide swamp, the feared all-out attack began. The sound of drums, horns and human voices was deafening, as spears flew out of the tall grass in showers. The bugles sounded and everyone knelt to pour shots at the unseen enemy in the undergrowth. 'I saw several lances pass within an inch or two of my wife's head,' wrote Baker afterwards. But Florence could only concentrate on firing her breech-loading rifle as fast as she could reload.

'My darling child,' she was to write later to one of her step-daughters, 'it is quite impossible to tell you about our weary march – I can only tell you that the entire population lay in ambuscades, and we had to fight for seven days through that dreadful country, where it was quite impossible to see the enemy – only showers of spears passed our faces . . .

'I was always *so* dreadfully afraid that something would happen to dear Papa. What should I have done in such a fearful case? Of course, I should have shot myself rather than fall into the hands of the natives. Everybody would have been killed without Papa, but he managed everything so well that there was never much time lost in acting . . .'

After three days of marching, two of the three donkeys could not keep going and to wait for them to be dragged along was an extra hazard. So the donkeys were shot and their loads thrown into the high grass. Soon afterwards a spear hit one of the horses and went completely through its body. Baker went to look at the animal, of which he was very fond, and knew at once that its hours were numbered, because its intestines were divided and hanging from its belly. But it could still walk, and carried its load until a halt was called after a sixteen-mile march. Then it fell to the ground and was finished with a revolver shot to the forehead. Everything in its loads that could be burnt was used to cook the evening meal; that night, Sam and Florence slept on the ground beside its body.

On the fourth and fifth days of the march the column ran into constant ambushes. In one attack, four men were hit in the legs and had to hobble forward on crutches; their loads were abandoned in the grass. The colonel, Abd-el-Kader, was badly wounded in one arm and a lieutenant took a spear through his shoulder-blade. The deaths went on: a boy leading the last horse was struck through the body and crawled up to Baker, pleading, 'Shall I creep into the grass, Pasha? Where shall I go?' He died a minute later. A young freed slave who belonged to Florence's 'family' fell dead in front of her after being hit by two spears simultaneously. 'He was such a good lad,' wrote Florence, 'he was always afraid something would happen to me.'

The soldiers began to learn the signals by which their hidden enemies organized themselves for an attack. The notes of a shrill bird-song were imitated on an antelope horn, then repeated several times. At once, all the column's rifles were cocked, ready to counter the spears. The march became more desperate and the numbers of the wounded rose with a sinister steadiness. One day, when a halt was made, Baker went off to scout for crops that might be seized to feed the column. On his return he learnt that several of his men had resorted to black magic, by cutting up the corpse of an African shot in the fighting and eating pieces of his liver raw. They believed that this would give them power to score a kill with every shot.

As the column fought its way nearer to the river, a new danger began to overtake it. Florence and the other women grew so exhausted that they had to be helped along. She recalled: 'My feet became very sore from marching, as we had to go sometimes sixteen miles through nothing but swamps two or three feet deep.' But there could be no pausing yet.

The most perilous fight took place as the expedition wound its way through a ravine, while Kabba Rega's warriors hurled their spears down from the rocks. One of Baker's 'Forty Thieves' collapsed in a pool of blood and was left for dead, brandy being poured down his throat as a farewell gesture – even though his heart seemed to have stopped beating; yet the spirit revived him, and there was amazement and rejoicing as he was seen staggering into the camp, supported by two men of the rearguard.

After seven days the column reached the edge of Bunyoro and the ambushes became less frequent. A roughly stockaded camp was formed, so that several days' rest could be taken, for everyone was at the limit of endurance. The losses on the retreat from Masindi had been ten killed and ten wounded; the survivors were left with scarcely any possessions and were suffering from hunger and exhaustion. Ammunition was running low. But the soldiers who formed the band had clung on to their instruments, so Baker told them to play some tunes, simply to impress the people of the surrounding villages with the idea that the expedition was in the best of spirits. Then he led off a work-party, to dig up sweet potatoes in a nearby field.

When the march began again it took only two days to reach the Nile, and only one more man was injured. The riverside district was abandoned and burnt, and to get away from it dugout canoes had to be made. These were used for a journey to the island stronghold of Chief Rionga, whom Baker now resolved to make the Egyptian government's agent, to rule Bunyoro whenever Kabba Rega might be overthrown. As a face-saver, this was all he could do.

It was to take eleven months to get back to Gondokoro. Most of this time was spent at Fatiko, in country Sam and Florence knew well from their first expedition. A powerful fort was constructed and after a nearby slave-trading camp had been destroyed it seemed to Florence almost possible to recapture the magic of those earlier years. She fussed over her array of African children, kept herself busy making dresses from cheap trade cloth, and regarded Fatiko as 'quite the paradise of Africa' – even though more than sixty rats were killed in one day when she ordered a clean-up of the kitchens.

This was to be her last home in Africa. She left behind there a legend of the 'Morning Star' who shone with friendliness and humanity. Among the stories of her that were passed around among the tribes for decades was the one of a young soldier condemned to death for desertion. It was said that Florence persuaded Sam at the last moment to commute the sentence; when he agreed she hurried to the parade ground. The firing party was already taking aim at the man, who was tied to a tree, when Florence arrived, raised her hand and ordered him to be released. 'It would make rather a pretty picture,' said a later traveller who was told the tale. In fact, there is some doubt about the truth of it, as with many stories passed down by word of mouth. In her diaries, Florence says that Sam himself commuted the sentence to fifty lashes: 'Poor fellow, he was so very grateful and thanked Sam very much for his great kindness to him. He is only nineteen years old . . .'

For Sam, there was a certain consolation at Fatiko that he was able to establish firm relations with many minor chiefs around the fort on behalf of the khedive, and give their freedom to several large groups of slaves. He also displayed that old delight in physical prowess, notwithstanding his age, by jumping regularly from one rock to another over a deep ravine near Fatiko.

Yet any illusions he may have harboured that his more serious activities were having a conclusive effect were wiped away as he travelled back down the Nile. Three boats containing seven hundred slaves were intercepted only a few days from Khartoum. Although Abou Saood had gone to Cairo, to rally support among the khedive's ministers, his henchmen were still active everywhere. Yet Baker did his best to put a brave complexion on his three years of effort: in a long letter to Wharncliffe in April 1873 he wrote boldly: 'The slave trade is at an end – and Egypt extends to the equator.'

When he reached Cairo, the khedive received him with every sign of cordiality and pinned on his uniform one of the highest decorations that could be bestowed in the Ottoman Empire. In return, Baker handed over a map, showing how the khedive's territory reached not merely as far as Masindi, but more than a hundred miles beyond, into the very heart of Africa – even embracing those unknown southern shores of Lake Albert. Along the limits of this great annexation, Baker had inscribed the words, 'Imaginary Line'. In all the circumstances, that fairly well summed things up.

CHAPTER 14

A Family Scandal

The return to Europe was a triumphant progress, rather at odds with what had actually been achieved. Sam and Florence were the hero and heroine of the moment, a telegram they had received in Egypt from the Prince and Princess of Wales setting the tenor of the welcome: 'We both heartily congratulate you on your safe arrival in Cairo, after all the dangers you have been exposed to in your long and arduous journey.'

They travelled to England from Egypt by the same route as they had taken nine years earlier, with a halt in Paris. The intention was to gather their strength, but they seemingly did not mind being interviewed by reporters from the London newspapers, who took down everything Sam was prepared to reveal of the expedition's adventures on the White Nile. The role of the 'gentle, though heroic' Lady Baker was given its full romantic due, one correspondent noting her amusement – and Sir Samuel's – at 'the legendary reputation she has most wrongly and undeservedly obtained for Amazonian qualities'.

Although Baker was full-bloodedly heightening the image of his victory over fearful odds, this does not alone explain the adulation which met him at every turn. Rather, it was because a skein of coincidence was casting him in an almost mystical guise – as the true confrère of David Livingstone, the man who symbolized Britain's crusade against slavery. Events closely linked to the old missionary's name had provoked a national upsurge of emotion about the 'evil trade'; it was at a peak at that very moment when the Bakers suddenly reappeared upon the scene. Although Livingstone's solitary wandering south of the African lakes was so unlike Baker's military onslaught to the north of them, both men were avowedly pursuing an

204

identical goal in the same continent; that was similarity enough for most people.

The news that the Bakers were on their way home came amid renewed rumours that Livingstone was dead, a martyr to his high purposes. It also coincided with Britain's boldest stroke yet against slavery in East Africa – an action precipitated by letters sent from Africa by Livingstone himself, in which he described the barbarities of the Arab traders. The letters had impelled Parliament to demand of the Sultan of Zanzibar that he should end all slave auctions in his domains. In the middle of 1873, after being threatened with a naval blockade, the sultan capitulated and signed a treaty with Britain.

Livingstone had indeed succumbed in the African wilderness, only a few weeks before the signing of the Zanzibar treaty. That would not be known for many months, but at the very moment when the struggle with the sultan was at its height false reports reached London that the Bakers had both died fighting against slavery.

This story, allegedly put about in Cairo by the trader Abou Saood, was a garbled account of events at Masindi. It was given much publicity and had even inspired a first leader in *The Times* that came close to an obituary: the 'lamentable tragedy' had happened, so it was said, when Sir Samuel was beleaguered and forced to surrender, whereupon he was murdered alongside Lady Baker, 'who first shared his adventures as a girl-bride equally fearless and feminine'.

Although the reports had fairly soon been disputed, and confirmation came that the Bakers were still alive (the telegram saying so was dramatically read out in Parliament), the parallels were too obvious to miss: Livingstone and Baker were brothers in a noble struggle. A full-page cartoon appeared in one of the popular weeklies, showing a tired and resolute Sir Samuel, surrounded by black children, and behind him the ghostly figure of Wilberforce, the first great fighter against slavery. Wilberforce gives Baker a pat on the back, with the words: 'Receive a nation's thanks, with mine, for fighting freedom's cause.' It perfectly caught the public mood. The writer Henry Kingsley had even forecast about Baker's expedition: 'The influence which it will have on the slave trade, and on Eastern manners and African civilization, is equally beyond guessing.'

As soon as he was home, Sam went to give an account of his labours to the Prince of Wales, who could well consider himself the *deus ex machina* of the expedition. The prince was delighted to be linked with actions which were calling forth so much approbation, because this was such an agreeable change from the scandals which tended to pursue him and the members of his 'Marlborough House Set'. So he made it known that he would attend the meeting of the Royal Geographical Society early in December, when Baker was to give a public address about his campaign to crush the White Nile slave trade.

Not only did the prince put in an appearance; he also made an enthusiastic speech, twice referring to 'my friend Sir Samuel Baker'. He ended by saying that Baker was renowned already as a traveller, sportsman and Fellow of the RGS, but was now appearing in a higher character still, 'for as a philanthropist he has carried out a great work for the benefit of human kind'. This won ready applause, the audience seeming to find philanthropy perfectly compatible with an accumulated stipend of £40,000, tax-free.

The newspapers gave these royal sentiments their proper due, and recorded the warmth with which Sir Samuel and Lady Baker were greeted by the packed audience. After all, it was only six months since the gallant pair had been given up for dead. Now here they were, upon a platform in Piccadilly: Florence looked 'just the thing' in a fashionable dress, complete with bustle, that she had bought in Paris on the way home.

Fittingly enough, the meeting was chaired by Sir Bartle Frere, who had been personally responsible for bringing the Sultan of Zanzibar to heel. Frere was the new president of the RGS (Sir Roderick Murchison having lately died); he told the audience that Baker was like a Crusader or a Sea King, coming back to tell of unknown regions.

When he rose to speak, Baker showed that he was more than ready to be cast in such a role. He gave a spellbinding narrative of his travels and said how proud he was, as an Englishman, to have played his part in the 'downfall of slavery'. He said nothing of his original plans – such as the one for a 'new Liberia' in the Sudan where freed slaves could grow cotton. He stressed instead the frustrations his expedition had struggled against, without being too precise as to its achievements. At the end, just before a burst of cheering for Lady Baker, he remarked how glad he was that an Englishman had been appointed to replace him, because 'a Turk would certainly have upset the work which he had done'. Regardless of the feelings of anyone who might be loosely categorized as a Turk, this was widely quoted.

The new man for the Sudan was a talented colonel in the Royal Engineers – albeit a rather eccentric one – known as 'Chinese' Gordon. He had won his nickname for commanding an army which put down a rebellion near Shanghai. (Sir Samuel did not reveal that he had suggested his nephew, Lieutenant Julian Baker, for the Sudan job; the khedive had politely declined.)

At first, relations between the khedive's outgoing pasha and the incoming one were to be far from smooth. Charles Gordon was a bachelor, an ascetic, much given to spiritual anguish; Baker was a very physical man whose interest in religion, as far as it went, was somewhat unorthodox. In the New Year of 1874 the two men had a brief 'baton-changing' meeting at Brighton, where the Bakers were being obliged to rest throughout the winter on medical advice. This was the unpromising start to what would ultimately become a history-making friendship.

Gordon soon showed his style by refusing to accept more than a fifth of the salary that Baker had thought fitting for a governor-general; he also let it be known that he was startled by all the fine wines and costly china and glass which he found in the palace quarters recently vacated by Sam and Florence in Khartoum.

Matters were exacerbated in the summer, when Baker learnt that Abou Saood was being taken on Gordon's staff. It seemed baffling that such a tireless Christian should want to employ the slaver *par excellence*; so Baker complained privately, then publicly, that this made nonsense of all his work in the Sudan. The result was a long letter in the columns of *The Times* from a friend of Gordon's named James Shaw. Apart from some muted complaints by the Aborigines Protection Society that there had been too much fighting, that was the first serious questioning of Baker's recent tactics on the White Nile.

'Sir Samuel Baker's policy was one in which we heard of nothing but the magnitude of his powers and of his office, of conquests here and battles and victories there . . .' argued Shaw. He went on to assert: 'Colonel Gordon told me that his express instructions from the khedive were to undo the mischief which Sir S. Baker had created.' The appointment of Abou Saood was justified by Shaw as part of a policy of patient conciliation, after Baker's quixotic methods.

Such criticism had appeared once before in *The Times* – coming from ex-Consul Petherick, who argued that Baker had 'started at the wrong end' by his outright attack on the slave trade, and should have first made good his position, rather than simply turn every man into an enemy. But Petherick was commenting while Baker was still in the middle of Africa, well out of range. The sniping from Shaw provoked an angry response from Baker by the next post. In a private letter to John Delane, the editor, he declared himself upset at the publishing of an attack he saw as both abusive and ill-informed. He ended: 'How it is possible for the khedive to decorate me before parting with his highest honour – and then to speak against my acts to others without in any way having communicated his displeasure to me, is beyond my conception of Oriental morality.' Baker also supplied, for publication, a weighty rejoinder to Shaw's attack.

The argument was to rumble on in the newspapers for weeks, with some of Baker's former employees joining in and Gordon trying to restore harmony by diplomatically assuring his predecessor that nobody could have done more than he to defeat the slave traders. It was, of course, beyond argument that Baker had laid the foundations upon which Gordon was able to build; for example, the fleet of British steamboats so painstakingly carried in sections to the Upper Nile during Baker's governorship were to prove invaluable to Gordon and his staff.

A convincing assessment of Baker's performance is in the private diaries of Nubar Pasha, the most senior of the khedive's ministers. (It was Nubar who had selected Gordon, after meeting him in Constantinople.) 'Baker did not possess the necessary aptitudes for a mission of this kind,' he wrote bluntly. 'He knew only how to drive himself hard and keep going forward.' With his Armenian subtlety, Nubar saw that an outright confrontation with slavery in all its forms was more than Egypt was ready for. One of Baker's misfortunes was in having been given too free a hand, too wide a mandate. Nubar blamed this on the khedive's eagerness to 'appear as a liberal ruler and to make himself agreeable to the Prince of Wales'.

Yet such niceties were lost in the general admiration for Sam and

Florence, who had risked their lives for the great cause. In meetings with the leaders of Victorian life, in lectures at universities, Baker's spirit and intelligence were always apparent. At that moment, in the middle of the 1870s, his reputation was at its apogee and the future seemed full of possibilities. Time had dispersed the cloud that had hung over his name after the marriage to Florence. Despite the lingering disapproval of Queen Victoria, only some unforeseeable calamity could now stand between Baker and still higher honours.

Confident of the future, Sam and Florence began looking around for a home suitable for entertaining their growing circle of distinguished friends – a place upon which to spend some of the wealth bestowed by the khedive. The Sudan had taken its physical toll, and both suffered for months from bronchial troubles, to the extent that they could not even attend Livingstone's memorial service in Westminster Abbey in the spring of 1874. So the draughty manor house in East Anglia was abandoned, and in the early autumn they based themselves in their old London haunt, Almond's Hotel, while they began their search. A few years earlier, Sam had hoped to return to the Highlands. But the climate did not appeal to Florence. In any case the Bakers were in no sense as rich as the aristocrats who owned estates in Scotland, and they could not have 'gone the pace' there without inviting bankruptcy. It was prudent to keep well away and choose a less fashionable area.

In October they settled upon Sandford Orleigh, a neo-Gothic stone mansion in south Devon – the warmest part of Britain. The house has forty rooms, fine staircases and ornate ceilings. It overlooks the River Teign near the town of Newton Abbot, and when the Bakers bought Sandford Orleigh it was surrounded by several acres of wooded grounds.

Months were spent in laying out the gardens, buying furniture, and hanging up countless hunting trophies on the walls. Sam was in the highest spirits. In a letter to his youngest daughter, Ethel, he mentioned the importance of that first essential of gracious living – servants: 'Could you look out for maids of all classes in your neighbourhood. They must be virgins with their lamps trimmed.'

Although the Bakers may have seemed to some of their friends to be burying themselves rather deeply in rural England, they would still, of course, be taking a house in London every year for the season. Moreover, there was no likelihood of being forgotten while Colonel

Valentine Baker was representing the family with so much dash. Sam and his younger brother were now often spoken of in the same breath, since both were known to be the friends of the Prince of Wales. Just after Sam and Florence came back from Africa, the colonel had returned from an adventurous journey to the remote Perso-Turkoman borders; during a visit to Sandringham – the Prince of Wales's country mansion in Norfolk – he had told of his discoveries about Russian expansionism in the region, so causing the prince to write to the government stressing the importance of his report.

Valentine was a leading member of the 'Set', that influential coterie whose bastions were Marlborough House, the prince's own residence, and Stafford House, that of the Duke of Sutherland. As if to underline its exclusivity, the set also had its own club, the Marlborough, at 52 Pall Mall. The moving spirit behind the club's founding in 1869 was the prince himself, and Valentine was a founding member. Although Sam contented himself with belonging to the more sedate Athenaeum, a hundred yards along Pall Mall, he was always welcome at the Marlborough: his old friends Lord Wharncliffe* and the Duke of Sutherland were two of the three trustees.

The Marlborough set was undubitably fast, and few were faster than the Duke of Sutherland. His Grace's love of adventure went so far beyond his better-known diversions – driving railway trains and riding on fire engines – that the duchess was even constrained to write to the Prince of Wales about one of her husband's more notorious affairs. The prince advised patience until passion wore itself out, but added sympathetically: 'It distresses me beyond measure that he should make such a fool of himself . . . It is certainly a thousand pities that a man in his position and at his age should outrage society as he does.' This was somewhat bland, coming from one whose own private life did not pass entirely uncriticized.

Although Valentine spent a great deal of time with the Duke of Sutherland and other friends among the spendthrift rich, his reputation in military circles was nonetheless formidable; and now, in his middle forties, he was at the height of his powers. Like Sam, he combined great physical stamina and charm with intellectual verve.

* A few years later, Wharncliffe was to assure himself of a measure of immortality by throwing the dinner-party at which Lily Langtry was introduced to London society.

Denied a thoroughgoing war in which to extend himself, Valentine sought every outlet for his energies. He lectured, wrote books and pamphlets, and made a considerable impression with a public attack upon the unsupervised schools known as 'crammers' for young men hoping to pass examinations to enter the army as officer cadets. In such places, he warned, the candidates 'associate together in numbers at a most dangerous age, without any decided control, and often acquire bad and desultory habits which affect the whole character of their after lives'. These sentiments were much appreciated at a time when many people were growing anxious about certain tendencies which public schools seemed to encourage among the flower of the nation's youth.

Yet it was above all upon his achievements as 'Baker of the Tenth' that Valentine's fame depended. The Prince of Wales, gazetted a colonel of the Tenth when he was twenty-one, took great pride in its reputation. A large portrait of him in full black and gold regimental dress hung at Sandringham, and in 1871 another grandiose painting was done, showing His Highness and Colonel Baker riding in manoeuvres near Aldershot, the army headquarters in Hampshire. The prince had given Valentine a massive white charger, which became such a feature of military parades that Valentine was commonly called 'The Man on the White Horse'.

Just after his journey to Turkoman there were signs that Valentine might soon be promoted to the topmost ranks of the army. The Tenth had been posted to India, and because of his seniority Valentine decided to give up command and stay in Britain: soon afterwards, he was appointed to the staff at Aldershot, as assistant quartermaster general.

So the stars of the two famous Baker brothers were rising side by side; both were expected to enhance their reputations still further with books they were engaged upon about their recent adventures abroad. The one noticeable distinction between them was that Sam, now well into his fifties, had grown more tranquil in his habits, whereas Valentine travelled constantly between the pleasures of life in town and his military duties at Aldershot. He was married, to the daughter of a North Country landowner; but members of the 'Set' generally took a relaxed view of such ties.

Summer was the time to enjoy Aldershot, for then the army lightened the tedium of drill and parades with a series of balls, cavalry races and champagne lunches in snow-white marquees. In 1875, one of Valentine's guests at Aldershot was his married sister, Ann Bourne: the manoeuvres would be a royal occasion, for the Prince of Wales's younger brother, Prince Arthur, was to be brigade major; the Queen was also to make a visit. 'There is no end to the gaiety,' wrote Ann Bourne to her daughter. 'If it were not for the perpetual dressing and planning one's dress, I should enjoy it very much . . .'

But the grand reception planned for the Queen was something of an anti-climax; a case of scarlet fever was reported among the troops, so she sent her apologies and stayed at Windsor Castle. That mischance denied Valentine the last opportunity of seeing his sovereign before the disaster that was to shatter his own career and give a fatal check to the expectations of his elder brother.

The first hint Sam received of the scandal to come was contained in a brief telegram from Valentine, one Friday in mid-June, when the Sandford Orleigh house was full of guests; Sam had to make his excuses and prepare for a hurried journey up to town. But even before he could leave, the newspapers were starting to reveal what lay behind that urgent message with its appeal for Sam's help: Colonel Baker, friend of royalty, had been accused of assaulting a young woman in a first-class compartment of a train travelling from Hampshire to London.

Appalled, Sam read the report in *The Times*: 'EXTRAORDINARY CHARGE OF ASSAULT' said the headline. It recounted the allegations of a Miss Kate Dickinson, who was aged twenty-one and of 'very prepossessing appearance'. She claimed that Valentine had tried to violate her just after the train had left a country station and was not due to stop again until it reached London thirty minutes later. Since they were alone in the compartment, in a carriage without a corridor, she was trapped, but after a struggle she had managed to open one of the doors and stand perilously on an outside running-board, with her attacker holding on to one of her arms: after ten minutes, during which she screamed for help to passengers staring from the windows of other compartments, the train was at last brought to a halt.

The girl's name meant nothing to Sam, but her social background was clearly much like that of the Baker family. One of her brothers was a doctor in Mayfair and another was a young army officer, based at Aldershot. Her family also included a prominent lawyer. Miss Dickinson had laid the charge herself and it seemed as though she meant to press it to the limit.

Sam knew that Valentine was about to be engulfed in a momentous scandal, one that would leave its mark on everyone connected with him.

During the weeks of ordeal that were to follow, Sam never wavered in his loyalty to Valentine, and looked for every way to excuse his conduct. But what he truly felt about his brother was summed up by one sentence in a letter to Lord Wharncliffe: 'I always knew that the "trousers" would be the fatal point.'

As soon as he had heard Valentine's own account, Sam began laying bare his innermost feelings in a series of letters to his old friend. He hid nothing from Wharncliffe, who as he said had always 'sympathized in both joys and sorrows' – and was also bound, as a trustee of the Marlborough Club, to be intensely concerned that one of its members faced public disgrace.

Sam explained how Valentine had confided in him and two army colleagues: 'But as you know in such a case, a man is at the mercy of a lady, as his tongue must as a point of honour be absolutely sealed in a court of law. At the same time, Val must allow that his best friend cannot defend even as much as he himself confesses.

'Then on the other hand, men are not all "Josephs" – and we must all admit that it was lucky for Joseph that he did not meet Mrs Potiphar in a railway compartment.' After this attempt at levity, he admitted to Wharncliffe that his brother's behaviour had been 'much too amorous, incautious, and rash to the last degree'.

By the time he was writing those words, all Britain was talking about the amorous colonel. The journalist William Howard Russell, although a close friend of Valentine, noted in his diary that somebody had remarked to him how unlucky the Prince of Wales was in his friends – 'b——rs, violators, cheap card-sharpers . . .' Russell commented: 'It is a dreadful scandal and I am inclined to think all probability is against him, but immense efforts will be made to get it "squared".'

Doubtless it would have been 'squared', by money or intimidation, if Kate Dickinson had been a mere shopgirl or a seamstress. As it was, several newspapers hinted that the Prince of Wales himself was trying to intercede for his friend. But the Dickinson family would not be deflected.

A week after Valentine's disastrous journey, Sam attended the preliminary hearing that would inevitably send the case on to a full trial. The courtroom was packed, journalists were there in force and it was small comfort that so many of Valentine's friends in the cavalry had come along to offer support. As Sam was to write to Wharncliffe: 'I am afraid I do feel this humiliation almost more deeply than Val himself.'

When Kate Dickinson gave her evidence, in a self-possessed style, Sam speculated on how much she was to blame. She was certainly pretty, in a demure black silk dress, adorned with lace, a black hat with a feather in it, and with her hands resting in lavender gloves on the edge of the witness box. Surely, Val could not have behaved as he did 'without some attractions that he accepted as an encouragement'. The witness told how she and her companion – whom she had never met previously – were chatting before the attack about books, the theatre, and social occasions at Aldershot; they had even discovered that both their families stayed at the same hotel, Almond's, when they were in London.

She went on to tell how Valentine came to sit beside her when the train left Woking station. She pushed him away, saying: 'Get away, I won't have you so near!' The colonel was not so easily deterred. He put his arm around her waist and kissed her on the cheek. 'You must kiss me, darling,' he said. She was not at all willing, and got up to pull the communication bell, only to find that it was not working.

At that, Valentine dragged her down, pressed her against the cushions of the seat, and stood over her. 'He kissed me on the lips many times. I was quite powerless.' Then came the moment which Britain so ardently wanted to hear about: 'He sank down in front of me, and I felt his hand underneath my dress, on my stocking, above my boot.' What of his other hand? 'I had an impression, nothing more.'

Kate Dickinson told how she then saw her chance, jumped up, opened the window, and began to scream. Although Valentine pulled her back, she got out on to the steps and clung there until the train drew up. As it stopped, the colonel pleaded: 'Don't say anything – you don't know the trouble you will get me into.'

So that was it. Miss Dickinson had not been violated, but she had been frightened enough to risk her life. There was also some damning evidence from a passenger on the train who had noticed immediately after the incident that Valentine's fly-buttons were undone. But when the magistrates said the case must go for trial there was a rush of fellow-officers eager to put up the two £1000 bonds for bail. In the end, the court accepted sureties from Sam and a young viscount who was a captain in the Tenth Hussars.

Black as things looked, the best lawyers were employed to try repeatedly, but in vain, to have the trial delayed. In time lay the best hope, for steady pressure on Kate Dickinson's family might eventually do its work. The weight was felt most acutely by her brother at Aldershot; he openly said that he wished the case could be dropped.

Public opinion was mainly at one extreme or the other: some thought the colonel was a debauched monster, but many people felt he was getting it thick for his 'light cavalry tactics' – for trying to kiss a pretty girl who foolishly took fright. In the main, it was a dubious asset to have the Prince of Wales as a friend in such a case. One newspaper sold out a huge run of one edition by speciously denying that Colonel Baker was really covering up for a 'high personage' who was the true assailant: in fact, the Prince of Wales had spent the crucial 17 June entertaining a German prince in the afternoon and going on to dinner with the Austrian ambassador.

Sam wrote sadly to Wharncliffe, thanking him for his sympathy, but forecasting that Valentine would 'bear the penalty of an outrageous insanity'. So it was to prove.

The trial was held in Croydon, in the town hall. The local police were taken aback by the huge crowd which came down from London in hopes of getting a seat in court. Even Sam had difficulty in forcing his way inside. As a local paper recorded, the town had never known such tumult: 'Some daring innovators, with a good notion of a capital joke, actually hoisted up two young women and succeeded in getting them in through one of the windows.' When the trial began, the uproar was so great that the eloquence of the lawyers could scarcely be heard.

After a day-long hearing, Valentine was found guilty of indecent assault and common assault. The judge said that a 'thrill of horror' had gone through the nation that an officer and a gentleman should have given way so utterly to his vile passion. The sentence was a year in prison, although it would be served without hard labour.

For Kate Dickinson the judge offered a warm tribute: 'She goes from this court as pure, as innocent, as undefiled as ever she was – nay, more, the courage she has displayed has added a ray of glory to her youth, her innocence and her beauty.'*

Not everyone liked the verdict. As the prisoner was taken away, sympathetic cries of 'Bravo, Baker!' were heard. One newspaper even dared side with him openly – fittingly enough, it was *The Sporting Times*: 'Colonel Baker has received a very large punishment . . . for placing his hand upon a lady's stocking, and he having evidently mistaken her sentiments.'

All the newspapers devoted columns to the implications of the case and there were some shrewd rapier-thrusts at the moral standards of the aristocracy. An agitation also developed about the design of British railway carriages, as to whether there should be large open saloons on the American pattern, rather than the 'snug coupés in which Englishmen delight'. A consequence of Valentine Baker's downfall was to be the introduction of corridors in trains.

One of the few light-hearted observations was in the *Spectator*, which suggested the formation of a body of 'Railway Cavaliers', to escort and amuse young ladies, who should sign at the end of each journey as to their experiences. Another joke, of a rather broader kind, was managed by Sam in March 1876, when his brother was nearing the end of his sentence. Writing to express his gratitude to Wharncliffe for making a visit to the prison, he remarked that Val's book, *Clouds in the East*, about his journey to Turkoman, would soon appear – events had somewhat held up publication. 'I believe that the title includes "Explorations of unknown parts in Central Asia". I hope that the result will be more happy than his exploration of "unknown parts" in a railway compartment.'

However he might try to put a brave face on it, Sam knew that Valentine's disgrace was a hammer-blow. Only two years before, there were real prospects that the family's high standing of earlier centuries was about to be restored. Now, such dreams must be forgotten. In particular, the 'Widow of Windsor' would feel herself well

---

* Kate Dickinson withdrew herself from the public eye after the case. She never married, lived until 1915 and occupied much of her time by painting in watercolours.

justified in having ostracized Sam and Florence, for she could now proclaim that a fatal streak of immorality must run through the whole family.

Victoria made no public comment upon the case. But a few days after Valentine's conviction she asked her personal doctor, Sir William Jenner, to send a letter to Dr Dickinson, the Mayfair consultant. It told him that the Queen wanted his sister to know 'how much Her Majesty felt for her in her great trial'. The letter added that the Queen desired to be sent a photograph of Miss Dickinson. Nothing can convey more plainly than this the extent to which the Prince of Wales and his mother lived in opposite camps.

CHAPTER 15

The Nile's Last
Temptation

During the inglorious publicity of 'Val's affair', the remoteness of
Sandford Orleigh from London proved a boon. It also encouraged
Sam Baker to behave like a typical member of the West Country
gentry. He was elected president of the Devonshire Association, and
became a town councillor in Newton Abbot. The local people viewed
him at first with curiosity, because of what had happened to his
brother, then with admiration for his individuality. He was no
ordinary squire. Self-reliant craftsmen always attracted him:
blacksmiths, wandering tinkers, road-menders and gipsies encountered in the lanes around the Sandford Orleigh estate would
often be invited by him for tea in the billiards room. One day a
travelling strong man came to town, and as part of his act wound a
chain around his biceps, then snapped it by flexing his muscles.
Would any member of the audience care to try? Sam was sitting with
Florence in the front row, and this was precisely the kind of challenge
he could never resist, even in advancing years. Fortune was with
him: he gritted his teeth, tensed his still massive arms – and the
chain broke.

Yet despite the harmless unorthodoxies of its new owner, Sandford
Orleigh had an aura of almost courtly opulence. A diary kept by one
of Sam's young nieces describes a visit there: 'Dinner at the usual
time. Aunt Florence looked quite lovely in a pale sea blue satin dress
with very rich maroon velvet beautifully let in and with a tiara of
diamonds and diamond ornaments elsewhere.' Florence was going
to a ball in Newton Abbot, but Sam preferred to be at home with
the children; he told them stories of Africa until bedtime. At the end

of her stay the niece wrote: '. . . our visit could not have been jollier. It has also taught us many things. I hope we shall try and follow Aunt Florence's methodical ways.' But when she went to Sandford Orleigh again some years later she was more critical: 'The worldliness and luxury enervate and oppress one.'

There were certainly few reminders at Sandford Orleigh of the spartan exploring days. An Abyssinian servant whom the Bakers had brought home from their last expedition was in reality a trophy, like the animal heads on the walls. Only now and then did the harsher methods of former times come to the surface, as when a footman, serving at table, spilt soup over one of the guests. 'You should be whipped,' said Florence – not so much angrily, but as if it were a statement of fact. She was, in practice, solicitous to her large staff, so that when a small boy who came to stay kicked the butler in the ankle he was sent up to his room for the day on a diet of bread and water. 'Servants are our friends,' were her parting words as he went upstairs. 'We don't kick our friends.'

Florence believed in good food, and even by Victorian standards she served up a great deal of it. A renowned judge of culinary abundance who sometimes called unexpectedly was the Prince of Wales, and one Monday before lunch he presented himself at the front door while Sam was away and Florence was busy in the linen room, giving instructions for the week's laundry. An agitated footman ran upstairs to tell a maid, who hurried to tell Florence. 'Oh,' she said, 'you go and tell the Prince that I am all dobs and durbies and cannot attend to him until I have finished.' This refusal to be intimidated by royalty was derived from Sam, even if his public declarations of loyalty had sometimes verged on the servile: when two of the prince's sons came to stay for a weekend – one the future King George V – he gave them a thrashing after they had broken the branches on a rare tropical tree which he had earlier forbidden them to climb.

For one of the Bakers, this new life was perfect. Although she always spoke English in a heavily-accented fashion, Florence was resolved to immerse herself in British ways and the comforts of wealth. She enjoyed going to London for grand occasions and did not mind accompanying Sam on well-planned journeys abroad, but she had made up her mind that she was never returning to Africa – and would not allow Sam to do so either. Egypt was bearable, the Sudan she never desired to see again.

Despite her declared wishes, Sam was always planning forbidden adventures. One part of his mind still dreamed of Africa, and in 1877 he was much agitated by the news that Lake Albert was far smaller than his own claims, which were based upon tribal lore and his own hazy sightings in 1864. (Ultimately, it was discovered that although the lake in no way compared with the Victoria as a Nile source, it did receive much water from the snows of the Mountains of the Moon, so confirming the legends dating back to Herodotus.)

In a letter to Henry Stanley, just back from his momentous journey down the Congo River, he wrote: 'If my wife were not too valuable to risk again in those parts, I would go myself, and thoroughly work out the Lake.' Later, he rather wistfully told Stanley: 'If I were a single man, I would go out at once . . .'

It was his nostalgia for Africa which made Baker correspond so eagerly with his successor Charles Gordon, who as a proof of their reconciliation sent him repeated invitations to visit the Sudan: 'Telegraph me, come at once!' he urged. The temptation was almost irresistible when the Bakers set off on a round-the-world trip in 1878 that was taking them to Cairo. By this time, one of the steamers brought out to the Nile in 1870 was on Lake Albert and Gordon optimistically averred that a trip down there would be sheer delight. Florence would have none of it. 'Lady Baker and I thank you very much for your kind invitation,' wrote Sam. 'I should not hesitate for an instant, personally, but she is, I know, afraid that if once I should get into the old groove, my visit would be prolonged; and she rather dreads a return to savage life.'

Ironically enough, while Sam hunted fretfully for some last adventure which Florence would countenance, it was Valentine who emerged from degradation to win honour in distant lands. As soon as he left jail, 'Baker of the Tenth' decided to become a mercenary officer in the service of the Ottoman Empire, which was preparing for war against the Russians. With a recommendation to the sultan in Constantinople from the Prince of Wales – never one to abandon a friend down on his luck – Valentine was made a major-general. He was given the very title of 'Baker Pasha' which Sam had formerly held.

So out of humiliation, Valentine gained the chance which Britain's lack of wars had long denied him: to prove that he really did possess brilliance in battle. He made his name by a delaying action in a wild part of Bulgaria: with 3000 men, their morale already shaken by repeated defeats, he managed to defy a Russian force of 40,000 for long enough to allow the main Turkish army to escape encirclement. Baker's force held its ground throughout New Year's Eve, 1877, amid the snowy hills surrounding the village of Tashkessan. He rallied his puny rearguard again and again with trumpet calls and Turkish battle-cries, repeatedly halting the Russians, then falling back from one defence line to the next until darkness gave respite. The main army survived, while Baker and the remnant of his force struggled through the mountains to north Greece and the sea. A British War Office historian, in a definitive account of the Russo-Turkish war, called the Tashkessan battle an 'act of military heroism rarely matched in any age'.

When the news reached London that Valentine had proved his mettle, friends toasted his health all around London's clubland. Within a few weeks, Valentine took advantage of an armistice to come home on leave, and the Duke of Sutherland held a 'complimentary banquet' for him at Stafford House. Sam came up from Devon for the occasion. In his speech of welcome, the duke called the guest of honour the 'connecting link between our old allies, the Turks, and England'. After the dinner there was a reception, attended by a resplendent array of peers and generals. But with a laboured decorum, no ladies were invited, lest they should feel disconcerted at meeting in public the man who had laid hands on Kate Dickinson.

The Prince of Wales dared not carry his regard for Valentine to the extent of being at the reception, but he was present at a committee meeting of the Marlborough Club the following morning. The main item on the agenda was 'a request for General Baker to be restored to membership' – his name having been struck off under the club rules when he went to prison. There was no dissenting voice.

Two days after the Stafford House banquet, Valentine and his wife Fanny went down to Sandford Orleigh with Sam for a holiday. There was little sympathy between Sam and Florence and Fanny, who displayed a stiff and overbearing manner, but they felt warmly towards Val and had eagerly read about his campaign in Bulgaria. The scene of his rearguard battle was in a part of Europe they had reason to remember vividly from long ago. Perhaps they also saw a similarity, even if on a far smaller scale, between their flight from

Masindi to the Victoria Nile and his epic retreat through the Balkans to the sea.

Valentine returned to Turkey in May 1878, and apart from helping to reorganize the Ottoman armies he wrote a two-volume work, *War in Bulgaria*, which earned high praise for the clarity and pace of its prose. Many of his admirers claimed that he wrote better than Sam.

At the end of 1882, Valentine was offered a position for which he seemed ideally suited: commander-in-chief of the Egyptian army. Immediately, he handed his resignation to the sultan and left Constantinople for Cairo to meet the khedive – only to be confronted by a barrier nobody had foreseen. The British government, which by now had effective control of Egypt, succumbed to the inevitable pressure from Victoria and ruled out his name. The Prince of Wales, who had recommended Valentine, wrote furiously to Gladstone: 'I must confess that Baker Pasha has been very unfairly treated ... To deprive him now of the important command which the khedive has conferred upon him is simply to ruin him.' Later, when it was suggested that Baker should become head of intelligence to Lord Wolseley, commander of the British troops in Egypt, this was again prohibited. The prince protested that 'nobody but the most narrow-minded person' could have raised any objection.

So 'Baker of the Tenth' was driven to the relative ignominy of becoming head of the Egyptian police, and was told he must try urgently to reconstruct this force on military lines. Egyptian control of the Sudan was slipping away in the face of a fervent Islamic nationalism led by the messiah-like figure known as the Mahdi. In a series of defeats, the Egyptian armies had yielded up province after province, until Khartoum was no more than a dangerously-exposed outpost.

While Valentine was trying to turn the dispirited rabble in his charge into a fighting force, another British officer, Hicks Pasha, led an Egyptian force of nearly 10,000 men to total annihilation during a reckless march westwards from Khartoum. The date was 5 November 1883. The shock was so great in London that Gladstone's Cabinet came to what it saw as the only practical solution: the Sudan must be evacuated, and a cool-headed man of proven military and administrative prowess must be sent to Khartoum to withdraw the garrisons and see to safety all civilians who could be in danger.

The tactical skill he had shown during the retreat in Bulgaria – not to mention his nearness to the theatre of action – might have made Valentine Baker the logical choice; but his past caused too many tremors. In the closing weeks of 1883, Gladstone and his Cabinet colleagues looked about for the right man. One name was several times mentioned in letters and memoranda between the ministers – General Gordon, whose work as Sam Baker's successor in the Sudan up to 1880 was well remembered. By this time, after occupying various other posts, Gordon was living in seclusion in Jerusalem. Nothing was said in public about the prospect of asking him to take on the delicate task in Khartoum, and it fell to Sam himself to give it wide circulation.

The Sudan was stirring so much anxiety by the end of the year that Baker sent a series of articles to *The Times* on the country and its history. On New Year's Day, 1884, his broad appraisal came to the immediate heart of the matter. Baker declared his view as to who should be sent to Khartoum, with a mandate to seize the reins: 'Why should not General Gordon Pasha be invited to assist the government? There is no man living who would be more capable or so well fitted to represent the justice which Great Britain should establish in the Soudan.' These two sentences brought into the open what was being asserted in private. It must be Gordon.

There was one serious obstacle. On the day when *The Times* printed Baker's suggestion, Gordon was in Brussels, completing arrangements to work for King Leopold. For more than a year, the king had been pressing Gordon to go out to the Congo, where the explorer Stanley was struggling to set up trading stations. Both Stanley and Gordon imagined then that Leopold's motives were purely philanthropic, and dedicated to spreading civilization (the king's real intentions – colonial exploitation – were yet to be revealed). So Gordon was now about to honour his promise to aid the exhausted Stanley in a seemingly noble labour. From Brussels, he sent Stanley a letter saying he would be on the next mail steamer leaving Europe for Banana Point at the Congo's mouth. He forecast that together they would deal the slave trade a mortal blow.

What had now been printed in *The Times*, and a private letter he had received from Baker on the same lines, may have gratified Gordon's ego; they did not deflect him. On 7 January he arrived from Belgium at Southampton and posted a letter to the War Office resigning his commission. This cleared his path to work for Leopold. But by now there was a national ground-swell; the editor of the crusading *Pall Mall Gazette* capitalized upon it by interviewing Gordon about the Sudan and, in an editorial, repeating Baker's idea that he was the man to send there. The interview created a stir – to the extent that many other London newspapers reprinted it verbatim.

Gordon was not yet retreating from his determination to go to the Congo. In the interview, he had played the ball straight back: 'Sir Samuel Baker, who possesses the essential energy and single tongue requisite for the office, might be appointed Governor-General of the Soudan and might take his brother as Commander-in-Chief.'

As the debate grew hotter about what should be done, Gordon went to stay for a week with a clerical friend, the Reverend S. H. Barnes, who lived in Exeter. Conveniently enough, this was only twelve miles from Sandford Orleigh, so that the two former pashas of the Sudan were able to ride in a carriage through the wintry lanes of Devon, each trying to persuade the other that he should go to Khartoum. It was a curious disputation, since neither had been invited by anybody in authority to take on such a duty; and the one more likely to be called was still insistent that he was about to sail for quite a different part of Africa.

On 11 January, two days after the *Pall Mall Gazette* published its interview, Gordon sent a letter to Sandford Orleigh repeating his views on how the Mahdist uprising should be tackled. Diplomacy, he urged, was more important than arms, although Baker should not overlook the military essentials. 'I take it, then,' he continued, 'that you will go; and I would recommend (1) permission to be got from the Sultan to engage 4000 of his reserve troops, both officers and men, which will be under your brother's command . . .' So he went on, point by point, setting out the programme for action.

If Gordon seemed to cringe from the limelight, Baker showed no such reticence. With alacrity, he posted this letter to *The Times* for publication, preceding it by a short covering note of his own, in which he avoided saying whether or not he wanted the role Gordon seemed to be pressing upon him. Perhaps Baker simply enjoyed being at the centre of the verbal excitement, while fully realizing that the idea of two Baker brothers representing Britain in Khartoum would be anathema to Gladstone and the Queen. Or perhaps the old ambition was coursing through him and he genuinely was after the appointment. However, before the letter appeared, on the following Monday, 14 January, Gordon decided to take the train from Exeter to Newton Abbot to press home his point.

Baker was on the station platform when his guest arrived, and ushered him to the carriage waiting outside. There was time to spare before tea, so despite the cold weather they took a roundabout route to Sandford Orleigh. By now, Baker seemed all enthusiasm. True, he was sixty-two and was putting on so much weight that he had become rather ponderous on his feet. But Gordon's proposals were irresistible.

Sam had reckoned without Florence. She knew exactly what was in the wind. As tea was being served she suddenly sat stiffly upright and said: 'You promised me that you would never go back to the Sudan without me. I do not go. So you do not go.'

Gordon was angry, and baffled that a man as forceful as Baker could so easily be floored. But then, Gordon never took much account of women. Baker soon led him from the drawing-room, saying sadly: 'My dear Gordon, see how I am placed – how can I leave all this?' The rest of the visit was passed in undisguised hostility between Florence and the distinguished guest, who next morning left by the first train.

Afterwards she said Gordon seemed like a wizard, with an almost hypnotic force in his pale blue eyes. But for the rest of her life she deeply resented the way he had tried to pass over to Sam, at his age, a mission that looked fated to end in calamity.

Denied what he knew was his last chance of taking the stage, Sam nonetheless managed to find room in the wings. Soon after Gordon had left for the Sudan – an inevitable capitulation to the British government's appeals – he and Florence followed him as far as Egypt; they chanced to arrive just as Valentine had flung himself into the struggle against the forces of the Mahdi, only to find that his men (Sam later branded them as mainly 'ragamuffin blacks kidnapped for service in the streets of Cairo') were totally unequal to the task. Before the police battalions would even board a train near their barracks in Cairo, they had to be threatened with an attack by three squadrons of cavalry brought on to the parade ground. Ultimately, Valentine got them to the port of Suakin, halfway down the Red Sea. Then they were marched inland to relieve a trapped Egyptian garrison, but were ambushed by the Mahdists and speedily routed.

At the height of the battle, many of Baker's men threw away their rifles and lay on the ground pleading for mercy, only to be stabbed to death in hundreds. Less than half the force was able to straggle back to the coast – two thousand were left for the vultures and huge amounts of equipment were abandoned. The garrison Baker was trying to relieve was totally wiped out.

This débâcle was partially retrieved when Valentine was dramatically – if only briefly – reunited with his old regiment, the Tenth Hussars. It was sailing home from India at the moment of his defeat, and the transport ship was ordered to halt at Suakin, where his well-remembered figure was waiting to greet it. To repeated cheers, Valentine went aboard, and said he could provide three hundred horses from his Turkish cavalry squadron to equip part of the Tenth for action. The hussars were eager to fight.

With renewed confidence, Valentine led his forces inland again, the Tenth following him across a plain littered with shrivelled corpses, relics of the recent defeat. As in days gone by, he rode a white horse, and when the battle of El Teb began, he headed the cavalry charge against the Mahdists with all his former *panache*. The years and the sadness fell away.

During the battle he was hit in the face by a bullet, which lodged below his eye, but fought on regardless. His victory at El Teb, although in military terms it could not have lasting results, awakened old sympathies in Britain for Valentine Baker. His reunion with the Tenth provoked *Punch* to publish an emotional piece of verse. One stanza read:

'Wounded and worn he sat there, in silence of pride and pain
The man who had led them often but was never to lead them again!
Think of the secret anguish – think of the dull remorse,
To see the hussars sweep past him, unled by the old white horse.'

It ended with the plea of a humble trooper:

'Give back to the Tenth their Colonel . . .'

But nothing was to come of that, any more than the limited victory at El Teb could help the man, far across the desert in Khartoum, whose peril was stirring the conscience of Britain.

Month by month throughout the year 1884, the net tightened on Gordon, while the politicians in London vacillated about how to save him. Their decision-taking was complicated by the nature of the man, for Gordon was more than half in love with the idea of martyr-dom; certainly, what he least wanted was to admit that all his years of effort in the Sudan were to end in an abject withdrawal. So while Gordon bided his time in the Khartoum palace, a belated relief operation worked its way up the Nile towards him. Mail could still find its way through, in spasmodic fashion, which allowed Sam Baker and Gordon to correspond throughout the year. While the Bakers were still in Cairo, they were even invited by Gordon to slip through the Mahdist forces and visit him in Khartoum: 'You and Lady Baker would enjoy the excitement.' No evidence survives as to Florence's reactions, but they may easily be imagined.

Gradually, Gordon's predicament became more acute. Baker snatched at the opportunity to write a passionate introduction to a book about the Sudan, in which he attacked British policy and suggested provocatively that Germany should 'occupy the deserted ground' and exhibit a wholesome contrast to Britain's decrepit attitude. He condemned the slowness of Lord Wolseley's relief expedition, as being 'a forlorn hope to rescue the one man who has represented the ancient chivalry of England'. Wolseley was quick to respond, blaming delays in London – 'the folly of Mr Gladstone' – for the position he felt himself to be in. Just as he received Wolseley's rejoinder, Baker had a farewell message from Gordon, dated 3 November 1884: 'Thank you for your kind letter of July 17th. We are about to be hemmed in here . . . all roads are cut off and we must eventually fall, and with Khartoum fall all other places . . . I have not time for more and doubt if you will get this, for we may expect the roads cut today or tomorrow. If the Nile was high it would be easier. Believe me, with kindest regards to Lady Baker, yourself and your family, Yours sincerely, C. E. Gordon.'

Against all expectations, including his own, Gordon was able to hold out for almost three months after that. Then as the steamers of the relief force were only two days away from Khartoum, the city finally fell to the huge armies of the Mahdists. Gordon was speared to death on the steps of his palace, and the relief force retired when it saw the Mahdist flags flying over Khartoum.

The news of this tragedy threw the British into paroxysms of grief. Gordon was the symbol of Christian self-sacrifice, of British virtue. But to Sam and Florence, reading the news in their Devon mansion, the fall of Khartoum also meant the obliteration of that vision of fifteen years before – an Egypt spreading right down to Lake Albert and the equator. The frontier was now rolled back nearly two thousand miles.

Although there were no more battles to fight, Valentine stayed on in Cairo, drilling his gendarmerie. His one hope of a return to Britain with honour, his commission restored, was if Victoria were to die. But she was the more tenacious. On 5 November 1887, he suddenly collapsed with a heart attack after a bout of malaria; two of Sam's daughters, in Egypt for a holiday, were with him as he died.

'Baker of the Tenth' was buried beside the Nile with full British military honours, on orders from London. The obituaries all agreed that he was Britain's finest cavalry officer in the second half of the nineteenth century, and that but for his moment of madness on a train to Waterloo Station he would probably have reached the pinnacle of his profession.

Memories of him lived on down the years in the British Army. There must have been many who felt his spirit was riding with them in the heat and passion of history's last great cavalry charge. That took place at Omdurman, across the river from Khartoum, in 1898, during the merciless battle by which Gordon was avenged and the Mahdist power destroyed. A young hussar named Winston Churchill who fought on that day later wrote his own tribute to Baker of the Tenth, in his book *The River War*. He called him a soldier of 'unshaken courage and high military skill'.

Sam did not live to read those words, which would have so touched his emotions; nor was he to survive to see the conquest of the Sudan by Kitchener – whom many years before he had met and singled out as a soldier of outstanding promise. Much of the old explorer's last years was spent in globe-trotting, Florence always by his side. They went bear-hunting in the American Rockies (Sam later protested that there was too much carnage just to collect pelts, with the bodies of the animals left to rot). They made several trips to India, where Sam became more interested in the training of tame elephants than in the shooting of wild ones. The Far East proved fascinating, and after coming home from there, Sam sketched a light-hearted self-portrait in the shape of a Japanese vase: he depicts himself as smiling and rotund, and underneath is scrawled his caption: 'Only half cracked.'

The Bakers decided to stay at Sandford Orleigh for the winter of 1893–4; Sam planned to spend the next year hunting lions in Somaliland. Yet although he was only in his early seventies, his spirit was no match for his ever-increasing bulk. He walked more slowly, suffered bouts of gout – and on 30 December 1893, death came quickly after a heart attack.

Florence was holding him in her arms. His last words were: 'Flooey, how can I leave you?' The verdicts of the obituaries upon his career were epitomized by a sentence in the *Pall Mall Gazette*: 'When he was not exploring he was hunting or fighting or writing.' All the newspapers made dutiful comments about Sam Baker's impact on Africa.

How significant was that impact? In 1888, fifteen years after the Bakers were last in what is now Uganda, the region around Lake Albert was visited by an Englishman named A. J. Mounteney Jephson. He wrote in his diary: 'One cannot help noticing how all the good and lasting things were brought into this country by Sir Samuel Baker, one often hears of him from the people and particularly about Lady Baker to whom all seem to have been devoted. Sir Samuel was very hard with the natives, and she always tried to mitigate their sentences.'

Shortly after Baker's death there was a tribute which would have appealed to his sense of the droll. The Sunday School Union brought out a book about him in a series called 'Splendid Lives'; all the other figures chosen for such eulogies were missionaries, a group with whom he rarely found himself in sympathy. The author was at times hard pressed to convert the story into a suitable inspiration for young Sunday School prizewinners, so it was perhaps fortunate that there were many personal details of which he was presumably unaware. But at the end there is a fine patriotic flourish, proclaiming Sir Samuel Baker's unquestionable right to 'a place among the "splendid lives" that have made Great Britain the envy and admiration of the world'.

EPILOGUE

Grande Dame
of Sandford Orleigh

Although Baker had so often sought aggrandizement in life, he
certainly did not look for it in death, because he asked that he should
be cremated with the minimum of ceremony. This shocked many of
his friends and all his family, with the apparent exception of Florence.
In the early 1890s, cremation was a most controversial last wish:
only shortly before Sam's death, a prominent surgeon had read a
paper to the Society of Arts in London, claiming that cremation was
an incentive to crime, a scientific fad, and even sometimes concealed
occultism.

The old explorer's remains were taken to Britain's only crema-
torium, opened two years earlier at Woking (whose name evoked
other poignant memories for the Baker family). As one of his nieces
wrote, it seemed 'very awful to think that all that remained of Dear
Uncle Sam' could be carried in a small sarcophagus.

Florence said three weeks after his death: 'I feel so forsaken and
lonely, and yet every moment of the day I think that I must see him
again and hear his voice.' But in her typically down-to-earth fashion
she still looked to affairs at Sandford Orleigh. After Sam had died,
a fifty-gallon cask of claret he had ordered was delivered to the house.
Florence gave it to the butler and told him to entertain his friends.
She felt Sam would have approved of that.

Florence was scarcely helped in adjusting to widowhood by some
members of the large regiment of Baker women, who showed their
antagonism now that her protector was gone. Their letters at this
time contain many barbed remarks: 'But it is very hopeful that
Florence is so softened and so humbled.' '. . . lead Florence gently to

see God's hand in all this.' 'From what you tell me, some day Florence will be a really happier woman.'

She did achieve a quiet contentment, with the dignity of advancing years. She was to live for almost another quarter of a century, the *grande dame* of Sandford Orleigh, changing nothing in the mansion from the way it had been in the 1870s. Whenever relations came to stay, she greeted them with her little jokes in broken English and huge Devonshire cream teas. Of course, they were all relations on the Baker side, for she never tried to find out about her own family in Hungary.

Yet she still held to some sentimental loyalties. In March 1914, a newspaper remembered that it was fifty years since the discovery of Lake Albert. In the course of a graphic reconstruction it mentioned Florence's Hungarian origins, and a reader sent her a picture of the national assembly building in Budapest, with the Hungarian flag flying over it in full colour. She carefully put the picture away among her treasures.

Florence died in 1916, during one of the bloodiest periods of the First World War. The house was sold, its furniture and trophies auctioned off, and much of Sam's correspondence destroyed: not one letter from Valentine was left.

With her death, it seemed that the last survivor from that diverse gallery of Victorian explorers who had sought the Source of the Nile was gone. She had long outlived them all. Yet one forgotten eye-witness of the events in Gondokoro in 1863 still lingered on.

Dr James Murie, the distinguished Scottish biologist who had travelled with the Pethericks, was to die in a broken-down cottage in Essex in 1925. He was ninety-three and half-mad. In his last years he refused all help, even rejecting his pension from a scientific society. What were his thoughts about that bitter quarrel between Petherick and Speke? What did he remember of Florence, the teen-age mistress whose existence must not be mentioned? We shall never know, because just before he died Murie took all his letters and journals into the garden, made a bonfire and burnt the lot.

Bibliography

MANUSCRIPTS

Baker Papers
There are three separate family collections: (1) Valentine Baker collection, Salisbury. The papers held by the namesake of the Victorian military figure include extensive correspondence addressed to Sam and Florence, letters exchanged between various members of the family, Lady Baker's diary of the Ismailia expedition (much of which appears in Anne Baker's *Morning Star*), texts of Baker's speeches, sketches, and assorted ephemera. (2) Dr John Baker collection, Lyndhurst, Hampshire. This includes correspondence between Baker and various members of his family; a large collection of original watercolours, most of them of African settings, by Baker; and assorted papers of Julian Baker including the diary he kept during the Ismailia expedition. (3) Erica Graham collection, Barton-le-Cley, Bedford. This contains letters between Sam Baker's sisters which chronicle the quarrel about Florence in 1865 and later give a family view of Valentine's downfall. Mrs Graham also has many Baker photographs.

Scottish Record Office, Edinburgh
In GD 261/51 there are six important Baker letters, all written in 1862. Five are to Admiral Henry Murray and one to Valentine Baker. There are also comments on Baker in letters from Murchison (GD 261/57) and Burton (GD 261/18).

Royal Archives, Windsor Palace
Of importance primarily for information on the connection between the Prince of Wales and the Bakers. In addition to correspondence, Queen Victoria's diary contains pungent comments on her son's relationship with Sir Samuel and Lady Baker.

Public Record Office, Kew
Material in the F. O. 78 (Ottoman Empire, including Egypt) and F. O. 84 (Slave Trade) series is of particular significance. Included is considerable information on Petherick as well as comments on Baker in correspondence from various consuls. F. O. 633 (Cromer Papers) contains Baker correspondence in later life.

National Library of Scotland, Edinburgh
The Blackwood papers contain significant correspondence from Speke and Grant, there are frequent references to Baker by Livingstone in the vast collection of manuscripts which forms the Livingstone Documentation Project, and the recently acquired Grant papers include an important series of thirty-one Baker letters.

British Museum, London
The Layard papers contain much important information on Speke's relationship with Murchison and other members of the RGS establishment, and there are scattered mentions of Baker and other explorers in these papers and other holdings.

Royal Geographical Society, London
This archive holds four volumes of diaries covering Baker's two expeditions to the Upper Nile, a number of Baker letters, and other material including press clippings, published and unpublished manuscripts and referee reports on same, African relics, and the like. The diaries, which originally were in family hands before being given to the Society, are indispensable for an appreciation of Baker's career. There are also numerous mentions of Baker in the official records of the Society and in the correspondence of various individuals.

Sheffield Central Library
The papers of Lord Wharncliffe contain a total of sixty-one letters from Samuel Baker spanning the period 1857 to 1891.

Bodleian Library, Oxford
The Clarendon papers contain the letters revealing Baker's abortive efforts to accompany Livingstone to the Zambezi. Also in the Bodleian are the records of the Windham and Marlborough Clubs.

Other Collections
Relevant material is in: Bulwer papers, Norwich; Sutherland papers, Stafford; Derby papers, Liverpool; *The Times* archives, London; Zimbabwe-Rhodesia national archives, Salisbury; Houghton papers, Trinity College, Cambridge; Wellcome Library, London; Rhodes House, Oxford; Library of Congress, Washington, D.C.; and Duke University, Durham, N. Carolina.

PUBLISHED SOURCES

Books by Samuel Baker

The Albert Nyanza. 2 vols. London and New York, 1866. Reprinted, with an introduction by Alan Moorehead, London and New York, 1962.
Cast Up By the Sea. London and New York, 1869.
The Egyptian Question: Being Letters to The Times *and* Pall Mall Gazette. London, 1884.
Eight Years' Wanderings in Ceylon. London, 1855.
Ismailia. 2 vols. London and New York, 1874.
The Nile Tributaries of Abyssinia. London, 1867.
The Rifle and the Hound in Ceylon. London, 1854.
True Tales for My Grandsons. London, 1883.
Wild Beasts and Their Ways: Reminiscences of Europe, Asia, Africa and America. 2 vols. London, 1890.

Other Contemporary Works

BARKLEY, HENRY C. *Between The Danube and Black Sea.* London, 1876.
BURTON, RICHARD F., and MCQUEEN, JAMES. *The Nile Basin.* London, 1864. Reprinted, with an introduction by Robert O. Collins, New York, 1967.
GALTON, FRANCIS. *The Art of Travel.* London, 1867.
GRANT, JAMES A. *A Walk Across Africa.* Edinburgh and London, 1864.
GREY, MRS WILLIAM. *Journal of a Visit to Egypt, Constantinople, the Crimea, Greece, etc. in the Suite of the Prince and Princess of Wales.* London, 1869.
HOTTEN, JOHN CAMDEN. *Abyssinia and Its People.* London, 1868.
LEJEAN, GUILLAUME. *Voyage aux Deux Nils.* Paris, 1865.
PETHERICK, JOHN. *Egypt, the Soudan and Central Africa.* Edinburgh and London, 1861.
PETHERICK, JOHN AND KATHERINE. *Travels in Central Africa, and Explorations of the Western Nile Tributaries.* 2 vols. London, 1869.
SPEKE, JOHN H. *Journal of the Discovery of the Source of the Nile.* Edinburgh and London, 1863.
TAYLOR, BAYARD. *A Journey to Central Africa.* New York, 1854.

Later Works

BAKER, ANNE. *Morning Star*. London, 1972.

CHURCHILL, WINSTON S. *The River War*. London and New York, 1899.

DOUIN, GEORGES. *Histoire du regne du Khedive Ismail*. Tome III. *L'empire africain, 1863–1869*. Cairo, 1936.

GEIKIE, ARCHIBALD. *The Life of Sir Roderick I. Murchison*. 2 vols. London, 1875.

GLADSTONE, PENELOPE. *Travels with Alexine*. London, 1970.

GRAY, RICHARD. *A History of the Southern Sudan, 1839–1889*. London, 1961.

HALL, RICHARD. *Stanley*. London and Boston, 1975.

HIBBERT, CHRISTOPHER. *The Royal Victorians: King Edward VII, His Family and Friends*. London and Philadelphia, 1976.

HILL, RICHARD. *A Biographical Dictionary of the Anglo-Egyptian Sudan*. Oxford, 1951.

JOHNSTON, HARRY H. *The Nile Quest*. London, 1903.

LOGIN, E. DALHOUSIE. *Lady Login's Recollections*. London, 1916.

LOMAX, ALFRED E. *Sir Samuel Baker: His Life and Adventures*. London, 1894.

MAGNUS, PHILIP. *Edward VII*. London and New York, 1964.

MAITLAND, ALEXANDER. *Speke*. London, 1971.

MIDDLETON, DOROTHY. *Baker of the Nile*. London, 1949.

MOOREHEAD, ALAN. *The White Nile*. London and New York, 1960.

MURRAY, T. DOUGLAS, and WHITE, A. SILVA. *Sir Samuel Baker: A Memoir*. London and New York, 1895.

OSWELL, W. EDWARD. *William Cotton Oswell: Hunter and Explorer*. With an introduction by Francis Galton. 2 vols. London, 1900.

SHUKRI, MUHAMMAD F. *The Khedive Ismail and Slavery in the Sudan (1863–1879)*. Cairo, 1937.

Articles

BAKER, JOHN R. 'Samuel Baker's Route to the Albert Nyanza,' *Geographical Journal*, CXXXI (1965), pp. 13–20.

CASADA, JAMES A. 'British Exploration in East Africa: A Bibliography with Commentary,' *Africana Journal*, V (1974), pp. 195–239.

COLLINS, ROBERT O. 'Samuel White Baker: Prospero in Purgatory,' in Robert I. Rotberg (ed.), *Africa and Its Explorers*, Cambridge, Mass., 1970, pp. 139–73.

GRAY, JOHN. 'Ismail Pasha and Sir Samuel Baker,' *Uganda Journal*, XXV (1961), pp. 199–213.

JENSEN, H. and ROSEGGER, GERHARD. 'British Railway Builders Along the Lower Danube, 1856–1869,' *Slavonic and East European Review*, XLIV (1968), pp. 105–28.

Newspapers and Periodicals

Nineteenth-century periodicals directly concerned with exploration, such as the *Journal of the Royal Geographical Society* and *Le Tour du Monde*, were frequently consulted. Much use was made of *The Times*, the *Pall Mall Gazette* and other London dailies. The Viennese newspapers for 1859–60 were carefully scrutinized. A wide selection of British periodicals, ranging from the *Illustrated London News* and *The Athenaeum* to *The Field* and *Tomahawk* were also selectively studied. Detailed references appear in the notes.

Notes and Sources

TABLE OF ABBREVIATIONS

AN   *The Albert Nyanza*, by Samuel Baker.
BARP   Barkley Papers.
BM   British Museum Additional Manuscripts.
BP   Baker Papers.
EYW   *Eight Years' Wanderings in Ceylon*, by Samuel Baker.
HP   Houghton Papers, Trinity College, Cambridge.
ISM   *Ismailia*, by Samuel Baker.
JDSN   *Journal of the Discovery of the Source of the Nile*, by John Speke.
JRGS   *Journal of the Royal Geographical Society*.
MS   *Morning Star*, by Anne Baker.
NB   *The Nile Basin*, by Richard Burton and James McQueen.
NLS   National Library of Scotland.
NTA   *The Nile Tributaries of Abyssinia*, by Samuel Baker.
PRO   Public Record Office, London.
RAW   Royal Archives, Windsor.
RGS   Royal Geographical Society Archives.
SSB   *Sir Samuel Baker: A Memoir*, by T. Douglas Murray and A. Silva White.
TCA   *Travels in Central Africa*, by John and Katherine Petherick.
TWA   *Travels with Alexine*, by Penelope Gladstone.
WBW   *Wild Beasts and Their Ways*, by Samuel Baker.
WCO   *William Cotton Oswell*, by W. E. Oswell.
WP   Wharncliffe Papers, Sheffield.

     UNPUBLISHED and PUBLISHED material are distinguished by the figures (1) and (2) respectively.

Chapter 1: Stag at Bay

Notes: Baker's interest in explosives began early. As a boy he almost blinded himself by accidentally setting off a roomful of fireworks.

     Family life in Scotland is recounted by Min Baker in a series of letters (1857–8) to her sister Annie. Lochgarry House stands beside Loch Rannoch.

239

Valentine's book, published in 1858, was *The British Cavalry; with Remarks on its Practical Organisation.*

Lord Wharncliffe (1827–99), a Grenadier Guards officer in his youth, became a second-rank Conservative politician; close to Lord Derby, prime minister in the 1860s, Wharncliffe was president of the Southern Independence Association, which rallied British support for the Confederates in the American civil war.

(1) RAW, WP, PRO, RGS, BP. Letters about Baker's hopes of exploring with Livingstone are in the Bodleian, Oxford (Dep. C 80).

(2) WBW; *The Field*, 11 September 1858; Bayard Taylor, *A Journey to Central Africa.*

Chapter 2: A Girl for Sale

Notes: Baker wrote several letters home about the Danube journey; none, of course, mentions Florence. The most vivid is to the Duchess of Atholl, 18 April 1859 (held at Blair Atholl, Scotland).

A biography of Duleep Singh, *Queen Victoria's Maharajah*, by Michael Alexander and Sushila Anand, is due for publication in 1980.

Florence's account of her purchase by Sam was told to a step-niece, Lady Wood, and is set down in an unpublished family memoir. The story was also heard by Mrs Erica Graham, now in her eighties; she is a grand-niece of Sam Baker and often visited Florence at Sandford Orleigh.

(1) RAW, BP, WP, PRO. Austrian references to the visit to Vienna of Baker and Duleep Singh are in the Austrian Haus-, Hof- und Staatsarchiv (1858 r. 2–9, K 480 *et seq.*).

(2) SSB, *Fremden-Blatt* and other Vienna papers, *Morning Post*, London, and *The Field*. Widdin is described by M. Lancelot in *Le Tour du Monde*, Paris, 1866. The prevalence of slavery is detailed by William Denton, *The Christians of Turkey*, London, 1863.

Chapter 3: Together to Africa

Notes: Duleep Singh was eventually married in 1864, to Bamba Muller, off-spring of a German trader. Bamba, aged fifteen, was being brought up at an American mission in Cairo. The story is given in *The American Mission in Egypt*, by Andrew Watson, 1898.

Despite intensive efforts, including a visit to Romania, it has been impossible so far to identify precisely where Florence was born.

Sam's rescue of the drowning man is mentioned by his first biographers, Murray and Silva White (1895); the fictionalized account is in *Cast Up By the Sea* (1869).

(1) BP, BARP, PRO, RGS, TCA. Relevant letters are also in the Bulwer papers, Norwich.

(2) The fullest account of the building of the Constanza-Danube rail-

way is by Jensen and Rosegger (see bibliography). The opening of the railway is reported in the *Levant Herald*, 10 October 1860 (file in Cambridge University Library); other material is in *The Railway Times*, *passim*.

Obituary of Admiral Murray: *Spectator*, 4 March 1865.

Chapter 4: On the Abyssinian Frontier

Notes: Most of the material in this chapter comes from Baker's unpublished diaries and his book, NTA. Early on in the diaries there are fairly regular references to Florence ('F'), but these suddenly stop.

The private papers of Colquhoun seem not to have survived, but there are numerous letters from him in the Bulwer papers. His attempt to make Sam become married to Florence is confirmed by James Grant's letter, 22 October 1866.

(1) BP, RGS.

(2) NTA, TCA, JRGS.

Chapter 5: The Gateway to Black Africa

Notes: The most convincing account of Khartoum in the 1860s is undoubtedly that of Lejean, *Voyage aux Deux Nils*. Also useful are Ferdinand de Lesseps, *Recollections of Forty Years* (1887), and George Melly, *Khartoum and the Blue and White Niles* (1851). A remarkably violent letter by Sam Baker, attacking the White Nile slave trade, appeared in *The Times*, 25 November 1862.

(1) BP, RGS, WP, PRO, SRO. Harriet Tinne's references to Florence are in her unpublished diaries. The diaries of the American, Dr Clarence Brownell, were in the hands of descendants in Connecticut in 1960, but now are untraceable.

(2) JRGS, AN, TWA, *Punch*.

Chapter 6: Rendezvous in Gondokoro

Notes: The Nile journey from Khartoum to Gondokoro is just short of 1100 miles.

The lay missionary Franz Morlang abandoned Africa, and died in South America in 1875. His diary was published by a Catholic mission press in Bologna, Italy, in 1973.

The Scottish doctor, James Murie, did not write about the Sudan until the 1880s, when he contributed a chapter to *The Story of Africa*, edited by Dr George Brown. The best account of his life is a long obituary in *The Southend Standard*, 31 March 1932.

Speke's love affair in Uganda was known to the Church Missionary

Society and Burton's co-author, James McQueen, had plainly heard of it. It is clearly described in his journal (Ms. 243/4873, Blackwood collection, NLS).

(1) BP, RGS, NLS, PRO.

(2) AN, TCA, JDSN, Grant's *A Walk Across Africa*, JRGS. A biography of the Maltese trader, Andrea de Bono, was written by Salvino Galea (Empire Press, Malta, 1933).

Chapter 7: Florence on the March

Notes: Soon after leaving Gondokoro (just north of modern Juba), the Bakers crossed what is now the northern border of Uganda.

A Venetian wanderer, Giovanni Miani, had travelled some way beyond Gondokoro up the Nile, but fame eluded him. Miani died in 1872, 300 miles west of Gondokoro. He had made his own coffin and his body was laid in it, wrapped in a carpet. But the local chief cut off his white beard to make a girdle and the grave was robbed. '. . . they would certainly have taken the body itself to eat, if they had not objected to the flesh of white men.' Wilhelm Junker, *Travels in Africa* (1891).

(1) BP, RGS.

(2) AN, MS, JRGS.

Chapter 8: The Way to the Lake

Notes: At the point where they crossed the Victoria Nile, Sam and Florence were about 120 miles north of Kampala, the modern Ugandan capital.

Since they were by now out of contact with all other Europeans, the sources are solely Baker's own writings.

The Albert Nyanza (lake) is also called the Muitan Zige.

Chapter 9: Tarnished Heroes

Notes: A pithy characterization of Sir Roderick Murchison is in a letter from the orientalist, Lord Strangford, to Max Muller: 'The very incarnation of all jobbing.' (Dep. d 171, Bodleian, Oxford).

The debate about how Speke died goes on. Given his emotional instability, there is good reason to think that he committed suicide.

Richard Burton's correspondence with Houghton reveals much about the former's nature. Houghton, who was to represent the RGS at the opening of the Suez Canal, was Burton's strongest supporter in the Establishment. The Houghton papers (Trinity College, Cambridge) also contain letters from Petherick and Baker.

(1) BP, RGS, PRO, BM, HP, NLS. Speke's revealing letter from Paris

(20 April 1864) was to Colonel Christopher Rigby, later to be best man at Grant's wedding (Rigby papers).

(2) A useful analysis of Speke's quarrel with the RGS is by Roy Bridges in *Uganda Journal*, XXVI, 1962. Other published material: AN, JDSN, JRGS, NB, *Athenaeum, The Times*. A copy of Peter McQuie's leaflet (Liverpool, 30 December 1863) is in Kew Gardens archives.

Chapter 10: Sailing the Inland Sea

Notes: Baker's diaries have had a number of passages scissored out, probably by one of his daughters, but the entry on a financial provision for Florence was overlooked.

Petherick's involvement with the Austrian consulate in Khartoum is recorded in a series of despatches to the consul-general, Alexandria (Austrian State archives, LXII, 9462 *et seq.*).

(1) BP, RGS, WP, PRO.

(2) JRGS, AN, TWA, TGA, *The Times*.

Chapter 11: The Ideal Englishman

Notes: The marriage certificate is in the St James's Church records, Westminster Central Library, London. The licence is in the archives of Lambeth Palace.

The dinner with Murchison on the day of the wedding and the commissioning of a painting of the Murchison Falls are both mentioned by Baker in a letter to his daughter Edith, 30 October 1865.

The Derby papers (Liverpool Record Office) reveal how Lord Stanley pressed both Disraeli and Lord Derby to give Baker a knighthood.

There is nothing in Victoria's diaries and correspondence to reveal how she heard that Florence had been Sam's mistress. Her matter-of-fact diary entry about the bestowal of the knighthood suggests that she did not know then.

The intensity of Grant's fury is well documented in his papers (NLS). More than a year after his first outbursts, he ordered his wife to refuse an invitation to stay with the Bakers.

(1) BP, RGS, NLS, WP, RAW, PRO.

(2) AN, WCO; and a wide range of newspapers and periodicals.

Chapter 12: Friend of the Prince

Notes: Although Baker called Livingstone his 'old friend,' there is no evidence that he ever met him.

The memoirs of Nubar Pasha, edited by Mirrit Boutros Ghali of Cairo, are due to be published in Paris in 1980. Excerpts kindly made available by Mr Ghali illuminate Baker's relations with Nubar.

(1) BP, WP, PRO, RAW. The exchanges between the prince and Victoria about the Bakers are in Windsor Add. A3/113/121/125. Florence's letter to Lady Colquhoun is in the Wellcome Library, London.

(2) MS, NTA, *Cast Up By the Sea*. Various biographies of Edward VII recount the journey to Egypt. Also useful are the published diaries of William Howard Russell and the Hon. Mrs William Grey.

Chapter 13: A Ring of Spears

Notes: The acute misfortune for Baker in 1870 was the appearance of a solid barrier of *sudd*. This was to block the Nile until 1874.

The major manuscript sources for the Ismailia expedition are the diaries of Sam, Florence and Julian Baker.

By 1870, European traders such as Thibaut and de Bono had been driven out of the Sudan by Egyptian rivals or died of disease.

(1) BP, RGS, WP. There are also important letters from Baker to editor John Delane in the archives of *The Times*, London. Gladstone's letter to Baker is in BM Add. Mss. 44536.

(2) MS, ISM, JRGS.

Chapter 14: A Family Scandal

Notes: Although Baker and Gordon were ultimately lavish in their praise of one another, the former was bitterly critical of his successor in letters to Delane of *The Times*. Gordon was likewise withering about Baker while writing to Grant.

The Prince of Wales gave Valentine letters of introduction to the Grand Duke Michael at Tiflis (*Clouds in the East*, p. 7). The prince's advice to the Duchess of Sutherland on her errant husband is in family papers, Stafford record office.

The quotation about Valentine from Russell's unpublished diaries was supplied by Alan Hankinson, currently working on Russell's biography.

Sir William Jenner's letter (17 August 1875) on behalf of Victoria is in the possession of Mrs Alex Heape.

(1) BP, WP, RAW, RGS.

(2) Apart from the published writings of the Baker brothers, recourse has been had to a wide variety of contemporary newspapers.

Chapter 15: The Nile's Last Temptation

Notes: Not only did Valentine go to the Balkans in the 1870s, but James Baker travelled there and wrote a book on his experiences (*Turkey in Europe*).

All biographers of Gordon have overlooked the part played by Baker in advocating his return to Khartoum. It is intriguing to speculate what might have happened if Baker himself had gone back – how he would have sought to resolve the dilemma.

At the end of Sam Baker's life, the rescue of Emin Pasha by Henry Stanley compelled great attention. Stanley's criticism of Baker as an explorer is expressed in letters to Grant (NLS).

Much of the information about the last years of Sam and Florence comes from eye-witness accounts and oral tradition in the Baker family. Also valuable is an article by Edith Wheeler in *Mid-Devon Times*, 16 November 1968.

(1) BP, RAW, BM, H. M. Stanley papers, unpublished reminiscences of Robin Baily.

(2) SSB, Winston Churchill's *The River War*, *Vanity Fair*, *Whitehall Review*, *Echo*, and other contemporary journals. Vital for Valentine's later relations with the Prince of Wales is Sir Sidney Lee, *King Edward VII* (1925).

Index

Baker, Florence, Lady [*contd.*]
return to Europe, 204–6; rumours of death, 205; at SB's address to RGS, 206–7; at Sandford Orleigh, 218–19; restrains SB, 220, 225; and SB's death, 229–30; widowhood and death, 230–31

Baker, James (SB's brother), 16, 154, 158–9, 165–6

Baker, Sir John (SB's ancestor), 13

Baker, John (SB's brother), 72, 133–4, 165

Baker, Julian (SB's nephew), 188–9, 191–3, 207

Baker, Louisa (James's wife), 157–9, 165

Baker, Min (SB's sister), cares for SB's children, 16, 158; letters from SB, 26, 32, 44, 150; kept in ignorance of Florence, 33; and SB's marriage, 158–9, 164–5; own marriages, 166–7

Baker, Sir Samuel White, kills stag, 11–12, 51; background, 12–13; first marriage, 13, 23, 32; children, 13, 16, 32, 157–9; invents rifle ball, 16–17; appeal of Africa to, 14–15, 17–18, 38, 44, 220; interest in entering church, 16; elephant hunting, 17–18, 39, 42, 56–7, 108–9; Danube trip with Duleep Singh, 20–7, 30; views on non-Europeans, 20, 52–3, 63, 81–2, 117, 166; contributions to *Field*, 21, 37, 40, 42–3; buys Florence at slave auction, 27–9; early relations with Florence, 31–5, 39–40, 43, 45; works on Danube Railway, 32–5, 40; rescues shipwrecked sailor, 36, 179; plans African expedition, 38–41, 43–4; 1861 journey up Nile, 45–6; painting and sketching, 46, 52, 81, 91, 105–6, 117, 160–1, 189; dress, 52, 100, 105, 188; medical treatment by, 53–4; and slavery, 54–5, 63–4, 66, 68, 166,

185–6, 202–4; relations with servants, 55–6; expedition to Gondokoro, 74, 77, 82–3; repels boar, 76; will, 77; health, 79, 109–11, 116, 143–4; and Speke-Petherick quarrel, 93; plans to leave Gondokoro, 94–9; quarrels with Petherick, 98; march towards Luta N'zige, 100–12; makes wine and spirits, 108; and Kamrasi, 113–14; reaches Luta N'zige, 123–4, 134, 163; reputation, 133, 209; awarded RGS gold medal, 134, 150; Murchison supports, 134; navigates Luta N'zige, 136–40; discovers Murchison Falls, 142–3; and Kamrasi's war, 144–6; decides to keep Florence, 146–7, 149, 151, 153; first mention of Florence in diary, 149–50; marriage to Florence, 154, 156, 158–62; homecoming, 155; addresses RGS, 160–1; writing, 163–4, 172; elected to Athenaeum, 164; knighted, 167; proposes second expedition, 170, 181–3; honoured in France, 171; friendship with Prince of Wales, 173, 178, 180; trip to Egypt with Prince of Wales, 178–82; Queen criticizes, 180; given Egyptian support and rank, 182, 185, 187; second expedition, 184–203; trapped in Masindi, 190–6; retreat from Masindi, 197–200; honoured by khedive, 202–3; return to Europe, 204–6; rumours of death, 205; addresses RGS on Nile slave trade, 206–7; and Gordon, 207; settles in Sandford Orleigh, 209, 218; and scandal of brother Val, 212–13, 215–17; restlessness to return to Africa, 220; on Mahdist uprising, 223–5, 227–8; later world travels, 228–9; death, 229; achievement, 229; cremation, 230. WORKS: *The Albert Nyanza*, 163, 166, 172; *Cast Up By the Sea*,

ABOUT THE AUTHOR

RICHARD HALL is the author of five previous books on Africa, including his noteworthy biography of Henry Morton Stanley. The former editor of the *Observer* magazine, Hall is at present a columnist for the *Financial Times*. He lives in London.